Perception
and
Persuasion

*A New Approach to
Effective Writing*

Perception and Persuasion

A New Approach to Effective Writing

Raymond Paul
Pellegrino W. Goione

Montclair State College

 THOMAS Y. CROWELL COMPANY
New York   Established 1834

Library of Congress Cataloging in Publication Data

Paul, Raymond.
    Perception and persuasion.

    Bibliography: p. 236.
    1. English language—Rhetoric. I. Goione,
Pellegrino W., joint author. II. Title.
PE1408.P28   808'.042   72-11812
ISBN 0-690-61413-6

Design by W. P. Ellis

Manufactured in the United States of America

1 2 3 4 5 6 7 8 9 0

PE1408
P28

For Anne and for Marie

Preface

When this project was in its infancy, its working title was *A Crash Course in How to Survive in College*, and in many ways the title remains apt. We teach two essential and inseparable skills: perceptive reading and persuasive writing. *Perception and Persuasion* was developed and tested in the classroom with students varying widely in ability and interest. In its initial form the course was designed to bring students with substandard admission credentials to a viable level of academic competition. Subsequent classroom experience proved that these methods were progressively more effective as levels of preparation and ability increased.

"The first thing you are going to do is write, as spontaneously, as imaginatively and as much as you can." Section I, "Thought, Imagination and Writing," is introduced by this sentence, and is designed for this purpose. Without regard for mechanical errors (at this point) the student produces as much written material as he can, all in the form of first drafts, which will be rethought and rewritten as he proceeds through Sections II and III. The segment on propaganda makes the student writer aware of his reader and of the necessity of consciously attempting to *control the reader's response* to what he writes.

Section II, "The Dynamics of Language," demonstrates that *the function of language is the communication of ideas*. We deal first with the meaning of a word, and the dependency of its meaning on the context. Punctuation is discussed in terms of its functions. (All detailed explanation of punctuation is left to Appendix A, to which the student may be directed at any point in the course.)

In Section II the relationship between a word and its context is emphasized with an examination of groupings of words into sentences and sentences into paragraphs. We stress the correlation between the eye's physical perception of word-groups and the mind's perception of their meanings. The jargon of rhetoric is kept to a minimum, but segments on deception, equivocation, connotation and irony help the student experience the power of language to inform, persuade, amuse or mislead the reader. The detailed analysis of a complete essay as a succession of paragraphs, or *main ideas*, is included.

Follow-up exercises direct the student to reevaluate and revise his own earlier drafts in terms of new writing techniques as he masters them. That is, the student practices techniques as they are introduced, using his own writings as his "workbook." He develops confidence in his ability to edit his work, and he sees each assignment as a means of improving skills rather than as merely a factor in his final grade.

Section III, "Reading, Comprehension and Logic," moves the student closer to the problems of research by stressing (1) accurate reading and (2) the application of logical thought processes to the sorting out and evaluation of facts. We emphasize the distinction between fact and opinion, and the need for the student to draw logical inferences rather than to leap to assumptions which may be unwarranted. This section concludes with "The Locked Room Murder Case," an exercise in which the student, acting as a detective, must solve a murder by applying his skills of deduction to police reports and depositions of suspects.

This text aims at developing perception in reading and persuasion in writing. The activity which forms the logical bridge between these two skills is *research writing,* the subject of Section IV, "Projects in Investigation."

Phase I (Preparing Abstracts) of Section IV offers an article on how to prepare an article abstract; this article is itself abstracted. Abstracting provides useful experience in such basic researching techniques as close reading of sources, effective note-taking, paraphrasing, and objective evaluation of the source's scholarship and style. Our two basic themes of perceptive, or *defensive*, reading and persuasive, or *aggressive*, writing are reinforced by two follow-up articles—to be abstracted by the student—on the trial of Bruno Richard Hauptmann for the kidnapping-murder of the Lindbergh baby.

Phase II (Introduction to Research) opens with a discussion of "What a Research Paper Is Not," an effort to dispel some standard misunderstandings. Segments on "The Questions Most Asked about a Research Paper" and "The Questions Most Asked about Footnotes" provide resource materials on the procedures for compiling research data. Phase II concludes with source materials on two famous events, the Salem witch trials and the Lizzie Borden case.

Phase III (The Independent Research Project) turns the student loose on a full-scale independent research project, the Sacco-Vanzetti case. Here the student, although encouraged to consult earlier instructional material, is essentially on his own. Four articles provide the basic social and historical background of the case while assessing the guilt or innocence of the accused.

The independent research project is the appropriate culmination of a course built around this text: the student is required to separate fact from opinion, and the inferences of his sources from their assumptions. He must also separate his own inferences from his own assumptions, avoid making false assumptions and perpetrating outright deceptions, and, having achieved all this, persuade his reader to accept his view of the truth.

The appendices are designed for the student's independent reading. Appendix A, "Punctuation and Grammar," should be read as the class works through Section II. Appendix B, "Preparing the Research Paper," is most useful if read when the class begins Phase II of Section IV. Appendix C, "Using the Library," is best read at the same time as Appendix B, but Appendix D, "The Dictionary and the Thesaurus," will be useful to the student from the beginning of the course.

For their assistance in gathering reference materials we wish to thank Paul Anderson, director of the Emerson Media Center; Vincent Jennings of the Montclair State College library; and student assistants Phyllis Volin and Lori Wilken. We extend our appreciation also to three Montclair State colleagues who helped to test these materials and offered many valuable suggestions: Butler Brewton, Grover Furr and especially Percy E. Johnston. We are grateful to Herbert Addision for his early and unfailing

Preface

faith and support, and to our tireless editor, Walter Brownfield, with whom it has been a pleasure to work during the development and production of this book.

Montclair, New Jersey   Raymond Paul
                                                            Pellegrino W. Goione

Contents

Contents

SECTION III

Reading, Comprehension and Logic

SECTION IV

Projects in Investigation

Appendices

Contents

Perception and Persuasion

A New Approach to Effective Writing

Section I

THOUGHT, IMAGINATION AND WRITING

Situation
Paragraphs

The first thing you are going to do is write, as spontaneously, as imaginatively and as much as you can. The materials used to stimulate your writings are called situation paragraphs, to be followed by argumentative paragraphs and propaganda paragraphs. In this initial stage, you will produce several unpolished first drafts. Later you will be asked to select some of these to edit and revise into final papers. As you write, be sure to skip lines on your paper. This will leave you space to make corrections and changes later.

The instructor will assign a situation paragraph to you. Read the paragraph and listen for the "response word" which the instructor will announce. Imagine yourself in the situation described in the paragraph and begin writing, making certain that you include the response word somewhere in your paragraph. At intervals of two or three minutes you will be instructed to stop writing and begin a new paragraph. Stop writing even if you are in the middle of a sentence. Listen for the next response word. Begin a new paragraph in which you continue your narrative, using the response word somewhere in your paragraph. Each exercise contains five response words, so you will begin five different paragraphs during the exercise.

Do not worry about leaving your paragraphs unfinished. Do not worry about errors of spelling, punctuation and grammar. You will have ample opportunity to correct these before any grade is assigned to your papers. Relax, and write whatever comes into your head. Follow the instructor's directions for the first exercise.

SECTION I: THOUGHT, IMAGINATION AND WRITING

THE GREEN DOOR

You step into the rickety old elevator in the crumbling tenement and press the button for the fourth floor. The car lurches and then rides upward. When the door slides open, you peer down the long, sixty-watt-lit hallway, toward the green door at its end. As you step out of the elevator, you fumble for the automatic pistol in the pocket of your coat, and you double-check to make certain it is loaded. Walking down the hall, you go over in your mind the events which led to this moment. Your eyes on the green door, you realize that in the next few moments you will face something you never faced before. You have arrived at the green door. You reach for the doorknob, turn it, and slowly the door opens and swings back. . . .

When you have completed the assignment, you will have produced a narrative paper in a very rough, unfinished form. Use this paper as the framework on which you create the first draft of a full-length narrative. *Do not worry about making mechanical errors yet.* The time to be concerned with spelling, punctuation and grammar is later when you are editing and revising your paper into a final draft. For now, *concentrate simply on telling the story as interestingly and entertainingly as you can.* Use the word you want to use even if you are not certain how to spell it. Write your sentences in a style that feels comfortable and natural to you without worrying about punctuation and grammatical mistakes. You will not be penalized for errors committed at this point. No grade will be given to any of your papers before you submit them in final form.

Notice that each situation paragraph in the next exercise presents a problem and asks you to imagine that you, yourself, are facing that problem. Be certain that, in the course of your paper, you *resolve* the problem, either by imagining a solution to the problem or by imagining that the problem has defeated you. For example, read the following paragraph:

You are on a crash diet, desperately trying to lose weight. You go to the diner intending to order a health salad, and you run into two friends who invite you to join them. They are just finishing a lunch of lasagna and preparing to wolf down two wedges of banana cream pie. As you sit there starving, the waitress asks you for your order.

The problem presented to you in this paragraph is obvious. The number of ways to resolve it are endless. Your willpower may triumph, or you may give in and order a big meal. You may order a big meal, but before you can eat it the diner catches fire or a plane crashes through the roof. You are both free and encouraged to imagine the wildest story you can, as long as during your story you resolve the problem one way or another.

When your first draft is completed place it in your folder with your other papers. You will be asked to revise it later in the course. If you have any questions, ask the instructor for help.

EXERCISE

Be sure to follow the instructor's directions in completing this exercise.

1. You are in a speeding car very late on a dark and windy night. You may be either the driver or a passenger.

2. You have studied very hard for an important examination. You are relieved to discover that you know the answers to most of the questions. Halfway through the examination, one of your closest friends begins asking you for the answers.

3. You have made a bet to spend the night in a house which everyone thinks is haunted. You do not believe in ghosts, but, as the old clock strikes midnight, you hear footsteps in the hall, approaching your room.

4. You have never used drugs before. At a party somebody offers you a couple of pills.

5. You are a member of the first crew of astronauts to fly to Venus. You have almost reached the planet when you receive a warning from Houston control of a malfunction in your landing craft.

6. You are playing on the varsity team of your favorite sport before a capacity crowd. The game is extremely close and in the last few minutes of play. Suddenly you realize the team is depending on you.

7. You have saved for months to buy a certain dress for the most important dance of the year. When you arrive at the dance, you see another girl wearing the same dress.

8. You have just witnessed a mugging from your window. The victim is probably still alive and in need of help. Yet you are afraid that you recognized one of the muggers as a friend of yours.

9. You are a policeman who has been ordered to be particularly hard on teen-age gangs.

10. You are a secret agent who has been sent to the Far East. Upon arrival, you discover that your contact has been murdered.

11. You have looked forward to a special date and a big party for weeks. On the day before the party, your parents catch you smoking and ground you.

12. You and a friend are driving to a rock music festival. For no apparent reason a police car flags you down, and the officers order you out of your car.

13. All at once you find yourself in a strange city. You do not know where you are or how you got there. Suddenly you realize that you cannot remember your name.

14. You receive a visit from the mayor. The city is being terrorized by a mad killer and you are the only person who can save it.

15. You are already late for a very important appointment. You just manage to catch the bus and then realize you have forgotten to bring your wallet.

16. You have just bought an expensive gift for your steady boyfriend. As you leave the store, you see him across the street, walking with his arms around another girl.

17. You are a volunteer worker for a "help line" where troubled people can telephone anonymously and talk to you about their problems. A caller has just told you she intends to commit suicide.

18. You are the only passenger in a small private plane. As the plane circles the field waiting for landing instructions, the pilot suddenly loses consciousness.

19. You and a friend are spending the weekend near a girls' school where your friend's girl has arranged a blind date for you with her roommate. You have just discovered that the roommate is fat and homely and that the school is full of beautiful, lonely girls.

20. You are the slickest jewel thief in Europe. At a hotel in Paris you learn that the famous Capetown diamond is being kept in the hotel safe, a safe so burglar-proof it has never been successfully robbed.

21. You are leading an expedition of explorers deep into the Amazon jungle. You suspect that the natives in the area may be cannibals.

22. You have a dinner date with someone of a different race from your own. At the restaurant you run into two friends of yours. Although you can sense immediately that they disapprove, your date suggests the four of you have dinner together.

23. You have just gone into a bar with a couple of friends. Your friends are of legal age but you are not. The bartender approaches you.

24. You have a terrible toothache, and a friend recommends a famous "painless" dentist. You no sooner sit down in his office than you hear a loud scream of agony.

25. You and a friend are lost while driving through Transylvania. You stop at a lonely castle to ask directions, and a strange man with a cape and sharp teeth invites you to spend the night.

Argumentative
Paragraphs

Listen for directions from the instructor. Read the assigned paragraphs and respond either by agreeing or disagreeing with the opinions presented. It makes no difference whether you agree or disagree with the point of view expressed in the paragraph as long as you argue what you honestly feel.

1. Teachers have absolutely no right to strike. Sure, they claim they're striking to improve conditions in the schools, but all they really care about is getting more money. All that teachers' strikes ever accomplish is to cheat the students of the education they have a right to expect. Instead of picketing, the teachers should spend their time improving their classes. Most of them are lousy anyway.

2. It's ridiculous to give the vote to youngsters under twenty-one. These kids are only children, not yet emancipated from their parents. As long as a kid is financially dependent on his family, he cannot be considered independent of them in any other way. Following this philosophy, you might as well let thirteen-year-olds vote as eighteen-year-olds if you're going to let children vote at all.

3. The reason so many kids are on drugs today is that the parents are too permissive. The whole structure of the family has broken down in this country. Kids need strict discipline and solid moral values, and they can only get them in the home. The police are doing everything they can to nail the pushers and stop the dope traffic, but it won't do any good until these permissive parents reassert their authority.

4. What really burns me up is Whitey going around pretending to love the black man. He hires a couple of token blacks for his business or gives a couple of bucks to some phony government

project and he thinks he's a great liberal. Just let a black family move into his neighborhood or start busing black kids to his fancy schools and he'll scream fast enough. He's not fooling anybody. He really doesn't give a damn.

5. When are we going to start cracking down hard on these so-called student demonstrators? What right have they got to occupy a school administrator's office or issue lists of "demands"? By disrupting school routine they're hurting the vast majority of students who want to get an education. They always claim they're demonstrating for peace and love, but all they actually want is an excuse to cut classes. The only way to deal with these characters is to expel them.

6. The government welfare system should be abolished at once. It's degrading for the people who must accept it. It discriminates against the working poor who sometimes earn less than they could get in government handouts. It's not fair to the taxpayers who have to foot the bills for deadbeats who could get jobs but won't. Welfare money would be better spent on job training and child care centers so the poor could get work and pull their own weight.

7. It's about time we lowered the legal drinking age to 18 throughout this country. It's ridiculous that a man of 18 can be drafted, be tried in adult court, even vote, but in most states he can't buy a can of beer. These stupid laws are just an excuse to put young people down. It's embarrassing and insulting to be asked for proof of age. Young people can handle liquor just as well as older ones, maybe better. When is the last time you saw a young wino?

8. Women must, at long last, demand absolutely equal status with men. This means equal pay for equal work, equal opportunities for jobs and education, and especially equal rights in marriage. Why should a woman change her name to her husband's when she marries? Why should she be trapped in the house with the kids all day while he has a career? She's a fool to marry as long as marriage serves only to destroy her identity and prevent her from self-fulfillment.

9. The only way we're ever going to put an end to drug use among young people is if the kids who are straight begin to come forward and volunteer information to the authorities. True, this idea violates the teen-ager's honor code which condemns "ratting" on a pal, but kids must start to realize that a friend who is a user needs

help. Turning him in is doing him a favor, as well as providing the police with the information they must have to clear the pushers off the streets.

10. All wars are evil. There is no such thing as a justifiable war. As long as there is a single American serviceman stationed anywhere outside our borders, we, as a nation, are disgraced. Violence never solved any problem, whether it was conducted on an individual or an international level. We may not be able to stop other nations from fighting wars, but we have no moral justification for becoming involved ourselves.

Propaganda
Paragraphs

Before we get into a discussion of propaganda and its techniques, test your reading comprehension by reading the following passage and answering the questions that follow it.

One of the reasons Jim Ferris has the number of friends he has is that, no matter when he sees you, he always greets you with a big smile and an interesting new story. People usually respond immediately to Jim's personality. He is the kind of guy who's always ready for a good time, but he has his serious side too. When you are feeling low, you can count on him to listen to your troubles. When you are getting nervous before a big exam, Jim is the first one to suggest that you study for the test together. With the girls Jim has quite a reputation, probably because he is known to have very high standards when it comes to dating. After we graduate, Jim and I may not keep in close touch, but I know I will never forget him.

Test your comprehension by answering these questions. You will not have to turn the quiz in, but for your information jot down your answers on a sheet of scrap paper.

1. Jim Ferris is (a) very popular (b) extremely unpopular.
2. People usually (a) hate Jim Ferris (b) like Jim immediately.
3. Jim Ferris is (a) a sympathetic listener (b) very unsympathetic.
4. Jim Ferris (a) likes to help friends study for exams (b) never helps friends study for exams.
5. Girls usually (a) refuse to go out with Jim Ferris (b) want to date Jim.
6. The writer of this paragraph (a) is a close friend of Jim Ferris' (b) hates Jim's guts.

SECTION I: THOUGHT, IMAGINATION AND WRITING

When you have finished answering the questions, check your answers against the following: 1*a*, 2*b*, 3*a*, 4*a*, 5*b*, 6*a*. If your answers correspond to at least five on the list, your results on the quiz are significant. But, just to be certain that your performance was not a fluke, test yourself again with the following passage. Read it carefully and remember, the results of the quiz are strictly for your own information.

One of the reasons Jim Ferris is so unpopular is that, no matter how hard you try to avoid him, he always manages to spot you and corner you. It is interesting how many sad stories he can invent in his constant effort to borrow money. His personality is so obnoxious that people usually hate him immediately. Jim is always ready for a good time, as long as you're paying for it. He loves to listen to your troubles and encourages you to tell him, because hearing them makes him feel superior and supplies him with gossip. Jim cuts most of his classes and never reads the assignments, but before every big exam, especially when you are getting nervous yourself, he always shows up to copy your notes and pick your brain. With the girls Jim has a very bad reputation, probably because he is so conceited that he thinks very few girls are worth dating. After graduation I am going to try to avoid Jim like the plague, but, knowing him, I may not be successful. One thing is sure. I will never forget the jerk.

Test your comprehension by answering these questions:

1. Jim Ferris is (a) very popular (b) extremely unpopular.
2. People usually (a) hate Jim Ferris (b) like Jim immediately.
3. Jim Ferris is (a) a sympathetic listener (b) very unsympathetic.
4. Jim Ferris (a) likes to help friends study for exams (b) never helps friends study for exams.
5. Girls usually (a) refuse to go out with Jim Ferris (b) want to date Jim.
6. The writer of this paragraph (a) is a close friend of Jim Ferris' (b) hates Jim's guts.

When you've finished answering the questions, check your answers against the following: 1*b*, 2*a*, 3*b*, 4*b*, 5*a*, 6*b*. Of course you have noticed that not only does the second paragraph deal with the same subject as the first, but it also appears to contradict the first in every respect. The important word in the last sentence is "appears."

Reread both passages very carefully. Notice that the first passage contains absolutely nothing contrary to the statements made in the second. What information has the writer of the first passage given you? Jim Ferris "has the number of friends he has." Of course he does. *All of us* have the number of friends we have. *You* have the number of friends that you have. You are also as tall as your height, as heavy as your weight, and just exactly as old as your age.

The statement that Jim "has the number of friends he has" obviously contains no information to tell you *what that number is.* Yet the chances are excellent that you answered the first question about the first passage by checking (a) Jim Ferris is very popular. If you did so, think for a moment about *why?*

Perhaps your answer is that you naturally assumed he was popular. After all, he greets people with "a big smile and an interesting new story."

But smiles may be unpleasant, and unpleasant people smile. And the interesting stories turn out to be sob stories to mooch money.

But it says that people "respond immediately to Jim's personality." Naturally I assumed this meant that people like him as soon as they meet.

There are many kinds of responses. The passage does not make clear how people responded to Jim, or if they responded in the same way.

But he is "always ready for a good time." That certainly makes him sound like a nice guy.

Yes, it *suggests* that he is a nice

guy, but it doesn't *state* that he is. Besides, it turns out that Jim's idea of a good time is leeching off others.

But I did not know that when I answered the first questions. We are not told any of the bad things about him until we read the second passage.

In other words, you formed your opinion of Jim Ferris on the basis of inadequate information.

That's not fair. I based my original opinion on the only information I had at the time. The first writer lied.

No he did not. Check every statement he made against the facts in the second passage. You will not find a single lie.

Oh? What about where the first writer says Jim is good with girls? The second one says he is not. Someone has to be lying.

The first writer never says Jim is good with girls. He says Jim has quite a reputation with the girls.

But "quite a reputation" suggests that his reputation is good, doesn't it?

Yes, it *suggests* it, but doesn't *state* it as a fact. The sentence is *ambiguous;* it could have more than one meaning. If you jump too quickly to assume the wrong meaning, that is your fault, not the writer's.

Wrong! It is the writer's fault too. He may not tell any lies directly, but he deliberately misleads the reader by not telling the whole truth. He only tells the parts he wants you to know. For example, he says Jim is always willing to study together for exams, but he leaves out the fact that all the guy wants is to copy other people's notes.

In other words, you formed your original opinion of Jim Ferris on the basis of inadequate information.

Well, I was tricked into it. By withholding important facts, the first writer forced me to assume false conclusions.

Wait a minute. Maybe he omitted a few important facts, but he certainly did nothing else to trick you.

Certainly he did. Look at the way he phrases some of his statements. As you said, many of his statements are ambiguous. But the way he words them makes you assume one meaning immediately, without even thinking about the other possibilities.

For example?

For example, the first sentence: "One of the reasons Jim Ferris has the number of friends he has is that, no matter when he sees you, he always greets you with a big smile and an interesting new story."

What is the matter with that sentence?

You're kidding! First he uses the

phrase "number of friends," which *suggests* a *large* number even though it may not specifically *state* it as a fact.

Well, obviously you have to be careful to distinguish between *stated facts* and *suggested assumptions.*

He is guilty of more than withholding facts and using suggestive language. That sentence has a cause and effect construction.

A what?

The sentence gives a circumstance and offers a cause or reason for that circumstance.

Oh, I understand. The effect or circumstance is that Ferris "has the number of friends he has."

Correct, and the cause or reason given is that "no matter when he sees you, he always greets you with a big smile and an interesting new story." Obviously the reader is led to believe that Ferris has many friends.

Because smiling and knowing good stories are normally signs of popularity?

Yes. And since the writer establishes his deception from the first sentence on, the reader is likely to be tricked by the entire paragraph.

You admit the writer tricked you? What do you mean?

I mean that he fooled me into believing something which was not true. By his choice of words and the way he phrased his sentences, he took control of my mind and actually controlled my thoughts.

Did you enjoy having your thoughts controlled?

Well, did you?

The most important skill to be learned in writing is the skill of using words to control the mental responses of your reader. Quite possibly your own responses were controlled to some degree during the last exercise. Now, why not test your skill at propaganda techniques by completing this assignment?

EXERCISE

Select someone whom you know well and give him a fictitious name. Write two separate paragraphs in which you describe this individual's appearance, habits, and personality. You must tell the truth in both paragraphs. You cannot lie, nor can you include any statements in the paragraphs which directly contradict each other. But, in the first paragraph, tell only those truths which will make the reader like and admire the person you are describing. In the second paragraph, tell only those truths which will make the reader dislike the person you discuss.

FOLLOW-UP

1. *Try repeating the above exercise with a different person being described. This time write the negative paragraph first, and then do the complimentary description. You may find that the assignment is more difficult when the order is reversed. As before, you cannot lie or make statements in one paragraph which contradict those in the other.*
2. *As a variation on these propaganda assignments, go back and reread the argumentative paragraphs. Select one and write two brief essays in which you support two opposing points of view. This assignment is most effective if you select a topic about which you do not feel particularly strongly. Support the point of view*

with which you feel least sympathetic in your first essay. As with all written assignments during this first section of the course, complete these papers only through first-draft form, and then place the drafts in your folder in the classroom.

Section II

THE
DYNAMICS
OF
LANGUAGE

Introduction

Before you begin the major portions of this section, test your common sense by answering the following brief quiz. Like all the other quizzes you will find scattered through the text, it is intended simply for your own information. You need not show the results to anyone, nor will your score influence your grade in the course. These quizzes are intended only to demonstrate some fact about language to you.

QUIZZES

Complete the following sentences by choosing the appropriate word or words. Note your answers on a separate sheet of paper.

1. Ouch, this water is (cold) (hot).
2. Congratulations, Mr. Johnson, your wife just had a (baby) (tooth pulled).
3. I am so exhausted that I almost fell (in love) (asleep).
4. Mary is not only intelligent but also (beautiful) (a dog).
5. Mr. Doaks does not need to go to the barber now that he is (bald) (wearing lifts in his shoes).
6. Do not trust Thelma because she never tells (a lie) (the truth).
7. Jim may be a good quarterback, but Donny is (worse) (better).
8. His doctor warned him to stop smoking (hams) (cigarettes).
9. Be careful or you will (fall) (win the raffle).
10. Your high grades in English are the result of your thorough and devoted study of (dangling modifiers) (sex).

Check your answers against those given at the bottom of this page. You should have answered all ten correctly, but a score of eight is passing. To be certain you understand these exercises, do five more. The directions are the same.

1. The weather today is certainly (beautiful) (lousy).

2. Miss Rogers, I must tell you that (I have never seen you looking lovelier) (your slip is showing).

3. I know George is good, but Chris is an even better (swimmer) (shortstop).

4. I have never read a more entertaining (article) (book).

5. Helen ate a breakfast consisting of (orange juice, bacon and eggs, home fries, flapjacks, rolls and coffee) (black coffee and melba toast).

These five are somewhat more difficult than the others, so take your time. When you are finished, check your answers against those on page 24 (at the top when page is turned).

Obviously there is a difference between the first ten sentences and the last five. The first ten sentences contained clue words which enabled you to determine logically which of the possible answers best fit the meaning of the rest of the sentence. In other words, you were able to infer the correct answer from its context. In the last five sentences the context offered no clues, and thus the questions were unanswerable.

The *context* of a word or phrase is simply the other words and phrases with which it is grouped. Often, though not always, the context of a word or phrase gives the meaning of that word or phrase. Some words may stand alone without a context, such as "hello" or "help." However, most of the time words are used as part of a context, or sequence of words:

Sinking rapidly in quicksand while the boa constrictor coiled ever more tightly around his throat, Herman shouted, "hello!"

When answering the telephone one should, in the most pleasant, musical tone of voice possible, carefully pronounce the word "help."

Answers: 1. hot 2. baby 3. asleep 4. beautiful 5. bald 6. the truth 7. better 8. cigarettes 9. tall 10. dangling modifiers.

It is not necessary for you to think those last two examples were funny. If you understand that they were supposed to be funny, you get the point we are trying to make.

Look back at the first quiz in this section. In sentence (1) the context for the word "hot" is the rest of the sentence: "Ouch, this water is . . . ." The clue word in the context which enabled you to answer correctly is "Ouch." To change the proper answer from "hot" to "cold," all you would need to do is change the clue word from "Ouch" to "Brrr." Sometimes the smallest alteration in the context will change the meaning of the entire statement.

To be certain you understand these concepts, take some time out now to complete the following exercises.

EXERCISES

1. *Take a sheet of paper. For sentences 2 through 10 of the first quiz (page 21) write down the clue word or words which specify the meaning of the sentence and indicate the correct answer. (Please do all quizzes and exercises on separate sheets of paper rather than marking up this book.) The answers are on page 24 (bottom group).*

2. *Add clue words to the five sentences in the second quiz, on page 22, so that one of the possible answers is clearly indicated as correct. This is more challenging if you change the context only by adding words to those already used. You may add as many words as necessary, but the fewer words used, the higher your score.*

There are innumerable ways in which Exercise 2 could have been completed. The greatest skill, however, lies in using the fewest clue words possible. Study these samples:

1. *Ugh*, the weather today is certainly (lousy).
2. Miss Rogers, I must *unfortunately* tell you that (your slip is showing).
3. I know George is good, but Chris is an even better *backstroke* (swimmer).
4. I've never read a more entertaining *magazine* (article).
5. Helen ate a *light* breakfast consisting of (black coffee and melba toast).

FOLLOW-UP

Create a clue word exercise modeled on the quiz on page 21. The trick is to make certain that you have not included any clue words in the sentence which will allow only one of the two possible answers to make sense in the context. Exchange your quiz for that of another student and test one another.

Answers: 2. congratulations 3. exhausted 4. not only; also 5. not 6. not; never 7. good 8. doctor 9. careful 10. high.

Answers: The quiz is a trick. None of the five questions can be answered.

Concepts of Language

We have seen that words are used in a context, and that the context of a word is the other words with which it is grouped. The smallest change in the context can change the meaning of the word, or force a change of the word itself, or even render the whole statement meaningless and ridiculous.

Words appear in two principal contexts: the sentence and the paragraph. The word and its context depend on one another to communicate meaning. If they fit together logically, then they make sense and they communicate a meaning clearly. The function of language is the communication of ideas.

Stop a minute and read that last sentence again. *The function of language is the communication of ideas.* The idea exists first, as a thought in your mind. The problem is to communicate that idea clearly to someone else so that your thought will appear in his mind exactly as it does in your own. To solve the problem, you translate the idea from a thought into a word and speak that word or write it. Someone else hears your word, or reads it, and he translates it back into a thought. Now *your* idea is in *his* mind, *exactly as you thought it.*

Let us assume, for the sake of argument, that man could think before he could speak, and speak before he could write. It may not be true (no one is certain), but it is a useful premise for understanding the function of language. Imagine the difficulty of communicating ideas without words. When caveman Oog wanted to discuss his horse with his neighbor, Zud, he had to bring the horse with him and point to it to make Zud understand. Since he never knew when the horse was going to come up in the conversation, Oog got in the habit of dragging the nag along whenever he visited Zud. It began to be very inconvenient.

Finally the two of them agreed that when one of them made the sound "horse" with his mouth, the other would picture the horse in his mind. The oral sound was substituted for the physical thing, the horse itself. The sound was used to stand for, or symbolize, the horse. When Oog thought of a horse, he spoke the sound they had agreed on and Zud thought of a horse too.

A few centuries later man began to realize it was going to be necessary to communicate ideas over greater distances than he could shout. An ancient Phoenician named Oog wanted to discuss his horse with his neighbor, Zud, but did not want to take the trouble of going all the way over to Zud's tent to talk to him. Oog reasoned that, if he could use a sound to symbolize a horse, he could use a written mark or sign to symbolize the sound.

The sound "horse" is actually a combination of four different sounds: "heh," "oh," "ar" and "ess." Oog and Zud agreed that the written sign *h* would symbolize the sound "heh." Then they agreed to let *o* symbolize "oh" and *r* stand for "ar," but they had a fight over "ess." Oog insisted that *s* should symbolize "ess," but Zud had his heart set on *s* as a symbol for "zzz." They compromised by adding an *e* which, though it did not symbolize a sound of its own, softened the sound of the *s* into "ess."

They noticed that they could rearrange these five symbols to represent many different oral sounds. Oog mentioned "shore." Then Zud contributed "rose" and "hose." When they invented the spelling of *horse,* they had agreed that an *s* would be pronounced "ess" when it was followed by a final, silent *e.* But Zud wanted the *s* to be pronounced "zzz" in all the words he invented, so they compromised again and wrote the First Law of Spelling: "An *s* which is followed by a final, silent *e* will always represent the sound 'ess,' except a lot of times when it will represent the sound 'zzz.'"

Then, since they were off to such an excellent start, Oog and Zud sat down and wrote the first grammar text, excerpts of which are here reproduced from the original manuscript.

1. A spoken word is a sound or sequence of sounds which communicate an idea to the mind of another person.

2. Letters of the alphabet are written symbols which stand for oral sounds.

3. In written language, letters are arranged in groups to symbolize a complete oral sound or word.

4. Therefore, written words also communicate ideas to the mind of the reader.

5. It is important in speaking and writing to communicate your ideas as accurately and precisely as possible.

6. Some words have very general, imprecise meanings; other words have explicit, specific meanings.

7. In order to communicate your ideas precisely, you should express them with precise words rather than general words.

8. The word *horse* is a general word, because it may communicate any one of a large number of ideas to the mind of someone else. When you hear the word *horse,* you may think of a thoroughbred or a pinto or a quarter horse; a palomino, a roan, a stallion, a mare; or a trotter, a Clydesdale, a gelding, a filly, a sorrel, a Percheron, a nag . . . .

9. Each word on this list is preferable to the word *horse,* because each is a precise word, one which communicates a specific meaning. The general word *horse* communicates all these meanings and many others as well.

10. We may conclude that, because words communicate ideas, precise words communicate ideas precisely. The larger your vocabulary, the less risk that you will be misunderstood.

11. Since most poor vocabularies consist overwhelmingly of general words, it is advisable to increase your vocabulary until it contains many precise words.

12. The basic words of a language are nouns and verbs.

13. Adjectives and adverbs are modifying words. They are used to modify or limit the meaning of nouns and verbs.

14. Because they limit the meaning of nouns and verbs, modifying words make the nouns and verbs more precise.

15. Adjectives limit the meaning of nouns and pronouns. Adverbs limit the meaning of verbs, adjectives and other adverbs.

16. To limit the meaning of the general noun *horse,* we could use

the adjective *spotted*. The words *spotted horse* communicate a much more specific idea than the general noun alone.

17. However, there is a precise noun which communicates the same meaning as *spotted horse:* the noun is *pinto.* Using the precise word is preferable to using the general word and a modifier.

18. *Run* is a general verb. You could use the adverb *slowly* to limit its meaning, but there are a number of precise verbs which communicate even more specific meanings than *run slowly.* For example: *jog, trot* or *lope.*

19. *Red* is a general adjective. You could use the adverb *dark* to limit its meaning, but there are a number of precise adjectives which communicate even more specific meanings than *dark red.* For example: *crimson, maroon* or *ruby.*

20. To be certain you have understood these ideas, and as a test of your own vocabulary development, do the following exercise. Take a stylus and a clean piece of parchment and . . . .

Here, unfortunately, the fragment of the ancient manuscript breaks off, forcing us to invent our own exercise. Take a pencil and a clean piece of paper and follow the directions.

EXERCISE

Each of the following pairs of words contains a general word and a modifier. For each one write as many single precise words as you can think of which communicate the same idea as the two words in the exercise.

1. walk slowly	10. terribly small
2. small building	11. intelligent man
3. very surprised	12. most unfortunate
4. rather silly	13. quite drunk
5. speak haltingly	14. extremely pretty
6. run fast	15. deliberate falsehood
7. extremely large	16. very talkative
8. bad defeat	17. dead body
9. walk drunkenly	18. speak loudly

19. poor man
20. terribly ugly
21. large ship
22. quite angry
23. very tired
24. close associate
25. great unhappiness
26. wicked man
27. extremely proud
28. evil spirit
29. terribly strong
30. very happy
31. great devotion
32. close together
33. extremely believable
34. all gone
35. quite immature
36. highest point
37. crazy man
38. quite uncivilized
39. many people
40. laugh softly
41. very old
42. somewhat late
43. very often
44. small town
45. extremely tall

Punctuation

Man, you will recall, could speak before he could write. In speech he used oral sounds to symbolize ideas. When he began to write, he had to create a group of graphic symbols called letters which represented the oral sounds. But man soon found that his alphabet of 26 letters was not enough. These letters could symbolize sounds, but sounds are only one of the three principle parts of oral speech. The other two are *inflections* and *pauses*. It was necessary to invent written symbols which could be substituted for voice inflections and pauses. These symbols are the marks of punctuation.

There are ten major marks of punctuation. You are completely familiar with most of them, but you may be unsure of one or two, so review them briefly.

.	the period	:	the colon
,	the comma	—	the dash
?	the question mark	...	the ellipsis
!	the exclamation point	"	the quotation mark
;	the semicolon	()	parentheses

Of these ten, all but the quotation marks and, occasionally, the parentheses, are used to substitute in written language for an oral pause. Four of these marks are also used to indicate voice inflection: these are the question mark, the exclamation point, the ellipsis and the dash.

We are going to discuss these ideas in more detail and deal with the most essential rules for punctuating. Before doing so, however, we ask you to consider the following:

1. Punctuation marks are written substitutes for oral pauses and voice inflections.

2. Many people have difficulty knowing when and how to punctuate their writing properly.

3. Nobody has any difficulty knowing when and how long to pause while he is speaking. When you are speaking, your oral pauses occur naturally, without thinking, from habit.

4. Most people are able to carry this natural skill over to reading aloud. When you read a written passage aloud, the odds are excellent that you will automatically pause in the right places, for the right length of time, *even if the punctuation marks do not appear in the passage.*

5. This means that before we even begin to discuss memorize and apply the rules of punctuation you should be able to punctuate simply by reading a passage aloud noting your natural pauses carefully and inserting the appropriate marks at the points where you paused.

6. Stop To prove this theory to yourself reread paragraph 5 Read it aloud in a normal tone of voice without being self-conscious There is a period properly placed at the end of the sentence but several commas are missing from the interior Do you hear yourself pausing automatically at certain points It will probably be necessary to read the sentence more than once When you have completed the exercise check your punctuation against the answer at the bottom of this page

7. test yourself again by reading paragraph 6 aloud in a normal tone of voice this time you must insert not only commas but also the missing periods question marks and exclamation points if any when you are finished check the answers at the bottom of this page

Answers: 6. Stop! To prove this theory to yourself, reread paragraph 5. Read it aloud(,) in a normal tone of voice(.) without being self-conscious. There is a period properly placed at the end of the sentence, but several commas are missing from the interior. Do you hear yourself pausing automatically at certain points? It will probably be necessary to read the sentence more than once. When you have completed the exercise, check your punctuation against the answer at the bottom of this page. (A period following ",Stop" is also acceptable.)

Answers: 5. This means that, before we even begin to discuss, memorize(,) and apply the rules of punctuation, you should be able to punctuate simply by reading a passage aloud, noting your natural pauses carefully, and inserting the appropriate marks at the points where you paused. (*Note:* the comma appearing in parentheses is optional.)

8. did you notice that while paragraph 6 helped you by using additional space and capital letters to indicate the ends and beginnings of sentences paragraph 7 provides no such clues read paragraph 7 aloud several times listening carefully for your pauses this time each pause will indicate either a comma or a period the answer is at the bottom of this page

9. Paragraph 8, the last of the exercises in this sequence, requires the insertion of three commas, three periods, and one question mark. The corrected copy is at the bottom of this page.

Thus far we have concentrated on the first four marks of punctuation listed on page 30. Three, the period, the question mark and the exclamation point, are the only marks ever used to end complete sentences. The fourth, the comma, is by far the most common and versatile mark of punctuation in the English language. Unlike the other three, the comma occurs only in the interior of a sentence, never at its end.

All four are written substitutes for pauses in speech. In speaking a language, it is common to pause longer at the end of a sentence than in the middle of one. Therefore, in reading written passages aloud, it is probable that you paused longer after each sentence ended than you did when a comma was inserted at any point during the sentence. The difference in the length of the pause could probably be measured only in fractions of a second, but it is easily perceptible to the human ear.

Few people have any difficulty determining whether a sentence should be ended by a period, a question mark or an exclamation point, because few people have a problem telling the difference between a statement, a question and an exclamation. Notice, however, that each punctuation mark not only substitutes for an oral pause, but also indicates a voice inflection. Voices may

comma or a period. The answer is at the bottom of this page.
listening carefully for your pauses. This time each pause will indicate either a
paragraph 7 provides no such clues? Read paragraph 7 aloud several times,
tional space and capital letters to indicate the ends and beginnings of sentences,
Answers: 8. Did you notice that, while paragraph 6 helped you by using addi-

ished(.) check the answers at the bottom of this page.
periods, question marks(.) and exclamation points(.) if any. When you are fin-
of voice. This time you must insert(.) not only commas(.) but also the missing
Answers: 7. Test yourself again by reading paragraph 6 aloud in a normal tone

be inflected in two basic ways: pitch and tone. For our purposes, the term *pitch* will mean the degree of loudness or quietness with which a word is spoken. The term *tone* will mean the degree of softness or harshness with which a word is spoken.

When you are talking, it is easy to speak loudly or quietly, softly or harshly. But how do you communicate pitch or tone when you are writing? Part of the answer lies in the use of the appropriate punctuation. Study the following examples:

1.   ugly?
     Selma
   Is

The question mark, of course, ends a sentence which requests information. It also suggests, but does not require, a rising pitch of voice, as indicated here.

2.
Is *Selma* UGLY!

The exclamation point indicates strong feeling, either loudness or harshness, or both. (Notice that the words of the two sentences are the same. Only the punctuation mark changes the meaning of this sentence.)

3. Selma is ugly.

The period indicates a simple statement of fact. Sorry, Selma.

Purposes of Punctuation

Study these statements carefully.

1. The best way to learn punctuation is not to memorize a list of rules and attempt to apply them in quizzes and review exercises. It is much more effective to study what a mark of punctuation actually does in a sentence.

2. Although it may sometimes seem that the reason written language must be punctuated is to give you a bad time, the real purposes of punctuation are these:

   (a) To separate the thoughts contained in a passage into clearly identifiable units for the convenience of the reader.

   (b) To serve the writer. No less than words, marks of punctuation are tools a writer uses to express his ideas with as much clarity, emphasis and persuasiveness as possible.

With regard to purpose (a), all you need to do to understand how difficult it would be to read without the aid of punctuation is look back at the unpunctuated paragraphs given earlier. As another example, look at this paragraph:

remember that reading is not only a mental but also a physical process you read with your eyes your eyes must be able to distinguish units of words from one another just as your mind must be able to distinguish one thought from another in writing a unit of words is a thought if your eye cannot see separate units of words your mind cannot see or understand the writer's thoughts punctuation aids the eye not only in distinguishing one thought from another but also in understanding the relationship between separate thoughts

Note the difference between the preceding paragraph and the same passage punctuated:

Remember that reading is not only a mental but also a physical process. You read with your eyes. Your eyes must be able to distinguish units of words from one another, just as your mind must be able to distinguish one thought from another. In writing, a unit of words is a thought. If your eye cannot see separate units of words, your mind cannot see or understand the writer's thoughts. Punctuation aids the eye, not only in distinguishing one thought from another, but also in understanding the relationship between separate thoughts.

Make certain you understand the ideas expressed in this passage and that you see how the two paragraphs demonstrate the validity of these ideas.

The second purpose of punctuation is to serve the writer. At first glance that may seem obvious to you or, even more likely, it may strike you as a typical textbook cliché. In fact, however, it is neither obvious nor trite. The writer, especially the student writer, sometimes feels forced into becoming the tool of the punctuation, especially if the rules he must follow seem obscure or old fashioned.

It is easy to ridicule some punctuation rules as obscure or archaic. It is also unfair to penalize writers, especially beginning writers who have troubles enough, for failing to observe such rules. This is true so long as the "violation" in no way interferes with the clear communication of the idea. However, do not jump to the conclusion that all, most, or even many rules of punctuation fall into the categories of obscure, archaic or pedantic. Punctuation is the referee of written language. It preserves order. Like the referee you may hate it, but without it you have chaos.

For further discussion and exercises to help you improve your feeling for and use of punctuation, turn to Appendix A, which begins on page 239.

The White Space
and the Paragraph

Reconsider this paragraph, which appeared on page 34:

> Remember that reading is not only a mental but also a physical process. You read with your eyes. Your eyes must be able to distinguish units of words from one another, just as your mind must be able to distinguish one thought from another. If your eye cannot see separate units of words, your mind cannot see or understand the writer's thoughts. Punctuation aids the eye, not only in distinguishing one thought from another, but also in understanding the relationship between separate thoughts.

Look back at page 34 where the same paragraph appeared without punctuation or capitalization. Obviously it is considerably harder to distinguish the sentences from one another, and therefore more difficult to understand the ideas the writer is trying to communicate. But at least there are white spaces between the words so your eye can tell one word from another. Without those white spaces, it would be virtually impossible to read the paragraph:

> rememberthatreadingisnotonlyamentalbutalsoaphysicalprocess
> youreadwithyoureyesyoureyesmustbeabletodistinguishunitsof
> wordsfromoneanotherjustasyourmindmustbeabletodistinguishone
> thoughtfromanotherifyoureyecannotseeseparateunitsofwordsyour
> mindcannotseeorunderstandthewriter'sthoughtspunctuationaids
> theeyenotonlyindistinguishingonethoughtfromanotherbutalsoin
> understandingtherelationshipbetweenseparatethoughts

We may draw certain conclusions. One of the most important functions of punctuation is to separate the thoughts contained in a passage into clearly identifiable word-units, easily seen by the reader's eye. White spaces which separate words, sentences and paragraphs from each other are, if possible, even more important for this purpose.

White spaces are seldom discussed, probably because they are so obvious a part of written language that we take them for granted. There are almost no fixed rules to govern white space. Margins determine the amount of white space framing the written text on each page. In typing you hit the space bar twice after a period or other mark ending a sentence, but only once after individual words or internal punctuation. This indicates a longer pause between sentences and separates sentences more clearly for the reader's eye. White space also sets off paragraphs. Usually you indent the first line of a paragraph five white spaces to indicate the beginning of the paragraph. Usually, too, there is white space left at the end of the paragraph's last line.

Merely capitalizing the first word of a group and putting a period at the end does not make that word-group a complete sentence. The same is true of paragraphs. Setting off a group of sentences with white space may make the group *look* like a paragraph, but reading may make it clear that it is not. Before we say any more about paragraphs, check your ability to recognize them by reading each of the following sentence-groups and deciding whether it is or is not a paragraph.

1. Whenever I am near anybody who smokes, the wind always seems to blow the smoke in my face. This is especially true at baseball games. I enjoy football better than baseball, although football tickets are more expensive. Since I am usually broke, I watch the games on television. My friend Frank watches a lot of television because he is still in traction after his motorcycle accident.

2. My favorite season of the year is spring. The many small yet wonderful miracles conjured by Nature as she rouses herself from the death-sleep of winter have never failed to fascinate me. Still, winter is also an interesting season. I enjoy lots of winter sports, especially skiing and ice skating. Snow, too, can be beautiful, particularly when it is newly fallen and still glistening on the bare branches of the old elm in our front yard.

3. There are three things that really irritate me: crooked television repairmen, people who gossip, and bigots! My Aunt Jean has a

thing about men with moustaches, probably because she had a crush on Clark Gable when she was a kid. My history teacher was a Democrat, and he slanted all his lectures to make the Democrats look good and the Republicans look bad. Green is my favorite color, although I also like yellow and blue, but I cannot stand red. Every time it rains for more than two days, my ankle swells up where I broke it two years ago.

4. Gozorgenblatt Inc. manufactures the worst typewriters ever passed off on unsuspecting and hapless customers. Having had one foisted on me nine months ago, I consider myself in a position to know. Their guarantee is good for ninety days; on the ninety-first day the machine collapses. Oddly enough, the first keys to go are the ones used the least, the Z, the Q and the ½. In a short time the X and ? begin to stick. The tabulator never works, the space-bar jumps and the T and Y become obstinate. When the G and the ¢ are gone, do not bother to call a repairman. Just dig a hole in your yard and give the expensive monster a decent burial.

5. Anyone who does much driving in this state knows how badly many many of our principal highways are in need of repair. This is especially true of Route 78 in the vicinity of Burtonsville, where three fatal accidents occurred last year alone. Additional funds are also desperately needed by our schools and public institutions, where overcrowding and a lack of qualified staff have created intolerable conditions. Nobody likes to pay taxes. But the people of this state must realize that the only alternative to the proposed state income tax surcharge is the complete collapse of vital state services.

Only passages 4 and 5 are paragraphs. The first three are not, although they are set off by white spaces to look like paragraphs. Passage 3 should have given you the least trouble because not one of its five sentences bears the slightest relationship to any of the others. *The sentences in a paragraph should have meanings which relate to one another.* A bunch of sentences on unrelated subjects is no more a paragraph than a bunch of unrelated words is a sentence.

In the first two passages, the sentences have at least some relationship in subject matter, but a second requirement for a paragraph is missing. In passage 1 the writer bounces from one idea to another in a form of free association of words. Smoking reminds him of baseball which suggests football which reminds him of expensive tickets which brings up television which suggests his friend Frank. The sentences are almost as unrelated as those of passage 3. The writer has no central, important idea which he is trying to communicate. *To be a paragraph, a passage should attempt to communicate one central, important idea.*

A paragraph should also have a discoverable plan, a logical reason for the order in which its sentences are arranged. Passage 2 has neither a plan nor a central idea. The writer begins by praising spring for two sentences and then abruptly changes the subject completely and spends the last three sentences on the entirely separate topic of winter. Only passages 4 and 5 meet all three basic requirements of a paragraph.

Usually a paragraph contains what grammarians call a *topic sentence,* a sentence which communicates the central idea of the paragraph. For your convenience, the topic sentences of the three preceding paragraphs have been printed in italics. Note that the topic sentence may appear at the beginning, the end or the middle of the paragraph. Having a central idea is one of three basic requirements of a paragraph.

Study these statements carefully:

1. A paragraph contains a topic sentence which communicates the central idea of the paragraph.
2. The other sentences in a paragraph should be used either to explain or to support the central idea.
3. The topic sentence is usually placed at the beginning or the end of a paragraph because this is when the reader's attention is greatest.

In sample paragraph 4 the topic sentence is the first one. The writer's main idea is that Gozorgenblatt Inc. makes a bad typewriter. The second sentence establishes his authority to make this judgment: he has owned one of their machines. The rest of the paragraph is crowded with examples which support his main idea.

In paragraph 5 the writer chooses to give his supporting information first and place his topic sentence last. He plans his sentences in this order because he expects that his reader will not like the central idea of his paragraph. He feels that the reader will be more likely to agree that the roads need repair and the schools and public institutions need financial help. He can be positive that the reader agrees with the statement that no one likes to pay taxes. He hopes that, by getting the reader to agree with his supporting statements, he can influence him to agree with his unpopular main idea, the need for additional taxes.

Both paragraphs 4 and 5 communicate one central idea using sentences whose meanings are related and which are ordered according to a logical plan. These passages are, therefore, paragraphs. (For additional discussion of paragraphs see "How to Write an Abstract of an Article" in Section IV, pages 116–121.)

FOLLOW-UP

Working with another student as your partner, select some unedited paragraphs from your folder and his. The instructor will have copies made. Go over the paragraphs in each other's papers to determine if they are really paragraphs or not. Do they meet the three basic requirements? Discuss each other's paragraphs and rewrite where you agree it is necessary. Then go over both the first drafts and the rewrites with the instructor.

The Essay: A Succession of Main Ideas

We have established that a paragraph should communicate a central idea using sentences whose meanings are related and which are ordered according to a logical plan. By the same token, an essay should communicate a *central argument,* or *thesis,* using paragraphs whose main ideas are related and which are ordered according to a logical plan.

The total essay presents a central argument. The paragraphs in the essay should be used to *express, explain* or *support* the central argument. As in an individual paragraph, so in an essay the central argument is expressed at the beginning, or the end, or both, because this is when the reader's attention is at its highest.

A paragraph expresses a main idea. An essay is a succession of paragraphs, and therefore a succession of main ideas, intended to explain or support the essay's central argument. The essay on page 42 is designed to demonstrate the validity of these points. (The following footnote summarizes the Antigone myth.*)

* The Antigone myth on which Sophocles' tragedy is based tells how, after Antigone's father, Oedipus, tore out his eyes and was driven from his kingdom of Thebes, her brothers agreed to share his throne, each ruling in alternate years. When the elder, Eteocles, refused to give up the crown, his younger brother, Polynices, raised an army and declared war on Thebes. When Eteocles and Polynices killed each other in hand-to-hand combat, their uncle, Creon, succeeded to the throne and drove off the invaders. To test his power, Creon decreed that Eteocles be buried as a hero, but that Polynices be declared a traitor and left, unburied, to rot. Since the Greeks believed that the soul of a dead man could not enter heaven until his body had been buried, and believed, too, that failure to bury the dead was an insult to Zeus, their chief god, all Thebes was outraged at Creon's decree. But only Antigone dared to disobey her uncle and bury her brother in accordance with Zeus' law. Furious, Creon ordered her death. In defiance Creon's son, Haimon, who had loved Antigone, first tried to kill the king and then took his own life. Haimon's suicide brings Creon to his senses and leaves him broken with grief and remorse. [All direct quotations are taken from *The Oedipus Cycle,* Dudley Fitts and Robert Fitzgerald, trans. New York: Harcourt Brace Jovanovich, Inc., 1949.]

Creon: The Tragic Protagonist
of Sophocles' Antigone

[1] Sophocles' version of the Antigone myth is essentially a study of a man thrust suddenly into a position of authority utterly beyond his capabilities, who is driven to outrageous extremes of blasphemy and injustice by a pride born of his deep, and (as the action of the play demonstrates) justified sense of insecurity. Creon's edict that Polynices must rot unburied is not only profane but irrational, its sole purpose being to test the power of his office by determining whether a law, no matter how odious, will be obeyed simply because the king has decreed it.

[2] Creon's insecurity is evident. Though he announces to the chorus his awareness "that no Ruler can expect complete loyalty from his subjects until he has been tested in office," his immediate demand for unquestioning obedience betrays no such awareness, and his violent reaction to the news of Polynices' burial is nothing short of paranoic:

> No, from the very beginning
> There have been those who have whispered together,
> Stiff-necked anarchists, putting their heads together,
> Scheming against me in alleys.

[3] It is not only in his kingship, but in his position as head of his family, and in his very manhood, that Creon feels threatened. First one, then both of his nieces defy him. His son attempts to murder him. His wife dies with a curse for him. When he cries, "Show me the man who keeps his house in hand; he's fit for public authority," the irony requires no comment. He is deeply disturbed at being challenged by a girl. "Who is the man here, she or I, if this crime goes unpunished?" To his son he proclaims, ". . . no woman shall seduce us. If we must lose, let's lose to a man at least! Is a woman stronger than we?" It is possible that the description of marriage he gives to Haimon may be based on personal experience: "Your pleasure with her would soon grow cold, Haimon, and then you'd have a hellcat in bed and elsewhere."

Analysis of Paragraph Structure in Sample Essay

[1] The opening sentence not only serves as the paragraph's topic sentence but also introduces the main ideas of the first five paragraphs by citing all of Creon's important characteristics: inability to rule, blasphemy, injustice, pride and insecurity. Note that the writer dives right into his subject without wasting time on windy introductions. Instead of telling the reader what he is going to write about, he immediately begins to write about it. The second sentence moves the paragraph from a *general* discussion of Creon to the *specific* act which begins his downfall, his decree that Polynices be left unburied. Here is first mentioned the irrationality of this decree, an idea picked up again in paragraph 4.

[2] The brief opening sentence establishes the main idea. The second sentence *supports* the main idea by citing Creon's speeches and actions in the play. The main idea, Creon's insecurity, is further developed from its first mention in paragraph 1 as a cause of his inability to rule. The second quotation shows Creon's fear of a conspiracy against him, an idea picked up in paragraph 4.

[3] The opening, topic sentence establishes the *transition,* or change of main ideas, from paragraph 2 to paragraph 3. It refers back to Creon's doubts of his kingship (the main idea of paragraph 2) and forward to his uncertainty as a father and a man. Sentences 2 through 5 illustrate his weakness as head of a household, and the rest of the paragraph, his fears as a man. Paragraph 3 continues to develop the essay's themes of insecurity and inability to rule. Notice that the writer uses direct quotations to support his main ideas, and that he is careful never to "pad" his quotations, but limits them to what is necessary to illustrate his points.

[4] Even after Antigone's capture, Creon persists in his conviction of a conspiracy, ordering Ismene's arrest, accusing the sisters of "aiming at my throne," charging Teiresias with accepting a bribe, all without a shred of hard evidence to substantiate his assumptions. Because the actual motive for his edict is irrational, he cannot defend his action rationally. His argument to Antigone that Polynices, as a traitor, is undeserving of funeral honors collapses into rage before her calm self-assurance, and thereafter he can only rant against "anarchy." To Haimon he reveals his true position:

> Whoever is chosen to govern should be obeyed—
> Must be obeyed, in all things, great and small,
> Just and unjust!

[5] No one must question the wisdom of the king. Not the entire city for "The State is the King!" Not the gods, themselves, though the eagles of Zeus should carry the corpse "stinking bit by bit to heaven. . . ." Because, in his mind, Creon has risked the entire power of his throne on the validity of his decree, he does not dare to yield until it is too late.

[6] It is too simple to say that Creon's fall is the result of his pride. Antigone is no less haughty than he, no less contemptuous, no less obstinate, but her pride is the result of strength, his of weakness, and Sophocles makes it clear that in championing the higher law of the gods she is right; in defying them, Creon is wrong. This is partially why his suffering strikes us as tragic as her self-willed death does not.

[7] The play belongs to Creon. He is the tragic protagonist by Aristotle's definition, a man highly renowned and rich, yet not eminently good or just, who suffers a downfall and whom Fate forces to a realization of his crimes. Standing with the corpse of his son in his arms, Creon cries, "I alone am guilty. I know it and I say it."

> Lead me away. I have been rash and foolish.
> I have killed my son and my wife.

[4] Unlike the first three, paragraph 4 places its supportive material first and builds to the main idea, expressed in the final quotation, that, for Creon, might makes right and power is its own justification even when it decrees injustice. The ideas of Creon's paranoia and irrationality are picked up from earlier paragraphs to emphasize the depth to which the king has sunk. Notice that a direct quotation may be used as a topic sentence to express a main idea.

[5] The topic sentence is again placed at the end of the paragraph. The opening sentence repeats and clarifies the main idea of paragraph 4, which is then further clarified in the next two sentences. The last sentence, by spelling out Creon's essential dilemma, not only climaxes the paragraph but also sums up the main ideas of the entire essay to this point.

[6] As he moves to his conclusion, the writer has two more points to make: first, that it is not merely Creon's human pride but his blasphemous defiance of the gods that causes his fall. Second, that his capacity to suffer for his crimes is what makes him tragic. The opening sentence of paragraph 6 is the topic sentence, and the rest of the paragraph expands and clarifies the writer's first point. The last sentence provides a transition to the second point, the main idea of the final paragraph.

[7] It is often wise in the final paragraph of an essay to place the topic sentence last in order to leave the reader with your concluding main idea fresh and clear in his mind. That is the tactic followed by this writer (p. 46). He opens with Aristotle's definition of the tragic protagonist, having already shown that Creon fits the definition in all ways but the last. He then quotes the play to demonstrate that Creon, too, has been forced by fate to a realization of his crimes. He ends by expressing his final main idea, the idea toward which his whole essay has been moving.

> I look for comfort; my comfort lies here dead.
> Whatever my hands have touched has come to nothing.
> Fate has brought all my pride to a thought of dust.

It is in the agony of his remorse that Sophocles raises Creon above the pettiness of his crimes and fears to a measure of greatness. What makes Creon worthy of tragedy is that, corrupted by pride as he is, he has not lost his capacity to suffer.

SUMMARY

The writer's aim was to present an analysis of the character of Creon as the tragic protagonist of Sophocles' *Antigone*. He used his first paragraph to outline the main qualities of Creon as a character and pinpoint the fatal decree which signaled his downfall. Paragraphs 2 and 3 develop Creon's insecurity as king, head of his family, even as a man. Paragraphs 4 and 5 show how that insecurity has destroyed his ability to rule and driven him to paranoiac fears of conspiracy and the irrational conviction that his power position justifies any edict he decrees, even if it defies the laws of the gods. Not insecurity, not pride alone, but this blasphemous defiance is what brings Creon to his knees, as the sixth paragraph demonstrates by comparing Creon's pride with that of his niece, Antigone. Yet, as the writer concludes in paragraph 7, Creon is tragic because he is able to realize his guilt and to suffer for it.

FOLLOW-UP

Examine the draft of one of your own papers (or that of another student if assigned to you by the instructor). Attempt a paragraph-by-paragraph analysis similar to the one shown here. If the essay seems difficult to analyze, submit it to the following checklist:

1. Does each paragraph attempt to present a main idea?

2. Does each paragraph contain a topic sentence?

3. Do the other sentences in the paragraph clarify or support the main idea?

4. Could any sentence be removed without changing or weakening the main idea of the paragraph?

5. Is the main argument of the essay clear?

6. Could any paragraph be removed without changing or weakening the main argument of the essay?

7. Is the transition of main ideas from one paragraph to the next unclear at any point?

8. Can you write a summary of the entire essay similar to the summary of "Creon: The Tragic Protagonist of Sophocles' *Antigone*"?

If the answer to any of these questions is no, discuss the paper with your instructor. Be certain that the fault lies with the essay and not with your ability to analyze it. Then rewrite the essay to conform with the conditions which a well-organized paper should meet.

NOTE

Some students write entire papers without breaking their ideas down into paragraphs at all. If you or your partner has done this, your editing problem will be different. Instead of trying to decide whether the paragraphs in the paper meet the three basic requirements outlined on page 39, you will have to break down the huge chunk of material into workable paragraphs.

When you are faced with such a problem, try following this procedure. We know that a well-constructed essay presents a central argument through a succession of main ideas which clarify or support the argument. You should first read through the problem essay a few times to get a feeling for the main ideas the writer is trying to express.

When you have grasped his main ideas, identify the specific sentences in which they are expressed. These are the topic sentences around which the separate paragraphs can be built.

See which other sentences are related in meaning to these topic sentences. To be related, a sentence should *clarify, expand, illustrate* or *support* the main ideas. Group these sentences into paragraphs, each anchored to a topic sentence.

The last step is to reread the essay, making certain that the paragraphs follow each other logically and smoothly, and lead the reader to a full understanding of the central argument. If the succession of main ideas is not logical, check the order in which they have been presented. Do they build on each other in a rational, plausible design, or is some reorganization needed?

By the same token, if the essay does not seem smooth, be sure you have constructed transitions, or verbal bridges, between your main ideas. Eliminate sentences whose meanings are unrelated to their context. You should wind up with a clear, well-organized paper.

Words and Meaning

In considering words and meaning we will be guided by two basic principles:

1. If a word is to communicate a meaning clearly, there must be complete agreement between the reader and the writer on what the word means.
2. The most important goal of a writer is to control his reader's responses.

The first principle is simple common sense. If your reader does not understand the meanings of your words, you will be unable to communicate your ideas to him. Imagine the difficulty of communicating with someone who cannot speak or read English.

The second principle is crucial. The good writer selects and uses words which will produce in his reader the specific effect or response he desires. The four basic reader-responses are:

1. Conviction that the writer knows what he is talking about. (This is the response you aim for in every paper and examination you write for your instructors.)
2. Clear understanding of the writer's ideas.
3. Conviction that the writer's ideas are correct.
4. Misunderstanding of the writer's ideas.

The first of these is very important to you as a student since almost all the writing you do in school is assigned by instructors for the purpose of discovering whether you understand their subject matter. The second response is achieved through clarity and precision, the selection of words whose meanings are specific and comprehensible to the reader. Writing whose main purpose is to explain ideas clearly is often called *exposition* or expository writing.

The third response is more difficult to achieve. It requires that the reader not only understand your ideas, but also accept them as true. Writing whose main purpose is to convince the reader to believe an idea or to take an action is called *argumentation*.

The fourth response involves tricking the reader into believing you have said something you actually have not said at all. This writing is of two basic types:

a. *deception:* leading the reader to believe you have said one thing when, in fact, you have said something entirely different.

b. *equivocation:* leading the reader to believe you have said something when, in fact, you have said nothing at all.

As a student you have probably never been assigned to do this kind of writing, although you may have developed some skill in equivocation while attempting to bluff your way through essay examinations. A careful study of deceptive writing provides a useful experience in the power of words to mislead as well as clarify, to swindle while they convince.

Deception

Suppose you wanted to lose some weight and were planning to buy one of the "reducing belts" now on the market. Based on their advertising claims, which of these products would you purchase?

Acme Reducer Belt: We guarantee that our product will reduce your waist by up to three inches in the first two weeks of use or double your money back.

Zenith Reducer Belt: We guarantee that our product will reduce your waist by at least one inch in the first month of use or your money back.

If you read their claims carefully, you bought the Zenith. Note that the key words in the Acme advertisement, the words intended to catch your eye, are "three inches," "two weeks" and "double." If you read carelessly, you may have concluded that Acme promised to perform three times as effectively as Zenith in half the time or twice the refund.

The real key words in these advertisements are "up to" and "at least." Acme guarantees a loss of "up to three inches," that is, a loss of zero to three inches. If their belt does not work at all, they have fulfilled their guarantee. By contrast, Zenith promises "at least one inch" of flab will disappear. *Some* performance has been guaranteed.

Consider the claims made for Painos, a headache remedy:

Painos is like a doctor's prescription, that is, a combination of ingredients.

It is true that a doctor's prescription is a combination of ingredients. So is a salad. The advertisement is carefully worded so as to claim no greater similarity between the product and a doctor's prescription than that both are "a combination of ingredients." But the *implication* of the comparison is that Painos is as effective a painkiller as drugs available only by prescription.

The same product also claims the following:

Painos contains more of the one pain reliever doctors recommend most than the other leading extra-strength tablet.

Have you wondered why the writer uses so many words ("the one pain reliever doctors recommend most") when all he had to do was name the ingredient? The answer is that the ingredient recommended most by doctors is aspirin. Pure aspirin is one of Painos' chief competitors.

It is true that Painos has more aspirin than "the other leading extra-strength tablet." The reason is that the other tablet contains, in addition to aspirin, two drugs which Painos doesn't have at all. It is also true that Painos is "a combination of ingredients," aspirin and caffeine. You could get the same effect by dropping a couple of aspirin in a cup of coffee.

Consider the claims made by No-cav, a sugarless chewing gum:

> Four out of five dentists surveyed recommend sugarless gum for their patients who chew gum.

At first glance it may look as though No-cav conducted a large survey of dentists, four-fifths of whom recommend their gum. The implication is that the dental profession overwhelmingly approves of chewing No-cav. But read the copy closely. No-cav "surveyed" only five dentists, otherwise the ad would read "four out of *every* five dentists surveyed." Of these five, four agreed that they "recommend sugarless gum for their patients who chew gum." This means, not that sugarless gum is good for your teeth, but that if a patient *insists* on chewing gum it is less destructive to chew gum which is sugarless. Note that these dentists do not specify the No-cav brand or recommend No-cav over other brands. The fifth dentist has been paid by No-cav *not* to recommend sugarless gum. The reason? If all five agreed, it would be obvious that only five had been surveyed.

You should be beginning to understand how words can be used to appear to have one meaning while actually meaning something entirely different. You should also see the need for careful, close reading, especially of advertising claims, political speeches, leases, contracts: of any paper whose author has a personal interest in convincing you of his ideas. As further reinforcement of this, study the following.

The chances are that at some time in your life you will have the experience of buying a used car. As a service, the authors present the five most common claims made by salesmen and a translation of their real meaning:

1. I was holding this dandy little model for an old friend, but I'll give you first crack at it. (*Translation:* I had a mark lined up but I'll unload this heap on the first sucker who walks in.)

2. This beauty is in such condition that I'll let you drive it right off the lot today as is for only $500. (*Translation:* I won't even guarantee this jalopy through inspection.)

3. I've never seen an engine in the kind of shape this one is in. (*Translation:* The motor needs a complete overhaul.)

4. I'll guarantee those tires unconditionally for the lifetime of the car. (*Translation:* The tires should last another month.)

5. My men have worked on this fine automobile until even its former owner wouldn't recognize it. (*Translation:* The car is hot.)

Equivocation

Equivocation is to appear to be saying something meaningful and profound while actually saying nothing at all. It is a favorite device of politicians and school administrators. The two tricks to remember are: (1) use the most impressive and formidable vocabulary possible and (2) be as wordy as you can. The average reader is easily cowed by words he cannot understand and tortured sentence constructions he cannot follow. The skilled equivocator knows that if his reader cannot figure out what he is saying he will assume it is because of his own ignorance. Study these excerpts from a recent interview with one of our nation's most important political leaders:

Q. Senator, are you in favor of lower taxes?

A. I have never opposed any reduction of taxes which would not leave the government lacking the basic revenues essential to underwrite the vital services which we must provide for the relief and comfort of the downtrodden, overburdened taxpayer.

Q. Senator, do you believe government military spending should be reduced?

A. I stand squarely on my well-known position that military spending should not under any circumstances exceed the maximum fiscal needs of the military.

Q. Sir, how do you feel about the racial issue?

A. Without fear of contradiction, I may say that the racial issue is one of the most significant and important issues facing our great nation today. There can be no question that my position on this issue is well known and, while it may have become controversial in certain quarters, I believe I can say without the least trace of equivocation that I, for one, have nothing to hide.

Q. Senator, what is your opinion of equivocation?

A. Well, on the one hand . . . .

FOLLOW-UP

1. *In Section I, while writing the exercise on propaganda, you practiced the technique of misleading the reader by the deliberate suppression of fact. In this section we have studied methods of misleading the reader by selecting words which seem to imply a meaning different from their literal one. Take your propaganda exercise from your folder and rewrite it as an example of deception. That is, instead of suppressing the unpleasant details about the individual you described, look for words which will express his faults while appearing to imply that they are virtues.*

2. *Carefully study the most recent speeches and statements of prominent political and other public figures. If the students at your school are holding an election, include those running for office in your survey. Also read commercial advertisements, newspaper editorials, announcements and pronouncements by your school administration. Collect the deceptions, equivocations and plain old double-talk you uncover.*

3. *Select a commercial advertisement or political speech which seems to you especially misleading, and write an analysis of the writer's use of deception and equivocation.*

4. *Reread the segment on the used-car salesman. Select some other kind of person who might use deception and create a group of typical claims or promises made by such an individual together with translations of his "real" meanings. Possible examples: (a) a teacher in the first class session explaining the requirements of the course, (b) an academic counselor describing your program, (c) a spokesman for the registrar's office explaining what improvements are planned for the next registration period, (d) a school administration official justifying the regulations imposed on the student body.*

Connotation

In the segment on concepts (pages 27–28) we dealt with the literal meaning of words, distinguishing between general words and words with more specific meanings, and arguing for precision of expression by expanding your vocabulary of precise words. In the segment just completed, we discussed deception and equivocation and tried to show how a close reading of the *literal* meanings of the words enables you to detect double-talk. Thus far we have been concerned only with a word's *denotation;* that is, its literal, explicit, dictionary definition.

In addition to their denotations, many words have connotations. A connotation is the emotional response the word creates in the reader. In a sense, it is the word's emotional meaning.

Let us take a simple example. You know a girl who is thin. You tell her that she is "slender." She is pleased. You tell her that she is "willowy." She is flattered. You tell her she is "skinny." She will not speak to you for a month.

There is little difference in the literal meanings of these three words. Basically they all mean "thin." The difference lies in their connotations, in the emotional response they cause in the reader or listener. Slender and willowy are pleasant, flattering words, suggesting beauty and grace. Skinny is a harsh word suggesting unattractiveness and awkwardness. Note that slender does not literally mean beautiful or graceful; it *suggests* the idea of beauty and grace. Note that skinny does not literally mean ugly or awkward; it *suggests* the ideas of ugliness and awkwardness.

We may conclude that another way of describing connotation is to say that *connotation is the meaning suggested by a word* as opposed to its literal definition. It is often true that the suggested, emotional meaning of a word is more important than its denotation. A single word with a pleasant connotation can make a person's day. A single word with an ugly connotation can start a fistfight.

Some points to remember

We have said that the most important goal of a writer is to control his reader's responses. This means emotional responses as well as intellectual ones. When writing you should be aware of the connotations of the words you are using and the probable emotional reactions of the reader. Careful selection of connotative words will add emphasis to your ideas and give emotional impact to your communication. This is especially important in argumentative writing.

Study the following passages. Each describes the same event. Notice that the first writer selects words with as little connotative meaning as possible in an effort at straightforward, objective reporting; the second and third writers use emotionally explosive language to communicate their own strong feelings about the event and to attempt to get you to share those feelings.

a. The student group took possession of Wilson Hall at the south end of the campus before dawn and held it through most of the day. Their leaders asked for a meeting with President Dillard, but the president declined until they would agree to vacate the building and return to classes. By noon a large crowd of students hostile to the demonstrators had gathered before Wilson Hall. Angry shouts were exchanged and there were brief outbreaks of violence. Fearing, as he said later, that "a riot was imminent," President Dillard summoned the police at 3:30. After some scuffling, police entered the building and arrested seven of the student leaders.

b. A mob of radical, long-haired hippies seized Wilson Hall before dawn and occupied it through most of the day. The ringleaders demanded a confrontation with President Dillard. The president offered to meet with them if they would restore order to the campus and put an end to their disruption of the proper functions of the college. The radicals rejected these terms. By noon, groups of moderate students had assembled here and there on the lawns. From the security of their bastion, the agitators screamed down abuse and profanity. To prevent a riot, President Dillard asked local law enforcement officials to intervene. The building was liberated with little difficulty, and seven of the insurgents were taken into custody.

    c. An organization of concerned young people entered Wilson Hall before dawn in an effort to dramatize their desire for social justice. Their spokesmen requested a conference with President Dillard, which Dillard refused, substituting instead the tired call for "law and order" and "business as usual." By noon a mob of student reactionaries had laid siege to the building, swarming about and hurling bigoted invective at its occupants. When this horde threatened violence to the liberals, Dillard seized the excuse to bring the pigs on campus. The protesters offered little resistance to the uniformed goons who stormed Wilson, seizing the building and imprisoning seven youths in the local Bastille.

A second point about connotation to keep in mind is that when a word suggests a strong *emotional* meaning its *literal* meaning may be obscured. Language which makes an aggressive attempt to stir strong emotional responses in the reader often sacrifices clarity of communication. A study of the three paragraphs above demonstrates this. Which of the three writers seems to give you the clearest and most accurate description of what actually occurred at Wilson Hall? Obviously it is the first because he brings to his report no prior bias for or against the principals. His viewpoint is objective and his language is dispassionate.

The first passage is an example of *exposition,* an objective explanation of facts. The second and third are *argumentation.* Their purpose is less to explain than to convince. Though ostensibly they, too, are explaining what happened at Wilson Hall, by their choice of connotative words they are seeking to convince you to understand and interpret these events from their respective points of view.

When writing argumentation, try to keep a balance between words of strong connotation and those without emotional impact. This is really another way of saying: Maintain a balance between *emphasis* and *clarity.* Remember that excessively emotional language can serve to destroy both the clarity and the accuracy of your writing, and some writers deliberately set out to do exactly that. Be suspicious in your reading of authors who seem to be making too vigorous an attempt to stir your emotions. This can be as effective a method of deception as those we studied earlier.

FOLLOW-UP

1. *Make a comparison and analysis of the connotative word and phrases used in the "Wilson Hall" passages.*

Writer *a* speaks of a "student group" occupying Wilson. Writer *b* calls the same group "a mob of radical, long-haired hippies" as well as "radicals," "agitators" and "insurgents." Writer *c* labels them "an organization of concerned young people," "liberals," "protesters."

The group's "leaders" are called "ringleaders" by *b* and "spokesmen" by *c*. Opponents of the demonstrators are, according to *b*, "groups of moderate students" who "assembled here and there on the lawns." Writer *b* makes it all sound as harmless as a Sunday-school picnic. In *c*'s view the same students are "a mob of student reactionaries" who "laid siege to the building, swarming about . . .", a description suggesting the beginning of a pitched battle.

It is evident from *a*'s description that both sides were responsible for the "angry shouts" and "brief outbreaks of violence." But *b* puts all the blame on the demonstrators: "From the security of their bastion, the agitators screamed down abuse and profanity." And *c* denounces their opponents as a "horde" which "threatened violence" while "hurling bigoted invective."

All three writers relate the communications between the demonstrators and the college president; however, *b* and *c* editorialize rather than report. According to *b* the demonstrators "demanded a confrontation," while *c* says they "requested a conference." Writer *c* characterizes Dillard's response as a "tired call for 'law and order' and 'business as usual,'" while implying that the president "refused" to meet them under any circumstances. Writer *b* paints Dillard as a reasonable man, willing to meet the dissidents if they will only "restore order" and end "their disruption of the proper functions of the college." Writer *b* assumes that Dillard's motive in calling in the police was "to prevent a riot," and therefore implies that a riot would have occurred if the police had not been summoned, whereas *c* leaves the impression that Dillard was only waiting for an "excuse" to call the cops. And note that *b* speaks of the police as "local law enforcement officials" while *c* dismisses them simply as "pigs" and "uniformed goons."

This comparative analysis of the three passages is by no means exhaustive, but it should provide a starting point for your own analysis. Contrast the three paragraphs sentence by sentence and phrase by phrase. Why do certain terms have a negative connotation and others a positive one? How would you characterize the prior assumptions and prejudices which have influenced the attitudes of b *and* c *toward the same event? What techniques of propaganda and deception do you find used by* b *and* c*?*

2. *Based on your knowledge of the assumptions and prejudices of writers* b *and* c, *write character sketches of each. Try to imagine the backgrounds and experiences of each which have produced the attitudes they now have. How old would they be? What do you suppose they look like?*

3. *From the newspaper, choose an objective report of a controversial event or dispute and rewrite it using connotative language to sway the reader toward first one and then the other contending point of view.*

4. *Reread any papers in your folder which were based on the argumentative paragraphs of Section I. Make an analysis of your use of connotative words in those papers. Rewrite at least one paper, attempting to improve your skill in employing connotation to control the reader's response.*

Formal English and Slang

Before beginning a discussion of slang and formal English, normally considered the two extremes of English language style, we offer examples of both. What follows are two versions of a timeless tale which most readers should find familiar.

A LITTLE BLONDE BROAD & THREE MEAN GRIZZLIES

One time there were these three mean grizzlies, Big Daddy, Big Mama and Baby Bear, who lived in this bad pad in the forest. One day Big Mama said, "Dig it, I just made some porridge."

"Far out!" said Big Daddy.

"Porridge is not relevant," said Baby Bear.

But when Big Daddy tasted the porridge he got uptight. "Oh wow! Man, this hominy is hot!" he shouted.

"Let's split to the pool hall and rap with the three little porkers and that cat with the fiddle while the gruel cools," said Big Mama.

"Right on!" said Big Daddy.

"Fiddles are not relevant," said Baby Bear. And the three mean grizzlies split.

Pretty soon along came this Little Blonde Broad on the biggest, baddest chopper in the forest. "Like wow!" cried the Little Blonde Broad. "I smell the scent of some heavy porridge coming from that bad pad."

She tasted Big Daddy's mush but it was too hot. She tasted Big Mama's but it was too cold. Then she dug Baby Bear's mush. "Far out," said the Little Blonde Broad. "This is just right!" And she grooved on that gruel.

"Man, I'm fagged out," said the Little Blonde Broad and she looked for a place to sack out. She tried Big Daddy's rack but it was too hard. She tried Big Mama's bed but it was too soft. Then she dug Baby Bear's bunk. "Groovy," said the Little Blonde Broad. "This is just right! I'll just stretch out until I get my head together." In a minute she was zonked out.

Soon the three mean grizzlies came back. "Dig it!" yelled Big Daddy, "Somebody's been swilling my porridge."

"No sweat," said Big Mama. "Somebody's been swallowing my porridge."

"Oh wow," said Baby Bear. "Like my mush is, like, gone."

"Dig it!" yelled Big Daddy. "Somebody's been sleeping in my bed."

"No sweat," said Big Mama. "Somebody's been snoozing in my bed."

"Oh wow," said Baby Bear. "Somebody's freaked out in my cot and she's still here!"

"Hey, Baby," said Big Daddy, "Are you jiving me?"

Just then the Little Blonde Broad woke up. She had no bread so she left her chopper to pay for the room and board. "Since I can't use your pad," said the Little Blonde Broad, "I'll rack out for awhile on the grass till I get it together."

"Right on!" said Big Daddy.

"Far out!" said Big Mama.

"Grass is not relevant," said Baby Bear.

THE GOLDEN COIFFURED DAMSEL AND THE TRIUMVIRATE OF QUADRUPEDS

In a bygone era there abided, in a miniscule but tastefully appointed cottage in the midst of a vast, wooded and rustic region, a triumvirate of ursine quadrupeds, bears to be precise. One splendid forenoon, the maternal quadruped announced to the paternal quadruped and their offspring, "I have recently prepared an exceptionally delicious gourmet cereal; to wit, porridge."

Alas, the mixture was exceedingly warm and the family, after considerable consultation, determined to venture abroad to the billiard parlor in anticipation of some enlightening conversation with the trio of petite shoats or a lively exchange of stimulating ideas with the feline with the violin. Their hope was that during their absence the appetizing mixture would cool sufficiently to be consumed.

Anon, the Golden Coiffured Damsel arrived. "Leaping lizards!" exclaimed she to the canine which accompanied her, "I fancy I do detect the delectable aroma of a delightful gourmet dish which wafts hither from yonder, charming cottage. Come! Let us . . . ."

But that's enough to give you the general idea. The topic under discussion in this section is titled "Formal English and Slang," because the normal assumption is that these two kinds of English stand at opposite ends of the spectrum of acceptable English usage.

Keep in mind the first principle of communication cited in this section: If a word is to communicate a meaning clearly, there must be complete agreement between the reader and the writer on what the word means. With this principle clear and the examples of formal and slang English fresh, we can consider the question of what "good English" is.

☐ *"Good English" is English which communicates clearly to the reader the meaning intended by the writer.*

Among other things, this definition implies that the writer's intended meaning must be expressed in words which are understood by his reader. If your ideas are presented in a vocabulary which your reader cannot understand, then obviously you will be unable to communicate them effectively.

A few basic points should be cleared up.

Slang

Though there are subtle differences between the terms slang and dialect, the two words are often used interchangeably. *Slang* is the special vocabulary invented by, used by, and understood by a particular in-group. The in-group identifies itself by having something in common which is not shared by the rest of the population. This common denominator is usually an occupation or membership in a specific age group or ethnic minority.

An important distinction exists between occupational slang and other kinds. The special language used by people in the same profession has a practical purpose. They need to invent terms to describe special equipment or activities peculiar to their occupation for which no expression exists in the vocabulary of general

English. Baseball players, for instance, use terms like "pinch-hit," "Texas Leaguer," "squeeze play," and "run-down." Some of these slang terms find their way into general use; a squeeze play has become a synonym for being caught between two opposing factions, and pinch-hit is widely used to mean substitute for. Other slang terms (Texas Leaguer, run-down) have no general use but remain part of the standard vocabulary of the profession. You do not need to be a baseball player to know what a Texas Leaguer is, or to understand phrases like "shoestring catch," "extra innings," "knuckle ball," "hit and run," "fielder's choice." Anyone with any interest in the sport understands these terms. This slang has remained unchanged for decades. It would never occur to a baseball player to find a new way of saying "knuckle ball" or "fielder's choice" simply because people outside the profession had caught on to their meaning. But this is not true of the slang of groups identified by age or ethnic or racial origin.

Unlike occupational slang, the slang of special age or ethnic groups is not invented for practical reasons but to reinforce the feeling of identification of each individual member with the group. It is important that this slang not be widely used or even understood by people who are not members of the in-group. These slang words are not invented because there is no word in the general vocabulary which communicates the proper meaning; they are invented to allow the in-group to communicate with each other without outsiders understanding their meaning. As a result, while occupational slang provides terms for which there are no equivalents in general English, the slang of special age and ethnic groups is invented to substitute for the most common English words and phrases.

Occupational slang terms have a very specific meaning. A Texas Leaguer is a ball hit just behind the infield and nothing else. A hit-and-run is a ball hit between first and second when there is a runner on first base. But other slang words normally have a wide variety of meanings depending on their context. To "dig," for example, may mean to become aware of, to appreciate, or to enjoy a great deal. To "rap" may mean to talk seriously about important, sensitive issues or to talk informally about nothing in particular.

Occupational slang is fairly permanent, but the slang of other groups changes constantly as soon as it begins to be used and understood by people outside the in-group. The chief pleasure of slang is being able to communicate in a language, a kind of code, which outsiders cannot understand. When the outsiders (the "older generation" for instance) starts to catch on, the in-group usually abandons old slang terms and adopts new ones.

The idea that the use of slang is evidence of ignorance or a lack of education has been discredited and is disappearing. It would be a serious mistake, however, to assume that slang dialects can now be used in all situations in place of general English vocabulary. We have seen that communication is impossible unless both reader and writer agree on the meaning of the words. We have seen that slang is by definition a vocabulary coined by a special group in order to communicate without the understanding of outsiders. It follows that when you *want* to communicate with "outsiders" you cannot use slang.

Formal English

Like slang, formal English has been misused and misunderstood. The term "formal" is unfortunate because it often implies to students a style which is either stiff and pretentious or excessively flowery. True formal English is none of these things.

Reread "The Golden Coiffured Damsel and the Triumvirate of Quadrupeds," but before you do, please understand that it is not a true example of formal English at all. It is an outrageous parody of formal English and of the errors most commonly committed by those who try to write it: wordiness, unnecessarily complex sentences, pretentious vocabulary.

There is no reason why formal English should ever be wordy, stilted or pompous. These are hardly requirements of a formal style, and they are not virtues in any kind of writing. English can be considered formal if it is (a) impersonal rather than casual, (b) serious rather than comic and (c) written with a reasonable attention to basic grammar and in a vocabulary adequate to expressing its ideas clearly.

FOLLOW-UP

1. *Make a list of ten current slang expressions and their definitions. How many of these terms were being used two years ago? What phrases, current two years ago, have disappeared?*

2. *Slang, we have said, is usually substituted for the most common English words and phrases. What are the most recent slang equivalents of the following?*

great!	beautiful	handsome guy
arrive	enjoy	don't worry
get together	understand	no kidding
leave	pretty girl	in good shape

3. *Slang, like any language, should always be under the control of the writer. Practice your control of slang by rewriting a children's story or very serious article.*

Irony

Before we get into a discussion of irony, try your hand at this exercise. Simply read the paragraph and answer the questions at its conclusion.

Old Professor Lindquist retired this year, and last week his colleagues on the faculty gave him a testimonial dinner. Throughout his career Lindquist often spoke out against ignorance and arrogance, and, truly, there exists no more eloquent testimony against ignorance and arrogance than Lindquist's own career. In a touching ceremony, the guest of honor presented the college with a complete file of his lecture notes, most dating back more than forty years to his first semesters of teaching. These remarkable documents will be laminated in plastic and prominently placed in the library near our collection of Hitler memorabilia. His students have voted Lindquist the Ichabod Crane award for pedagogy so often over the years that the faculty retired the trophy in his honor. Lindquist responded by regaling those assembled with fifteen minutes of readings chosen at random from the errata of his book and, in a typical fit of generosity, offered autographed copies to all present at six percent off the list price. The affair concluded with a spirited rendition of "Auld Lang Syne." There wasn't a dry eye in the house. Personally I haven't been so moved since the last time I saw a late-night television rerun of "Goodbye, Mr. Chips."

Before answering these questions, be certain you understand the meaning of each word used in the paragraph. Then answer true *or* false *to each of these statements:*

1. The writer has a high regard for his colleague, Professor Lindquist.

2. Lindquist has been careful to update his lectures over the years.

3. His students have always considered Professor Lindquist a good teacher.

4. The writer admires Lindquist's book as an example of precision and accuracy in writing and research.

5. The writer thinks Lindquist is a generous man.

6. The writer respects Lindquist as an enemy of ignorance and arrogance.

7. The writer was deeply moved by Lindquist's testimonial dinner.

The paragraph is written in an *ironic* style. There is a strong contrast between the writer's apparent meaning (the meaning which he at first appears to convey) and his intended meaning (the meaning he really intends, which you can discover by careful reading). Behind the *appearance* of praising Lindquist's career at its culmination, the writer's actual *intention* is a biting attack on Lindquist's ignorance of his subject, dogmatic attitude in the classroom, and slovenly scholarship. The correct answer to all seven questions above is *false*.

In preparation for further analysis of the paragraph study the following closely related definitions:

☐ *Irony is the contrast between a writer's apparent meaning and the meaning he really intends.*

☐ *Irony is the use of words to communicate the opposite of their literal meaning.*

Study the following examples:

1. Chicago is a fair sized little community.

2. Today we will study that great American hero, Benedict Arnold.

3. Only two F's this semester? You are becoming quite a scholar, Furguson.

It is essential that the reader be in on the joke. If he does not know that you intend a meaning opposite to the literal one, he just might take you seriously. There is no danger of misunderstanding the first two examples because you may assume the reader knows about Chicago and Benedict Arnold. Misunderstanding is avoided in the third by giving the reader the information that Furguson received two F's.

An ironic style of writing is used to treat a topic with satiric humor. The writer's attitude toward his subject may range from gentle humor to biting sarcasm. Ironic style is marked by the following:

1. The understatement of obvious facts. *Examples:* (1) Benedict Arnold is not exactly a national hero. (2) Medicine is occasionally a lucrative profession.

2. The positive statement of an obvious falsehood (at least obviously false to the writer.) *Examples:* (1) Why not visit Cuba, that glorious vacation paradise? (2) World War I was billed as "the war to end all wars" which, as we all know, is what it did.

3. A tendency toward stating ideas negatively rather than positively. *Examples:* (1) War is no picnic. (2) Lincoln was not a bad president.

4. The use of sentences with an abrupt, or unexpected, twist of meaning. *Examples:* (1) This is National Crime Prevention Week so take a second-story man to lunch. (2) Professor Jones is obviously getting tough; only 87 percent of the class got A's this term.

5. The use of the sarcastic simile. *Examples:* (1) He was tall and stringy with a face like a feedbag and a nose like a meathook. (2) He has the courage of a rabbit, the intelligence of a warthog and the compassion of a cockroach.

FOLLOW-UP

1. *Make a detailed analysis of the techniques of irony employed by the writer of the Lindquist paragraph. In your analysis consider these questions:*

a. In view of the writer's real attitude toward Professor Lindquist, what is the effect of using, as his superficial subject, the professor's *testimonial* dinner?

b. What is the effect of the abrupt, unexpected twist of meaning in the second sentence?

c. What is achieved by associating Lindquist's name with that of Adolf Hitler: Of Ichabod Crane? Of Mr. Chips?

d. What connotation of the word "pedagogy" tips off Lindquist's students' true feelings toward his teaching methods?

e. It is common when a respected educator retires to present him with an award commemorating his career. It is also common for him to donate important works to the college from his private library. How does the author use these traditional ceremonies to ridicule Lindquist?

f. The *errata* of a book is a list of errors made by the author and appended to the book. Normally this list is very brief. What is the writer implying about Lindquist's scholarship and writing skill when he says the professor did "fifteen minutes of readings chosen at random from the errata of his book . . ."?

g. In view of the writer's actual feelings toward Lindquist, what is the effect of his use of these phrases: "a touching ceremony," "the guest of honor," "remarkable documents," "a typical fit of generosity," "there wasn't a dry eye in the house"?

2. *Write a short essay of one to three paragraphs in an ironic style. Possible topics include a public figure or policy which you particularly dislike, or a bad film or television show.*

Section III

READING, COMPREHENSION AND LOGIC

Introduction

Almost everybody at one time or another has been tested for reading skills and comprehension. These tests are very important. You can tell they are important because they are timed with a stopwatch, like a horse race, and you cannot start until the teacher shouts "Go!"; also, you are given a special pencil, and it is a federal offense to make a mark on the answer sheet outside the little dotted lines. You can tell they are *very* important because, after you take the test, you are never told what your grade was.

The purpose of these tests is to discover how fast you can possibly read and still manage to understand what you are reading. To accomplish this, you are instructed to read paragraphs which are crammed full of interesting facts. Then you have to answer questions about those facts. In case you have forgotten what these examinations were like, test yourself on the following sample exercise.

SAMPLE EXERCISE

Read the paragraph and answer the questions on a separate sheet of paper. Read as fast as you can. Do not think about what you are reading; just understand it. Thinking wastes time. Ready? Go!

Hoboken, New Jersey, located on the Hudson River in the county of Hudson, was incorporated as a town in 1849 and as a city in 1855. The area in which the present city is situated was originally named by the Indians, who called it Hobocan Hackingh, "the land of the tobacco pipe." First settled by the Dutch West India Company in 1635, the area was purchased by Samuel Bayard, a New York merchant, in 1711. In 1784 the state of New Jersey confiscated the property and sold it to Colonel John Stevens, who established a town on the site in 1804. Early in the nineteenth century Hoboken became a popular resort. The town's public park, the Elysian Fields, was the site of the first professional baseball game in 1846. P. T. Barnum once staged a buffalo hunt there. Today Hoboken is an important center for the manufacture of varnish, iron castings, lead pencils, paper boxes, and chemicals. The nickname of Hoboken is "The Mile-Square City."

1. Hoboken is nicknamed (a) The Mile-High City (b) The Mile-Square City (c) The Eternal City (d) The Big Apple (e) none of the above.

2. Hobocan Hackingh means (a) the great swamp (b) the Elysian fields (c) the land of the tobacco pipe (d) the big apple (e) all of the above.

3. In 1784 Hoboken was confiscated by (a) the Indians (b) Colonel John Stevens (c) the Dutch West India Company (d) the state of New Jersey (e) P. T. Barnum.

4. Hoboken is a center for manufacturing (a) paper boxes (b) varnish (c) lead pencils (d) iron castings (e) all of the above.

5. Hoboken was the site of the first professional (a) Indian raid (b) buffalo hunt (c) baseball game (d) varnish factory (e) none of the above.

Time is up. The correct answers are *b, c, d, e* and *c*. If you got all five right, you obviously read the paragraph carefully and understood it well, so here are a few more questions. Why did the Indians call the area "the land of the tobacco pipe"? Why did the state of New Jersey seize Hoboken in 1784? What happened in the first professional baseball game? How could even P. T. Barnum possibly have staged a buffalo hunt in Hoboken?

Time is up. Have you answered the questions? Probably not, because the answers are not contained in the paragraph. Unlike the five questions in the sample exercise, these four questions are not *answered* by the facts in the paragraphs, they are *raised* by the facts in the paragraph. This brings us to our first major point. It is not only necessary to know facts in order to answer questions; it is also necessary to know facts in order to ask questions.

If you stop to think about it, you will find proof of this in your own experience. Almost every time you learn a fact, your first response is to ask a question. Your best friend just broke up with her steady: you ask what happened. You were just cut from the football team: you want to know why. Your car will not start: you want to know what is wrong with it. Your mechanic tells you what is wrong: you ask how much it will cost *this* time.

Perhaps the only time you ever learn a fact and do not ask a question is in school. If this is true, there are two possible reasons. First, your experience may have led you to assume that the principal job of a student is to answer questions, not to ask them. This is not surprising. In most of your classes your grade has been based largely on examinations, quizzes and class recital. Obviously all three require you to answer questions.

You may also assume that if your instructor makes a statement in the class or you read something in a book, it must be true. Possibly you feel that, whether you agree with the instructor or not, it is smarter and easier to go along with him than to ask questions in class or disagree with him on an examination. It is almost certainly true that, whether it ever occurs to you to question your teachers or not, you never question anything you have read in a textbook. Think about it for a moment. It has never entered your mind that a textbook author might write lies, has it? You have been assuming all along that everything you are taught and everything you read for a class is true.

If you agree—is it because you just read it in a textbook?

If you do not agree, if you still insist that you have an inquiring mind, let us test the theory. Recall the paragraph you read on Hoboken. You probably had little difficulty answering the five questions in the sample exercise. But what about the other four? While you were reading the paragraph, did any of those questions occur to you? Did you wonder about how Barnum promoted a buffalo hunt, or why professional baseball began in Hoboken? If you did, of course, you were not following instructions. Wondering about those questions would have meant that you were thinking about what you were reading, and you were specifically told not to think. There was good reason for this. Thinking takes time and would have slowed down your performance. On a test of this kind you would have read fewer paragraphs and answered fewer questions. The test is designed to reward the student who does not think. So you did not wonder why professional baseball began in Hoboken.

Did you wonder *if* professional baseball began in Hoboken?

When you come right to it, how do you know it did? How do you know whether any of the statements made in the paragraph are true? Did you simply assume they were true because you read them in a book?

But suppose you say that you knew the first ball game was played in the Elysian Fields because you had read about it before, or because one of your teachers confirmed it, or because you looked it up in an encyclopedia or almanac. In other words, you believed it because you found *corroboration* of the fact in more than one source. You have taken the first necessary step in research.

Not that you are doing anything you have not done before. We have seen that the natural response to learning a fact is to ask a question. The natural response when your question has been answered is to try to find out if the answer is true. Your best friend just broke up with her steady, and you ask what happened. She says he was two-timing her. Will you believe her and drop the subject, or snoop around finding out his side of the story? Your mechanic tells you it will take $200 worth of work on the engine to get your car back on the road. Do you hand over the $200 or go to another mechanic? The bank tells you that your account is overdrawn. Will you take their word for it?

But the bank account is important to you. Two hundred dollars is important to you. Baseball and Hoboken are not very important. If you think so, think again. The facts may not be important, but the principle involved is, because the principle is simply whether or not you care about being told lies. The method for protecting yourself against being deceived is the same whether you are testing a statement made by a teacher, a writer or a used-car salesman. That method is to confirm the truth by seeking corroboration of the fact from more than one reliable source of information.

The only alternative to mastering this skill is to spend the rest of your life believing every television commercial's claim, every politician's promise, and that every used car you ever buy was formerly owned by a little old lady who only drove it once a week to go to church.

FOLLOW-UP

If you took the reading exercise at the beginning of this section seriously, you probably answered at least four out of the five questions correctly. Now, why not test your ability to retain facts in your memory for longer than five minutes? Without looking back at the paragraph, answer these questions:

1. Hoboken is located in the county of (a) Bergen (b) Harrison (c) Hackingh (d) Bayard (e) none of the above.

2. The town of Hoboken was first established by (a) the Dutch West India Company (b) the state of New Jersey (c) Samuel Bayard (d) John Stevens (e) none of the above.

3. Samuel Bayard was (a) a colonel (b) a New York merchant (c) the governor of New Jersey (d) the president of the Dutch West India Company (e) an Indian agent.

4. Hoboken was a popular resort in (a) the late 19th century (b) the early 18th century (c) the early 17th century (d) the late 18th century (e) none of the above.

5. Hoboken was incorporated as a city in (a) 1855 (b) 1635 (c) 1066 (d) 1492 (e) 1776.

Check your answers now by rereading the paragraph. If you answered three or more questions correctly, you failed the quiz. Either you sneaked a look back at the paragraph, or you spent too much energy during your first reading on the memorization of tiny, obscure detail. It is true that this type of examination normally requires either memorization or cheating, but neither, as has been mentioned, is productive of thought. The ability to think is what we are now concerned with.

(In case you are interested, the Indians named the Hoboken area "the land of the tobacco pipe" because pipes were made there out of stone. [Indian names, you might notice, were wonderfully logical. But why do you suppose they made pipes out of stone?] In 1784 New Jersey seized Hoboken because the residents were outspoken Tories and the state government was controlled by the rebels. [Do you think the residents left the land quietly, or were their homes taken by force?] In the first professional baseball game, a team named the "New York Nine" overpowered another club called the "Knickerbockers." Of course P. T. Barnum never held a buffalo hunt in Hoboken. Never, even before the first European set foot on American shores, were there any buffalo running wild in New Jersey.)

We have been concentrating on two major ideas: first, that it is necessary to learn a fact before you can ask a question; and second, that in order to establish that a statement is true, you must find corroboration in more than one reliable source. With these in mind, read the following paragraph.

EXERCISES

During the Texan war for independence against Mexico, in December of 1835, Texan rebels captured a San Antonio fort called the Alamo. Colonel William Travis was ordered to hold the fort with a garrison of only 155 men, later reinforced by a mere 32 additional soldiers. In February of the following year, an army of about 4,000 under the Mexican General Antonio Santa Anna laid siege to the fort. Santa Anna, expecting the arrival of artillery, was content to surround the fort at first, avoiding a direct assault. The Texans, whose leaders included pioneer Jim Bowie, inventor of the bowie knife, and the legendary frontiersman and ex-congressman Davy Crockett, held out until March 6, 1836, when the Mexicans succeeded in breaching the walls of the Alamo and, in brutal hand-to-hand combat, slaughtered the garrison to the last man. Bowie, sick with typhoid-pneumonia, died fighting from his bed. There were only six survivors, three women and three children. Crockett also died, as did Colonel Travis, who had requested reinforcements from the Texan commander, General Sam Houston, in vain. Santa Anna moved on to confront Houston in the war's climactic battle at San Jacinto on April 21, 1836. Though completely victorious at the Alamo, the Mexicans had only 1,400 troops left to meet 800 Texans under Houston's command. Though outnumbered, the Texans routed Santa Anna's army, and the general himself was captured. The Texan battle cry at San Jacinto was "Remember the Alamo."

1. *To be certain that the "facts" contained in this paragraph are correct, double check them against at least two other sources.*

2. *Make a list of questions which are raised or suggested by this paragraph but not answered by it.*

3. *Next, read the following two paragraphs. To be certain the facts in each are correct, double check them against at least two other sources. Then make a list of the questions raised or suggested by each.*

1. In Dayton, Tennessee, in 1925, a young high school teacher named John Thomas Scopes agreed to test a new state law which forbade the teaching of Darwin's theory of evolution or any theory "denying the story of Creation as taught in the Bible." Scopes' defense was financed by the American Civil Liberties Union and led by the famous criminal lawyer Clarence Darrow, a champion of freedom of thought and an avowed atheist. The prosecution called on William Jennings Bryan, three times an unsuccessful candidate for President and a leading spokesman for fundamentalist Christianity. The trial turned tiny Dayton into a boom town and attracted national attention. Frustrated in his attempts to call scientific experts to the stand, Darrow called instead a self-proclaimed expert on the Bible, the prosecutor, Bryan. Darrow's relentless, often sardonic cross-examination forced Bryan again and again into absurd and contradictory statements about his own religious beliefs. He was left a broken man, called, by the acid-tongued H. L. Mencken, "pathetic . . . elderly and enfeebled . . . . Once he had one leg in the White House and the nation had trembled under his roars. Now he is a tinpot pope in the Coca-Cola belt and a brother to the forlorn pastors who belabor half-wits in the galvanized iron tabernacles behind the railroad yards." Five days after the trial ended, Bryan was dead, and to many it seemed that the "old-time religion" he trumpeted had died with him.

2. Since the mid-nineteenth century, a hot debate has raged over whether or not the works of William Shakespeare were actually written by the man from Stratford-on-Avon. His detractors castigate Shakespeare as a "drunken illiterate clown," "sordid money-lender," "ignorant butcher boy," "lying rascal," "miserly malt-hoarder," and "unlettered rustic." In turn they themselves are reviled by orthodox scholars as "a troop of less than half-educated people," "a wretched group of dilettantes," and "a succession of cranks." The "heretics" have offered an odd menagerie of alternative authors, including Francis Bacon, Walter Raleigh, Francis Drake and a dozen or so assorted earls, not to mention Shakespeare's wife, Queen Elizabeth and a monastery full of Jesuits. The claims made for their favorites are occasionally as outrageous as their evidence is flimsy. A few Baconians, for example, have credited Sir Francis not merely with the whole of Shakespeare,

but with works of Marlowe, Greene, Peele, Kyd, Nash and Jonson, plus *The Faerie Queen, Paradise Lost* and *Gulliver's Travels.* In the face of this sort of nonsense it has been easy to brand all anti-Stratfordians as idiots and crackpots, forgetting that many famous men have doubted Shakespeare's authorship, including John Greenleaf Whittier, Nathaniel Hawthorne, Mark Twain, Henry James and Sigmund Freud.

Incidentally, it is absolutely true that P. T. Barnum staged a buffalo hunt in Hoboken. Disregard all earlier statements to the contrary. Naturally there were never any herds of wild buffalo in New Jersey, but Barnum found ways other than natural of doing things. If you are interested in how he managed it, it would probably be a good idea to look it up.

Fact and Opinion

The first concern of this part is testing your ability to draw logical conclusions from what you read. Look closely at the brief quiz on this page. Read the questions and jot your answers down on a piece of scrap paper. You will not be required to turn the answers in. The quiz is strictly for your own information.

1. In what city was the Battle of Trenton fought?
2. How long did the Seven Years War last?
3. Who is buried in Grant's Tomb?
4. From what nation does Scotch whisky come?
5. On what hill was the Battle of Bunker Hill fought?
6. Name the home state of the American playwright Tennessee Williams.
7. In what country will you find the Swiss Alps?
8. Name the home city of the Chicago White Sox.
9. Who wrote *The Autobiography of Alice B. Toklas*?
10. Where was the Treaty of Paris signed?

When you are finished with the quiz, check your answers against those at the bottom of page 82. It has probably occurred to you that this was really a series of joke questions, with the answer clearly contained in each question. Obviously the Battle of Trenton was fought in Trenton, the Seven Years War lasted for seven years, and Grant is buried in Grant's Tomb. Still, for your own amusement, match your answers against those given and score yourself as follows: if one to three answers match, your score is *poor.* If four to five answers match, score yourself *fair.* If six answers match, your score is *good.* If you have matched seven to ten answers, your score is *poor.*

That is right: seven to ten is *poor.* If you assumed that was a misprint, it is not the first false assumption you have made since you began this section. You may have assumed that because some of the questions had obvious answers, they all did. On the other hand, you may have known that Mrs. Grant is also buried in Grant's Tomb, or that the Battle of Bunker Hill was actually fought on Breed's Hill, or that the home state of Tennessee Williams is Mississippi, or that the author of *The Autobiography of Alice B. Toklas* was Gertrude Stein.

Those of you who did answer any of the above four questions correctly: what did you think when you found a different answer given at the bottom of the page? Did you *assume* that the answer listed in the book must be right, and did you therefore *assume* that your answer must be wrong?

If you find that you have made any assumptions at all up to this point, this part of Section III is aimed squarely at you and its message is a simple one: do not make assumptions.

The first part of this section raised the question of whether or not the authors of textbooks ever write lies. No author of a legitimate text in any field will deliberately lie to you. However, the author will probably present you with opinions which are phrased in such a way that you will most likely be misled into assuming that these opinions are facts. The following sample sentence could be from a standard text in American history. Study it carefully.

(a) Because of his great humanitarianism, (b) President Abraham Lincoln issued the Emancipation Proclamation, (c) which freed the slaves.

The sentence contains three parts, identified as *a, b* and *c.* Do you see anything in any of the three which strikes you as particularly controversial? Does any assertion seem false or misleading? Does any assertion appear to be unquestionably factual?

Answers: 1. Trenton, New Jersey 2. seven years 3. Ulysses S. Grant 4. Scotland 5. Bunker Hill 6. Tennessee 7. Switzerland 8. Chicago, Illinois 9. Alice B. Toklas 10. Paris, France

Part *b* is not controversial. All historians agree that Lincoln did in fact issue the Emancipation Proclamation. However, both assertion *a* and assertion *c* can be hotly contested. Some scholars have argued that Lincoln's motives were not humanitarian, but political or military. Other experts, while acknowledging his humanitarian feelings, claim that these did not really influence his decision to issue the Proclamation. Even more controversial is the statement contained in part *c*. You are apt to agree at once with the assertion that the Emancipation Proclamation freed the slaves, yet it can be logically argued that there is a difference between declaring that slaves are free and actually freeing them. The slaves were not really free until three years later, when the war ended in Union victory. Some historians would probably point out that the Emancipation Proclamation did not free *all* the slaves, but only those in the Confederate states. Slaves held in areas which had remained loyal to the Union government, and slaves held in Confederate territory already occupied by Federal troops, were not set free by the President's decree.

You should now be beginning to understand the distinction between a fact and an opinion. Study the following sample sentence:

(a) On December 7, 1941, the Japanese bombed Pearl Harbor (b) in an attack which came as a surprise to the American government (c) and forced the United States into World War II.

One of these three assertions is an undisputed fact; the other two are highly controversial. Think for a moment and decide which of the three is the fact.

The question of whether or not the attack on Pearl Harbor was really a surprise to the American government is loudly debated. Some experts insist that our leaders had ample warning of the Japanese air attack through British intelligence reports and the fact that we had broken the Japanese secret code. These scholars argue that our government suffered the destruction of Pearl Harbor in order to inflame American public opinion to the point where it would not only support but also demand a declaration of war. Others claim that no American government would knowingly have sat back and permitted the terrible destruction of lives and war materials at Pearl Harbor had there been any advance warning of the attack.

Almost equally controversial is whether or not the attack on Pearl Harbor, by itself, forced the United States into World War II. Certainly it was the most dramatic cause of our nation's entry into the war, but historians can cite numerous political, economic and military causes as well. In the sample it is *a* which is the undisputed fact. No one would argue with the assertion that "on December 7, 1941, the Japanese bombed Pearl Harbor."

Look at the next exercise. It should be possible, using common sense, to determine which of the three assertions in each sentence is an undisputed fact.

1. (a) In the battle which proved to be the turning point of the American Revolution, (b) under the brilliant leadership of General Gates, (c) a rebel army defeated a major British force at Saratoga, New York.

2. (a) After exhaustive and completely impartial tests, (b) having produced results which cannot be scientifically disputed, (c) the United States Surgeon General's office has declared cigarette smoking dangerous to health.

3. (a) In a thorough investigation of all available information and testimony, (b) the Warren Commission declared the assassination of President John F. Kennedy to be the work of a single killer, Lee Harvey Oswald, (c) a verdict which has been generally undisputed.

4. (a) In recent years, much of the Saturday morning television fare aimed at children consists of cartoons in which the emphasis is on violence, (b) creating a situation unquestionably both harmful and dangerous for the youthful viewers, (c) whose own inhibitions to commit violent acts are broken down by their viewing of cartoon violence.

5. (a) In a move which was long overdue (b) and which is certain to have a profound impact on the American political scene, (c) the Constitution has been amended to permit eighteen-year-olds to vote in national elections.

Check your answers to this exercise against those given at the bottom of page 86.

This time you can trust the accuracy of the answers. In sentence 1 it is assertion *c* which is indisputable. Historians would disagree over which particular battle could be called the single turning point of the American Revolution. As for General Gates, though he was the winning commander, some experts would argue that Saratoga was won in spite of his stupidity, not because of his brilliance. Others would claim that the real hero of Saratoga was Benedict Arnold. That, of course, was while he was still fighting on our side.

The attack against cigarettes launched by the Surgeon General's office has produced tremendous controversy, as has the report of the Warren Commission on the Kennedy assassination. The only statements in sentences 2 and 3 which would be universally recognized as factual are the declarations of the findings of these two investigations (2c and 3b). The degree to which television violence is harmful to children is very much in dispute, as is the wisdom, and the political effects, of the eighteen-year-old vote.

If you had difficulty with the last exercise, it may be because some of the opinions expressed in the sentences are so widely believed, or so often repeated, that people, including you, tend to accept them as facts. To test this theory, read through the following ten statements and note whether each asserts a fact or an opinion. Make sure you understand these two definitions first:

☐ *Fact: a statement which is proved and indisputable, or at least undisputed and uncontroversial.*

☐ *Opinion: a statement made with complete confidence but not definitely proved true. It is a statement based on incomplete evidence or evidence which could be questioned.*

1. Most kids who begin smoking marijuana regularly wind up using hard drugs.
2. Martin Luther King was murdered by a lone assassin, James Earl Ray, who is now in prison for the killing.
3. Cigarette smoking causes cancer.
4. Watching violence on television stimulates children to commit violent acts themselves.
5. The most effective and safest way to control your weight is through exercise, not dieting.
6. In any kind of automobile accident, the man wearing a seat belt is less likely to be injured than the man who is not.

7. John F. Kennedy was murdered by a lone assassin, Lee Harvey Oswald.

8. Marijuana is less harmful than alcohol because it is not habit forming.

9. Young people under thirty are more liberal politically than their elders.

10. Crime is much more of a problem in urban than in rural areas.

Which of these ten statements assert facts? Which express opinions? Note your answers on a sheet of paper and put it to one side. We will return to a consideration of these sentences later.

You should by now have noticed that there are certain circumstances under which it is especially difficult to distinguish between fact and opinion. For example, it is hard to identify an opinion when it is widely believed or often repeated. If a great many people accept it as true, or if you have heard it asserted many times, you are very likely to assume it is fact. Many of the statements in the above list fall into one or both of these categories.

It is also difficult not to accept an opinion as factual when the opinion expressed is one with which you personally agree. Naturally you are much more likely to assume the truth of an assertion if you *want* it to be true. The danger here is that wishful thinking replaces logic. Because you want to believe the statement, you not only refuse to question it or seek for proofs, but you also refuse to listen to anyone who *does* question it, whether his arguments make sense or not.

Reread the last paragraph. Ask yourself whether or not you are guilty of this sort of closed-mind thinking. Try this experiment: first, think of the longest running, bitterest disagreement you have ever had with your parents. If possible, use an argument which is still going on. Now, write down your side of the dispute in as few words as possible. Put it in the strongest language you can. Remember how unreasonable your parents have been. Get angry!

When you have expressed your own point of view, write down your parents' argument as you imagine they would explain it.

Answers: The factual assertions are 1c, 2c, 3b, 4a, and 5c.

Try to recall how they expressed their attitude on the subject during your last argument with them. After you have both sides of the conflict down on paper, put them aside for the moment; we will come back to them.

Pick up the sheet on which you identified the ten statements listed before as either fact or opinion. *Every one of these statements is an opinion;* that is, an assertion made with confidence but lacking final proof or universal acceptance. If you labeled any of the ten as facts, ask yourself why. Is it because the assertion is generally accepted as true? Or have you heard it reiterated so often that you simply assumed it must be true? Or is it a statement you want to believe?

If you defined all ten statements as opinions, you are developing an appropriately skeptical attitude. But be certain you understand the other circumstances under which an opinion can easily be mistaken for a fact. An opinion can be mistaken for a fact when it is presented in close proximity to a well-established fact. Reread the sentences dealing with the Emancipation Proclamation and the bombing of Pearl Harbor, used as samples earlier. In both sentences there is one assertion which is unquestionably factual. *The recognition of an undisputed fact in the sentence leads the reader to assume the truth of the other assertions made in the same statement.* In other words, since you know that Lincoln issued the Emancipation Proclamation, you are apt to assume that the rest of the statement is also true. Since you know that the Japanese bombed Pearl Harbor, you will probably accept the truth of the rest of the sentence.

Any accomplished liar can tell you that an untruth is much more likely to be believed if it is closely connected in the telling to an obvious truth. For example, when you were a child and needed an alibi for some stolen cookies or broken furniture, you had better luck claiming you were playing with some neighborhood friend when the "crime" was committed than you had asserting you had been kidnapped by pirates. The neighborhood friend at least existed, and that fact gave some semblance of reality to your story.

An opinion is not an outright lie, but neither is it a self-evident truth. You cannot accept an opinion as true until you have found evidence to support it; that is, until you have found facts from which the opinion may be logically inferred.

SUMMARY

A fact is an assertion which is indisputable or undisputed. An opinion is an assertion which is disputable. Though it may be stated with complete confidence, an opinion is controversial and must be supported with facts before it is accepted as true.

You may be misled into accepting an opinion as a fact if the opinion is (a) widely believed, (b) constantly repeated, or (c) expresses a viewpoint you want to be true. You may also be confused if the opinion seems closely connected to an undisputed assertion. Or, as was demonstrated in the first part of this section, you may assume that opinions are true because they are stated by an authority figure such as a teacher or textbook author.

FOLLOW-UP

1. *Reread the papers on which you expressed your side of your longest running disagreement with your parents and then attempted to give their viewpoint. Since these papers are argumentative, it is likely that almost every sentence contains at least one assertion. Identify all the assertions in your own argument and determine which are facts and which are opinions. Do the same with the opposing argument.*

   If you have been honest with yourself, it is probable that very few assertions can be labeled as facts. If that is the case, then it should now be obvious to you why you have had trouble winning the argument. Go over your parents' arguments to determine what their major contentions are and what facts you will need to prove them wrong. Decide what your major contentions are and what facts will be necessary to support them. Then gather the facts. Your instructor may require you to write a paper presenting and defending your point of view. But the final test of whether or not your fact-finding has been successful will be the next time you argue over the issue with your parents. You just might win.

2. *The most effective way to learn how to distinguish fact from opinion is not to take a lot of tests like the one back on page 84, but to practice writing sentences similar to those in the test. Try writing five sentences like those on page 84. Each sentence should contain three assertions, of which one is an acknowledged fact*

and the other two are controversial opinions. Take your time with this and be certain that your "facts" really are undisputable.

3. *Review the opinions listed on pages 85–86 and select the one which most interests you. (If you have not already noticed it, you might now note that research is less of a disagreeable chore when you are researching a subject in which you already have an interest.)*

When you have chosen what you consider the most interesting opinion, do three things. First, write down the reasons you are interested in this particular topic. Does it involve you personally? Do you particularly want to believe that it is true, or that it is false? (Recognizing that you have a prejudice for or against an assertion will help you to compensate for that prejudice and evaluate the assertion fairly.)

*Second, make a list of at least four questions raised by the assertion which you feel would have to be answered before you could decide whether the assertion is factual or not. (Remember that even if you come to a conclusion about the truth or falsehood of the statement, it remains an opinion, not a fact, because it remains controversial. Whether you agree or disagree with the assertion, there will be people who will take the opposing view. Thus, the assertion may become **your** opinion, but it will remain opinion, not fact.)*

Third, research the answers to the questions you have listed. The instructor may require you to write a paper in which you present your point of view.

Inferences,
Assumptions
and Implications

Read the following narrative carefully and answer the questions asked. As usual, you will not be required to submit the results of the quiz to the instructor. It is entirely for your own information.

Rusty and Pete have been close friends since they met in the seventh grade. They went all through high school together, both starring in athletics, though in different sports. The boys received athletic scholarships to the same college and roomed together during their freshman year. Pete had trouble with his grades and, though he did not flunk out, he lost his eligibility and with it his scholarship. After the freshman year he dropped out and enlisted in the service.

They continued to correspond regularly, but, on the morning that Rusty received Pete's telephone call, they had not seen each other in a little more than a year. Pete was on leave and in town. The Green Bay Packers were also in town for a regular-season game with Los Angeles, and Pete suggested they take in the game. But Rusty explained that his college team was opening its season that afternoon, and he invited Pete to come out to the campus. After the game they could have dinner and talk over old times. Pete accepted.

The game was hotly contested and decided only in the last moments of the second half when Rusty, playing center, scored the winning goal. Afterwards Pete went down to the locker room and congratulated the team members, many of whom were old friends.

They drove to the restaurant in Rusty's car, stopping briefly while Pete bought a pack of cigarettes. It was hot and they rode with the top down. Both were dressed casually, the younger boy in a white turtleneck and green shorts, the other in a yellow sport shirt and light-brown slacks. The restaurant Rusty had chosen specialized in Italian food, good but inexpensive, and Rusty had remembered that Pete was crazy about Italian cooking.

They ordered something to drink, but the elderly waitress, eyeing Rusty suspiciously, asked for proof of age. Then she disappeared into the bar. When she returned she was carrying one Scotch and soda and one bottle of Coke.

Although this is not the conclusion of the narrative, you are asked to pause in your reading and test your powers of logic and comprehension by answering the questions that follow. Base your answers on the information contained in the portion of the narrative you have just read. Write your answers on a separate sheet of paper. It is not enough simply to answer the questions; for each answer, write your reasons for giving that answer. Understand that each of your answers is a conclusion you have reached based on evidence in the narrative. In writing your conclusion, give the evidence on which it is based. Do not be afraid to give the answer "I don't know" to a question if you feel the narrative does not contain enough evidence to form a conclusion. If that is your answer, explain what evidence you feel is missing from the narrative. Take your time in answering the questions. You may look back at the narrative as often as you wish. You may find it helpful to quote parts of the narrative in explaining the evidence on which you have based a conclusion.

1. How many years have Rusty and Pete been friends? (a) seven years (b) eight years (c) nine years (d) I don't know.

2. Which boy flunked out of college in his freshman year? (a) Pete (b) Rusty (c) neither boy (d) I don't know.

3. Which boy smoked? (a) only Pete (b) only Rusty (c) both boys (d) I don't know.

4. What sport does Rusty play? (a) basketball (b) soccer (c) ice hockey (d) I don't know.

5. What kind of car does Rusty own? (a) sedan (b) convertible (c) pickup truck (d) I don't know.

6. What branch of the service is Pete in? (a) the Army (b) the Air Force (c) the Coast Guard (d) I don't know.

7. In what state is Rusty's college located?   (a) Wisconsin (b) Florida (c) California (d) I don't know.

8. How did Pete contact Rusty?   (a) by telephone (b) by letter (c) by telegram (d) I don't know.

9. Which boy starred on his high school football team?   (a) only Pete (b) both boys (c) neither boy (d) I don't know.

10. Which boy now lives on a college campus?   (a) only Rusty (b) neither boy (c) only Pete (d) I don't know.

11. Which boy was asked for proof of age?   (a) only Rusty (b) both boys (c) only Pete (d) I don't know.

12. Which boy wore green shorts and a white turtleneck?   (a) Pete (b) neither boy (c) Rusty (d) I don't know.

When you have completed the quiz put your paper aside. Before you begin reading the second part of the narrative, glance back over the first part briefly. Then continue reading the narrative. At its conclusion you will find some additional questions.

Sitting at the table, Pete and Rusty reminisced about their days in school and brought each other up to date on what had happened since they had last been together. Pete had been stationed in the Far East for almost a year. His enlistment was up in less than a year, and he was planning to return to college. Rusty had been dating the same girl during half the time he had been an undergraduate. Lately they had started talking about marriage, but not before Rusty graduated.

The waitress came back and waited while they studied the menus. One of the boys ordered lasagna and a repeat on the Coke. The other asked for veal parmigiana and switched from Scotch and soda to beer.

While they ate, Pete talked about his plans for the future. He had been in touch with his old college coach, and there was a chance of getting his scholarship back. They discussed Rusty's car. He was paying it off with money earned during the summer as a lifeguard and expected to own it free and clear about the time he turned Pete's age. They exchanged information on old friends and classmates; which ones were in college or in the service or in jail.

It was almost midnight when they finally yielded to the restaurant owner's plea that they get out and let him close up. One of the boys wanted to continue the conversation, but the other had an 8 o'clock class the next morning. Instead, as they got into the car, they agreed to meet on the following day near the campus for lunch.

Answer these questions, following the same instructions as those given for the earlier quiz. In formulating your answers, look for information in both *parts of the narrative, not just the second part.*

13. How long has Rusty been dating the same girl? (a) about 14½ months (b) about nine months (c) about a year (d) I don't know.

14. Which boy ordered lasagna? (a) Rusty (b) Pete (c) neither boy (d) I don't know.

15. Which boy could not swim? (a) Pete (b) both boys (c) neither boy (d) I don't know.

16. Which boy suggested they keep talking after they left the restaurant? (a) neither boy (b) Rusty (c) Pete (d) I don't know.

17. How many roommates did Rusty have during his freshman year? (a) none (b) one (c) four (d) I don't know.

18. Which boy got top grades in college? (a) Rusty (b) neither boy (c) Pete (d) I don't know.

19. Which boy was the last to arrive home? (a) Rusty (b) Pete (c) they arrived at the same time (d) I don't know.

20. Which boy paid the check for the dinner? (a) Rusty (b) Pete (c) they had separate checks (d) I don't know.

After you have completed this part of the quiz, look over your answers to the first twelve questions. Look first at those questions to which you responded with "(d) I don't know." Is there any additional information given in the second part of the narrative which now allows you to answer those questions? If so, write your new answer at the end.

Once you have finished this, recheck all your other answers and make certain that no evidence appears in the second part of the narrative which would cause you to change your original response. It is important to be sure that you have answered each question as accurately as possible.

Before we review the results of this quiz, take a moment to study the following definitions:

☐ **Inference:** *a reasonable conclusion based on sound evidence.*

☐ **Assumption:** *a conclusion reached prematurely on the basis of insufficient evidence.*

☐ **Implication:** *a conclusion indicated but not confirmed by the evidence.*

From now on we will be using these three terms a great deal, so it is important that you know and understand them. You may wish to review the exercises on propaganda (Section I, pp. 11–17) before continuing. Study these two sample exercises carefully:

1. Selma borrowed Eve's new pantsuit to wear to the party, but when she tried it on it fit too tightly in the hips and waist, and she had to return it.

   QUESTION: Which girl is heavier?   (a) Selma (b) Eve (c) they weigh about the same (d) I don't know.

2. George had left his hat on the top shelf of the closet. He could not reach it and asked Charlie to get it for him.

   QUESTION: Which boy is taller?   (a) George (b) Charlie (c) they are about the same height (d) I don't know.

In the first sample you know that Eve's pantsuit was too small for Selma, therefore you can reasonably conclude that Selma is heavier than Eve. Such a conclusion is an *inference*. It is very difficult to imagine a circumstance under which Eve's clothes would be too small for Selma if Selma were lighter in weight.

In the second sample you know that George could not reach the closet's top shelf, and you know that he asked Charlie to get his hat down. If, on the basis of this evidence, you answered that Charlie is the taller, you made an *assumption*. You reached a conclusion too quickly and on the basis of insufficient evidence. It is easy to imagine circumstances under which George could be taller and yet unable to reach the hat. For example, suppose he had been injured and was confined to a wheelchair. Then, too, you have been told only that George *asked* Charlie to get the hat. You do not know for certain whether or not Charlie was able to reach the shelf.

The facts given to you in the second sample do not supply enough information to enable you to *infer* an answer. Those facts do strongly *suggest* that Charlie is taller, but they do not confirm it as true. Therefore, there is an *implication* that Charlie is taller. An implication of a conclusion should lead you to seek additional evidence which will allow you to draw an inference of fact. But do not confuse an implication with solid evidence or you may assume a totally false conclusion.

The facts in the second sample imply that Charlie is taller, but they might just as easily support the conclusion that George is a seven-foot giant confined to a wheelchair and Charlie is a four-foot midget who had to stand on a chair to reach his buddy's hat. The correct answer to the question is "I don't know."

Study this sample and answer the question:

3. Joe had left his hat on the top shelf of the closet. He was too short to reach it, but Bill reached it easily without standing on a chair.

    QUESTION: Which boy is taller? (a) Joe (b) Bill (c) they are about the same height (d) I don't know.

This time the question is much easier. We know why Joe cannot reach the shelf: he is "too short." So we can infer that Bill must be taller because he "reached it easily" while standing on the floor.

Be careful. You have not been told that Bill was standing on the floor, only that he was not standing on a chair. It is possible that poor little Bill was so short that he had to climb on a table to retrieve that hat. Do not be tricked into making false assumptions. The proper answer again is "I don't know."

Look at one more sample before we review the quiz questions:

4. Jack had left his hat on the top shelf of the closet. He was too short to reach it, but Dave reached it easily while standing on the floor.

    QUESTION: Which boy is the tallest? (a) Jack (b) Dave (c) Harry (d) I don't know.

Think about that one while we go over your answers to the quiz. Check your conclusions and the reasoning which led you to them against the following list of correct answers. Notice that, whether you were aware of it or not at the time you took the quiz, you were making *inferences* and *assumptions,* and dealing with *implications.*

1. Rusty and Pete have been friends "since they met in the seventh grade." They would have spent six years together in junior high school and high school. Add one, their freshman year in college, after which Pete dropped out and enlisted. Since then the boys did not see each other until the time of the narrative, "a little more than a year." Six plus one plus one equals eight years of friendship. You may *infer* that the correct answer is *b*.

2. This question tests the care with which you read and think. The narrative states that Pete "did not flunk out," but "dropped out" after losing his scholarship. If you read carelessly you answered *a*, Pete. If you read with care you knew that the correct answer was *c*, neither boy.

3. This question may have trapped you into making a false *assumption*. We know from the narrative that "Pete bought a pack of cigarettes." From that fact we may logically *infer* that Pete smoked, which eliminates answer *b* from consideration. But which of the other three answers is correct? You are given no information at all as to whether or not Rusty smokes. You may have assumed he did not because he is an athlete in training, but many athletes smoke and the facts are hardly conclusive. The only reasonable answer you can give is *d*. If you answered with *a* you have made an assumption which cannot be confirmed with the known facts.

4. We know that Rusty plays a team sport, that his position is center, that a score is called a goal, and that a game is divided into halves. If you know nothing about sports, you probably had trouble with this question, but very little research would have told you that you could eliminate *c* immediately. Ice hockey is played in three periods, not in halves. But all the terms used in the narrative are used in both basketball and soccer. You may, therefore, have answered with *d*, but you should not have.

   Since the Green Bay Packers, a professional football team, is playing a regular-season game, the time of the narrative must be autumn. Basketball is a winter sport, but soccer is normally played in the fall and Rusty's team is just "opening its season." The right answer is *b*.

5. This one is simple. The boys rode in the car "with the top down," so it had to be a convertible.

6. Originally you should have answered with *d* because there is not sufficient information in the first part of the narrative to reach a conclusion. After reading the second part, however, your thinking should have gone like this:

   Eliminate *c* at once. If he were in the Coast Guard, Pete would not have "been stationed in the Far East." The time element provides the clue to this question. Pete enlisted. He has been in the service "a little more than a year," and his enlistment will be up in "less than a year." Only the Army offers two-year enlistments. The answer is *a*.

7. Since the Packers are "in town" to play the Los Angeles team, you may infer that Rusty goes to school in California.

8. This is answered by a direct statement in the narrative, "Rusty received Pete's telephone call." The answer is *a*.

9. Since we know the boys played "in different sports," we can eliminate *b* right away. Possibly, because you knew that Rusty's sport was soccer, you assumed that the answer must be *a*, only Pete. But there is no evidence to support any conclusion in either part of the narrative. The correct answer is *d*.

10. Once again there is great danger here of leaping to an unsupported assumption, and if you answered *a*, that is exactly what you did. Obviously Pete does not live on a college campus. Obviously Rusty goes to college. Since the boys "roomed together during their freshman year," it would be plausible to suppose that Rusty still rooms somewhere other than his home. But there is no evidence on which such a conclusion can be founded. If you doubt this, reread the narrative carefully. Although there is an *implication* that Rusty lives on campus, there is no basis for such an inference. This question must be answered by *d*.

11. The answer to this question is *d*. The tricky part lies in the fact that one sentence in the narrative seems to say more than it actually does. "They ordered something to drink, but the elderly waitress, eyeing Rusty suspiciously, asked for proof of age." Clearly it was Rusty, not Pete, whose youthful appear-

ance aroused the woman's suspicions. But this does not mean that she asked for proof only from Rusty. The narrative may *imply* answer *a* but it does not confirm it; *b* could also be true. Thus *d* is the only possible answer.

12. This question is closely related to the preceding one. The only fact we are told about the boy in the turtleneck and shorts is that he is the younger of the two. The clue to which boy is younger lies in the problem of figuring out who got the Scotch and who got the Coke. The temptation is to assume that Rusty is younger, since we know he looks younger, and wearing short pants could increase the youthful effect of his appearance. But, although answer *c* is strongly implied, you cannot infer it from the evidence contained in the first part of the narrative. True, a fact given in the second part of the narrative confirms that the correct answer is *c*; however, your original answer, given before you read the second part, should have been *d*.

Study the final paragraph of the first part on page 91 carefully. It states that the boys "ordered something to drink," which implies that both ordered liquor but does not state as a fact that they did. (Recall the distinction between suggestion and statement stressed at the conclusion of Section I of this book.) It then states that Rusty, and possibly Pete, were asked for proof of age. Finally it states that one boy was served Scotch, the other Coke. The strong implication is that Pete drank whisky while Rusty got a soft drink, but an implication is not grounds for an inference.

An inference can be drawn only if you cannot imagine a plausible alternative conclusion from the known evidence. But, given the evidence in this paragraph, there is a plausible alternative conclusion. A Coke is "something to drink." It is possible that the sequence of events was: (1) Rusty ordered Scotch and Pete ordered Coke. (2) The waitress asked Rusty for proof of age. (3) Rusty proved he was over twenty-one and was served. If this explanation is correct it could imply that Pete was under legal age, and therefore ordered cola.

Yet another interpretation can be imagined for the facts offered in the paragraph. (1) Both boys ordered whisky. (2) Because Rusty looked too young, the waitress asked both for proof of age and discovered that it was Pete who was underage. (3) Rusty got the liquor and Pete got the soft drink.

Notice that we now have three completely different versions of what happened in that restaurant, not one of which violates the facts given in the paragraph under discussion. Those of you who initially answered question 12 with *c*, assuming that Rusty was the lad with the warm neck and the cold knees, should take particular note that two of these three thoroughly plausible explanations support the opposite conclusion.

The right answer is *c*, but this is not clearly proved until the statement in the second part that Rusty was paying off his car "and expected to own it free and clear about the time he turned Pete's age." Thus, obviously he is not yet as old as Pete. This reduces the number of possible versions of what happened to one. (1) Both boys ordered liquor. (2) The waitress did not think Rusty was of legal age. (3) Either she asked only Rusty for proof or she asked both boys, and Pete was able to produce it. (The answer to question 11 remains *d*.) (4) Rusty is younger than Pete and therefore the proud possessor of the green and white wardrobe described in the question.

13. Rusty has been dating the same girl "during half the time he had been an undergraduate." The problem is to discover how long he has been an undergraduate and divide by two. Since the end of his freshman year "a little more than a year" has passed, and we know it is autumn at the time of the events in the narrative. It must be the fall of his junior year. He has been an undergraduate for two full years, and the correct answer is *c*.

14. Having struggled through the painfully complicated problem of question 12, this one should be easy. According to the narrative, one boy "ordered lasagna and a repeat on the Coke." Since we know that Rusty drank the original Coke, the answer must be *a*.

15. We are back to one of those questions which lures you into a false assumption. We know that Rusty is an excellent swimmer, since he works as a lifeguard, but we know nothing about whether Pete can swim or not. The only possible answer is *d*.

16. The key statement from the narrative is this: "One of the boys wanted to continue the conversation, but the other had an 8 o'clock class the next morning." Though Pete might attend classes in the army, he is now on leave. It must be Rusty with the early lecture, so the only possible answer is *c*.

17. Hopefully by this point in the quiz you are beginning to recognize an attempt to trap you into an illogical assumption when you see one. If not, then you answered *b* to this question, knowing that during his freshman year Rusty had at least one roommate, Pete. There is no information on whether any other guys shared their rooms. The right response to this question is *d*.

18. Eliminate answer *c*. Had Pete gotten "top grades" he would not have lost his scholarship. But there is no evidence to support the notion that Rusty received "top grades," or that he did not. All we know is that he got satisfactory grades. Another trap for those who tend to leap to conclusions. The answer: *d*.

19. This answer should, by now, be easily inferred. Since Rusty drove, he would have to drop Pete off where he was staying before returning home himself. The logical answer is *a*.

20. No evidence is given to indicate the answer to this question. The proper response is *d*.

FOLLOW-UP

1. *Study again the definitions for inference, assumption and implication on page 94. Then try creating your own exercises like the ones in this section. Begin with simpler quizzes consisting of a paragraph and one or two questions, such as the samples on page 94. Form teams and test each other with your own exercises. You should find it easier to learn by writing your own exercises than you would be taking more tests.*

2. *For an even greater challenge, create a longer and more complex exercise similar to the Pete and Rusty narrative.*

3. *Look back at the fourth sample quiz on page 95. Which boy is the tallest?*

Clearly Dave is taller than Jack, however, if your answer is *b* you have not understood this section. You have been given no information about the third boy, Harry, and you have no way of determining whether Harry is taller or shorter than the others. The answer must be *d*.

4. *"The Locked Room Murder Case," which follows, is designed to let you test the skills you have been developing through the exercises in this section. In order to solve the murder, you need to be able to distinguish fact from opinion, to tell the difference between a logical inference and a hasty assumption, and to recognize deliberate deception.*

The Locked Room
Murder Case

Wealthy Gideon Channing has been found murdered at his country estate under mysterious circumstances in a room locked and bolted from inside. You are one of a team of detectives brought in by the completely baffled police to attempt to solve the crime. There were only three people in Channing's mansion with him at the time of the murder. Each of them has a motive, yet it seems impossible to the police that any of them could have killed him. It seems equally impossible, however, that Gideon Channing could have committed suicide. So impossible, in fact, that the police are convinced it must be murder, and yet they cannot conceive of any way in which murder could be committed inside a locked room. For this reason they have consulted you and your team of investigators to solve the crime.

The police have turned all their evidence over to you, including their own report on the circumstances of the murder and the suspects' backgrounds, the coroner's report on the cause of death, and the depositions of the three suspects. Keep in mind that *only one of the suspects, the murderer, is lying. The other two are innocent and are telling the truth to the best of their knowledge.*

It is now your job to sift through the evidence and determine who murdered Gideon Channing and how the crime was committed.

Police report on the death of Gideon Channing

Sunday, July 10. At 2:35 a.m. police were summoned by telephone to investigate a possible homicide at Briarwood, the country home of millionaire Gideon Channing. At 2:50 officers arrived and were admitted by Scotty Channing, 22, resident of the house and nephew of the deceased. Waiting in the library were two other men, both weekend house guests. One, Nigel Penwarren, 45, was the deceased's long-time business partner. The other, Jonathan Mayhew, 51, has been the deceased's attorney for sixteen years. All three asserted that they had discovered the body together and had not been out of each other's sight since. They stated that the body had been found at approximately 2:25 a.m. and that nothing in the murder room had been touched or altered. All three insisted that, at the time the body was found, the murder room was locked and bolted from inside, making it necessary to break in.

Officers went to the second-floor bedroom of the deceased and found the corpse of Gideon Channing, 44, lying face down on the floor with its head near the center of the room and its feet toward the door. Channing had been wounded twice in the back. The apparent murder weapon, an ivory-handled knife, protruded from one of the wounds. On the floor near the body lay the parts of a steel bolt lock which had been ripped from the door and wall. An examination of the room's single window showed that it, too, was bolted from the inside. There was no evidence of any attempt to force entry through the window.

On the desk were miscellaneous business papers. The body was clad in pajamas and a robe, but the bed had not been turned down, leading the officers to conclude that Gideon Channing had been awake and working at his desk prior to his death. The room showed no signs of a struggle, nor was there any evidence to indicate that it had been searched. Channing's wallet, containing over $2,000 in cash, still lay in plain sight on the desk. Robbery, therefore, was ruled out as a motive.

There was evidence that the victim had been drinking heavily. Standing on a small bar in one corner of the room was a nearly empty bottle of Scotch whisky. A pair of heavy sterling silver ice tongs, badly scratched from heavy use, stood in an empty ice bucket, and on the desk was a glass which still contained two ounces of pure whisky. The deceased's fingerprints were found on the glass.

The entire murder room was checked for fingerprints, but the only clear sets found belonged either to the victim or to his housekeeper,

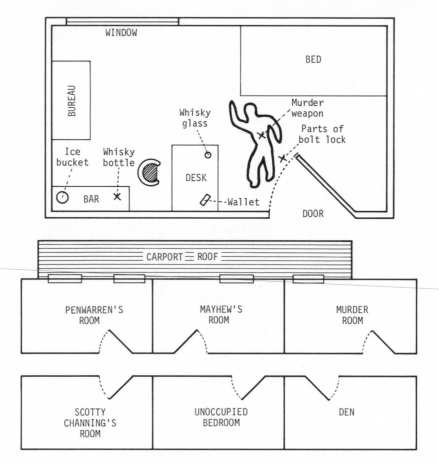

Details, murder room (top); second-floor bedrooms (bottom).

Mrs. Irene Poulty, 64. Police ascertained that Mrs. Poulty had been given the weekend off and spent the murder night visiting her sister thirty miles away. Mrs. Poulty later verified that the victim normally slept with his window locked because he was fearful of burglars. He had had the entire house air conditioned seven years before and had since left standing orders that every window and door in the house be secured at night. At the same time, he had installed heavy bolt locks on most of the rooms, including his bedroom. The housekeeper also testified that Channing kept a desk in his bedroom because he suffered from insomnia and often worked late into the night. She identified the murder knife as a letter opener kept on the desk.

A thorough investigation of the house and grounds not only showed that all doors and windows had been locked from inside, but also produced no evidence to suggest the recent presence of prowlers or any attempt to gain illegal entry. Police are convinced that no one except the victim, his nephew, his business partner, and his attorney were in the house on the night of the murder.

All three suspects had ample motive for murdering Gideon Channing. Nigel Penwarren, as surviving partner, stands to inherit the victim's half of Channing-Penwarren Enterprises stock, which is valued in the millions of dollars. Scotty Channing, the dead man's only relative, comes into the victim's personal fortune, estimated at more than half a million dollars. Police have learned that the young man has gambled and lost heavily, and he is believed to be in debt to loan sharks for over $50,000. Jonathan Mayhew's wife, his third and a woman considerably younger than he, has often been seen in the company of the deceased in recent months. A number of reputable witnesses have testified that Mayhew has had several violent quarrels with Gideon Channing on this account and has actually threatened the victim's life on two occasions.

The three men have been questioned closely. Their testimony and the evidence of the medical examiner constitute the remainder of this report.

Report of the medical examiner

An autopsy was performed on the body of Gideon Channing on Sunday, July 10, at 10:00 a.m. The victim had been stabbed twice in the back. The murder weapon was an ivory-handled letter opener left in the second wound by the killer. After it was removed by the medical examiner, it was examined by the police laboratory, which determined that the handle had been wiped clean of fingerprints.

The first wound entered the victim's back to the right of the right shoulder blade and continued downward toward the center of the spine but did not sever the spine. This wound by itself would not have been fatal. The second wound, which was fatal, entered slightly left of the spine above the heart and drove downward and to the left until it penetrated the heart.

The position of the wounds makes it impossible that they were self-inflicted. There is no question but that the victim was murdered.

Medical evidence indicates the victim died sometime between 1:00 and 3:00 on the morning of July 10, since the effects of rigor mortis became evident at approximately 6:00 a.m. An analysis of the stomach contents revealed that the victim had indulged in heavy drinking before his death.

Deposition of Scotty Channing, nephew of the deceased

My name is Scotty Channing, age twenty-two. Gideon Channing was my uncle. I lived with my uncle at Briarwood. I am not employed at present. I flunked out of Yale two years ago. I have never been employed.

On the morning of Saturday, July 9, I first became aware that my uncle had invited two house guests for the weekend. The housekeeper, Mrs. Poulty, informed me of this. She also informed me that she would be away that evening visiting her sister. She showed me food she had prepared for dinner that night. I was not annoyed that Mr. Penwarren and Mr. Mayhew were invited for the weekend. I knew both of them well. I had known them for years. They often visited my uncle to discuss business matters.

Mr. Penwarren arrived about 2:00 p.m. on Saturday. Mr. Mayhew perhaps an hour later. Mrs. Poulty had left around noon. The men met with my uncle in the library until supper at 6:00 p.m. I don't know what they discussed. My uncle was always very secretive about his business dealings, and I was never involved in his business.

Nothing unusually unpleasant occurred during dinner. My uncle may have mentioned my gambling debts. I really don't remember.

Question. How deeply in debt to the gamblers were you?
Answer. Not too bad.
Q. As much as $100,000?
A. No. Maybe half of that, no more.
Q. Had you asked your uncle to pay your gambling debts?
A. I think I had asked him for a loan.
Q. What was his response?
A. My uncle gave me anything I wanted.

After dinner Mr. Penwarren went up to his room as I remember. He took a bottle of brandy with him. Mr. Mayhew went into the library with Uncle Gideon. I couldn't hear what they were saying. I could tell they were arguing about something; their voices were very loud. Maybe they were talking about Mr. Mayhew's wife.

Q. Did you listen at the keyhole?
A. Certainly not. But everyone knew Uncle Gideon had been dating Mrs. Mayhew. It was in all the columns.

I went to my room about 10:00. I don't know whether anyone else had gone to bed yet or not. I went to bed about 11:00. I'm certain I locked all the doors before going to bed. My uncle was very particular about locking the house; he was afraid of someone breaking in. Yes, I'm sure Mr. Penwarren and Mr. Mayhew were aware of this. I've heard both of them kid him about it.

I did not sleep very well. I awoke a few minutes after 2:00. I lay awake for about twenty minutes. I decided to go down to my uncle's room to discuss something with him. My uncle was often awake very late at night.

Q. What did you want to discuss?
A. Something of importance.
Q. Possibly the fact that your uncle had refused to pay your gambling debts?
A. He had not refused.
Q. Suppose I said that we had testimony to prove he had?
A. You may have testimony to show he *said* he'd refused. I told you, my uncle gave me anything I wanted, sooner or later.

I passed my uncle's room at about 2:22. I know the time because I looked at my watch to see if he was still likely to be up. When I saw a light under his door, I knocked and called his name. There was no answer. I knocked once or twice more without response. Then I became alarmed.

Q. What did you do then?
A. I began to pound on his door and shout. I tried the knob and then

started to shove my shoulder against the door. I must have wakened the others because I remember seeing Mr. Mayhew running down the hall, mopping his forehead with his handkerchief, and behind him Mr. Penwarren. The door broke in and I saw my uncle lying on the floor. I may have shouted. I don't remember.

I was not the first person to enter the room. In fact I did not enter the room at all. To my best recollection Mr. Mayhew was the first person to enter the room. Mr. Penwarren followed him. Mr. Mayhew knelt beside my uncle's body. He said my uncle was dead.

Q. Why didn't you enter the room?
A. I saw my uncle lying on the floor.
Q. How did you know he was dead?
A. I didn't until Mr. Mayhew said so.
Q. What did Mr. Penwarren do or say?
A. He said the window was locked. Then Mr. Mayhew said my uncle was dead, and Mr. Penwarren said we had better call the police and leave everything as it was.
Q. You mean that during all this time you never entered the room?
A. I've never seen a corpse before. But I wasn't afraid; not for a minute.

I swear that I never entered the murder room. I swear that Mr. Mayhew and Mr. Penwarren were behind me. I know of nothing to suggest that either of them murdered my uncle. I have no idea how my uncle died. I swear that the door of my uncle's room was locked until I broke it open. I had no idea of how much money I stood to inherit from my uncle's will. I did know that his private fortune went to me, but I did not know how much money it would involve. I did know my uncle kept an ivory-handled letter opener on his desk. To the best of my knowledge, both Mr. Penwarren and Mr. Mayhew knew this also. My uncle often used his bedroom as an office, and both had been involved in conferences there.

Deposition of Jonathan Mayhew, attorney of the deceased

My name is Jonathan Mayhew, age fifty-one. I am a member of the firm of Lawrence & Mayhew. I was the attorney of the late Gideon Channing for the past sixteen years. I handled his personal matters. On Friday,

July 8, Channing summoned me to a business conference to be held over the weekend of July 9 and 10 at Briarwood, his country home. This was not unusual.

I arrived at Briarwood about 3:00 in the afternoon of Saturday, July 9. I was admitted by Channing's young nephew. Normally I had been admitted by the housekeeper; I understood the housekeeper had been given the weekend off. I found that Nigel Penwarren was also in the house.

Q. Were you surprised to find Mr. Penwarren had been invited?
A. I didn't expect to see either Penwarren or young Scotty.
Q. Why not?
A. Because I'd been given to understand that the reason for the conference was that Mr. Channing wished to change his will.
Q. And?
A. Well, I'd drawn up Channing's original will. His only heirs were his partner and his nephew. I assumed he intended to cut one of them out of the will by changing it.
Q. Why did you assume Channing had invited you to Briarwood to change his will?
A. Because, damn it, he told me so on the phone on Friday.
Q. Which of his two heirs was he planning to disinherit?
A. I have no idea.

Channing, Penwarren and I conferred on business matters in the library from 3:00 until about 6:00. Channing and Penwarren were drinking. I never take an alcoholic drink. I was never alone with Channing during this time. Channing did not mention his will during this conference. The business matters we discussed were routine. Dinner was served at 6:00. Since the housekeeper was away, it was served by Channing's nephew as I remember.

At dinner Channing mentioned his nephew's gambling debts. These amounted to about $50,000 as I recall. It was my understanding that the boy had asked Channing for the money and that Channing was being difficult about it.

Q. Did this disturb the nephew?
A. Yes, I would say that the boy was upset.

Q. Did he make any threats against his uncle?
A. No, I don't recall that he threatened Channing in any way.

After dinner Channing and I continued to confer in the library. I don't know what happened to the other two. Channing and I had business matters to discuss. I left Channing in the library about 9:45 and went to my room. I saw no one else at that time. I retired at about 10:30. I was very tired.

I was awakened at about 2:20 by shouting and a loud pounding noise. I got out of bed and put on my robe. I went into the hall to see what the disturbance was about.

Q. When you entered the hall, what did you see?
A. I saw young Scotty pounding on his uncle's bedroom door and shouting.
Q. What was he shouting?
A. His uncle's name. Then he began shoving his shoulder against the door. I ran down the hall toward him. Just before I reached the door, Scotty broke it in.
Q. What did you do next?
A. I looked into the room and saw Gideon Channing lying face down on the floor. He was dead.
Q. How did you know he was dead?
A. There was a knife in his back. I mean I assumed he was dead at first. I went into the room and examined the body. It was obvious he was dead.

To the best of my memory Scotty Channing never entered the room. Penwarren did enter, perhaps a few seconds after I did. It might have been thirty seconds later. The boy stayed in the hall. I don't recall that he seemed unusually upset under the circumstances.

Q. Did Mr. Penwarren touch the body?
A. No, I don't believe Penwarren went near the body.
Q. What did Mr. Penwarren do?
A. He went to check the window. He asked me if Channing was dead and I said he was. Then Penwarren said the window was locked from the inside. I then checked it; it was locked. Then Penwarren suggested we go to the library and call the police. That is what we did.

I repeat, after dinner Channing and I went to the library to discuss matters of business. He did not mention any changes in his will. My wife was never mentioned during our conversation. As I recall we did not argue about anything.

Q. Isn't it true that Channing had been seeing your wife recently?
A. They may have met by accident.
Q. Didn't you confront Channing and warn him to stay away from your wife?
A. I may have suggested to him that it was indiscreet for them to be seen in public together. I certainly did not suspect my wife of being unfaithful to me, if that's what you mean.
Q. On the night of Channing's murder, did you discuss your wife with the victim at all, in any connection?
A. Certainly not.
Q. On the evening of the murder, did you have an argument of any kind with Gideon Channing?
A. I told you: we talked business.

Deposition of Nigel Penwarren, partner of the deceased

My name is Nigel Penwarren, age forty-five. I was Gideon Channing's business partner for almost twenty years. My reason for being at Briarwood on the night of the murder was that Channing and I had business matters to discuss. I knew that Jonathan Mayhew would be at Briarwood. I am well aware that I inherited Gideon's stock in the business when he died. Channing and I had similar wills. If either of us died, the company would become the sole property of the other. I am certainly unaware of any intention by Channing to change his will.

I arrived at Briarwood at about 2:00. Channing's housekeeper was not there. Channing's nephew opened the door for me. I first saw Mayhew at 3:00 or thereabouts. He came into the library and the three of us met until about 6:00. I did not see Scotty again until dinner.

Q. What was the atmosphere at dinner?
A. I should say it was tense.
Q. Why?
A. Well, Gideon never did get along very well with his nephew. The boy

was in hock to gamblers for a large sum. Gideon was being difficult about paying the debt. Then there was the business about Gideon and Mayhew's wife.

Q. Did Mr. Channing argue with Mr. Mayhew concerning his wife?

A. Not while I was around. Of course they may have discussed it after dinner.

Q. Weren't you around after dinner?

A. Hell, no. I could see Gideon was warming up to a fight. He always turned mean when he'd been drinking. I didn't want to be around when the battle started. I took a bottle of his best brandy and went to bed.

Q. With whom did you think Mr. Channing would argue?

A. You mean Mayhew or Scotty? It could have been either one.

Q. You said Mr. Channing had been drinking. Hadn't you been drinking as well?

A. I always held my liquor better than Gideon.

I couldn't swear to exactly when I fell asleep. I woke up sometime after 2:00 because someone was shouting. It must have been closer to 2:30. I also heard a pounding sound. I put on my robe and went out in the hall. Mayhew came out of his room just ahead of me. Scotty Channing was further down the hall, beating on Gideon's door and yelling his name. Just as Mayhew started toward him, the boy seemed to break the door in. I went down the hall. I saw Scotty step back from the open door and bury his face in his hands. Mayhew went inside just before I got there, 30, maybe 40 seconds later.

Q. When you reached the door, what did you do?

A. I saw Gideon lying on the floor. Mayhew was kneeling beside the body, wiping his forehead with his handkerchief. I believe he said that Gideon was dead, and I said that nothing was to be touched. I looked at the window in the room and it was locked from inside. As I recall I then suggested calling the police.

I had no grudge against Gideon Channing. I don't believe, in almost twenty years, that we ever had an argument. I have absolutely no idea how he might have died.

Section IV

PROJECTS IN INVESTIGATION

Preparing
Abstracts

The materials in this Section are designed to introduce you to the fundamental techniques of writing research papers. The initial segment, dealing with abstracts of articles, provides experience in taking good notes on what you read and distinguishing a writer's major points from his secondary and supportive material. It also demonstrates the need for a critical reading of sources; that is, reading not simply for comprehension, but to judge the validity of the author's arguments.

To abstract an article is to write a condensed summary and critique of the piece. It is an effective first step in learning to do research because the skills it fosters, such as close, analytical reading, effective note-taking and paraphrasing, are also essential to successful research.

Study "How to Write an Abstract of an Article," and be certain you understand the points its author is making. After each paragraph you will find a sample note which might have been taken by someone preparing to abstract this article. Immediately following most of the sample notes are further instructions (in italics) for abstracting. At its conclusion appears an abstract of the article which has been composed from these sample notes. Our aim is to explain the process of abstracting and simultaneously to demonstrate it.

Abstracting is not only a way of learning research techniques but also an increasingly common assignment on its own, required by teachers in widely varied disciplines. When you have reviewed the samples thoroughly, you will be asked to test your skill by abstracting two articles.

How to Write an Abstract of an Article
by Albert Colombo

Scholastic Skills. Chicago: Dalton Press, 1962. Pp. 33–35.

> *Make certain you have recorded all the information needed for a bibliographical entry. Copy this information even before beginning to read the article. Here, notice that Colombo's article appears in his book,* Scholastic Skills.

The abstract of an article is a summary of the most important points the author has attempted to make. Its relationship to the article is similar to that of a book report to a book. It tells the reader in abbreviated form what the article is about and helps him to decide whether it will be worth his time to bother reading the entire article. To achieve this second purpose, the abstract should be written in two parts: in addition to a summary of the article's main points, it should include a section of comment and evaluation in which you give your own opinion of the author's arguments and his writing skill in expressing them.

[p. 33]   Article abstract in 2 parts: summary of author's major arguments and comment evaluating his article yourself.

> *Notice that the page in* Scholastic Skills *on which the noted information appears is written in the left margin of your notebook.*

The summary should represent the author's arguments in a straightforward and objective manner even if you do not agree with them or feel he has phrased them poorly. Reserve your subjective judgments for the comment and evaluation section of the abstract. In this way your reader receives a fair idea of the article's content uncolored by your own personal opinion. Keep in mind, too, that your comments should give a balanced view of the article by presenting both its strengths and weaknesses.

[p. 33]   Summary gives main points "in a straightforward and objective manner"—"comment and evaluation" gives good and bad criticism.

Abstracting an article provides practice in recognizing what an author's major points are, and in distinguishing between his major points and the secondary points he uses either to explain or to support them. Usually a writer places his most important statements at the beginning or the end of his paragraphs because this is when his reader's attention is most acute. Knowing this, good authors of detective stories tend to bury their most important clues in the middle of long paragraphs, where the reader is least likely to notice them.

[pp. 33–34]   Writing abstracts teaches how to identify main arguments and tell them from secondary ones.

Notice that Colombo's third paragraph is a good example of the ideas contained in it. His most important statement is made in his first sentence. His second sentence is used to explain *his first statement by clarifying it (telling where to look for a writer's major points and why they are usually put there). His third sentence is used to* support *his first statement (by giving an example to prove his argument). Look at Colombo's other paragraphs to see if they bear out the major statement made in this paragraph.*

If a writer considers a statement to be especially important, he may give it added emphasis by isolating it in a brief paragraph of only one or two sentences.

[p. 34]   Short paragraphs may be used for special emphasis.

Notice that Colombo's fourth paragraph is a good example of the point he is stating in that paragraph.

Learning to write abstracts is a good method of developing skills in note taking. The most difficult and dangerous temptation you will face is to take notes on the articles in the author's own words. This is difficult because, when you write the summary based on your notes, you will probably find it very hard to explain the author's ideas without using his language. It is dangerous because you may be further tempted to go ahead and actually use his wording in your paper. If you do, there are only two possible results, both bad. Either you will simply string together a bunch of direct quotations and produce a paper in which very little of the wording is your own or, worse, you will use the author's language without giving him credit and without using quotation marks to indicate that the wording is not your own. This is plagiarism, one of the most serious forms of academic dishonesty.

[p. 34]   Don't quote author in your notes. This can lead to too many direct quotations in your paper, or to plagiarism.

Plagiarism is sometimes committed unconsciously by students who, having recorded their notes in the author's language, cannot think of better or even different words to express his ideas. To avoid this writing trap, take your notes down as much as possible in your own words. If you find this difficult at first, try taking notes in the lousiest, most ungrammatical English possible. By this method you not only avoid the temptation to quote the author, but also guarantee that you will be able to think of better language in writing your paper than you used in your notes.

[p. 34]   Plagiarism can be unconscious. Take notes in your own words. If this is hard, "try taking notes in the lousiest, most ungrammatical English possible."

As an example, here is a note in "lousy" English: Abstracts learn you to take good notes. Don't take no notes in direct quotes. If this ain't easy for you, put notes in rotten English.

Quote the author in your notes only when you expect to use the quotation in your paper. Usually there are two principal reasons for quoting a writer: (1) when he has expressed an idea in particularly striking and unique language (either uniquely well or uniquely badly) or (2) on those rare occasions when rephrasing the author's idea into your own words might cause your reader to misunderstand or misinterpret that idea. This is not an excuse for excessive direct quotation, however. Most of the time you should be capable of explaining the author's ideas clearly to your reader.

[pp. 34–35]   Only quote when you plan to quote source in your paper. Only quote if writer used unusual language or if (p. 35) failure to quote author's ideas might misrepresent them. These are the "two principal reasons for quoting a writer." (p. 34)

Notice that when a paragraph begins on one page and continues onto another, you must take special care in recording your note so that it is clear to you what specific information appeared on which page. In the previous sample, "(p. 35)" is inserted to show that the second reason for quoting a source appeared on a different page from that recorded in the margin. However, since the direct quotation comes from the original page, that must be indicated by placing "(p. 34)" after the quotation.

Notes for an abstract can be most conveniently recorded on a page or two in your notebook. They should be complete enough so that you can compose your abstract entirely from them without having to consult the article itself once you have begun writing. Although it is not necessary to use footnotes in an abstract since, unlike a research paper, you are working with only one source, it is still a good idea to develop the habit of including in each note the exact page number or numbers of the source from which the information or ideas in that note were taken.

[p. 35]

Notes should be so thorough that "you can compose your abstract entirely from them." Record article page numbers in notes even though they aren't needed for abstract.

Mastering the techniques of article abstracting is an important first step on the road to successful research writing. The student who takes that step is on his way to discovering the joy of learning which lies at the end of that road.

In addition to a summary, it is necessary to comment on and evaluate the article. To prepare for this, you should record your own impressions of the author's ideas and style. When abstracting a very long article or doing a book report, these impressions should be noted as you read, as soon as they occur to you, and marked with the letter "C" (for comment) next to the page number in the margin. When you are abstracting a brief article such as the one by Albert Colombo, it is best to read the entire article and then jot down your reactions to it immediately. Study the following commentary notations to Colombo's article.

[C]

Directions for abstracting are clearly explained. Main points (identifying major arguments and dangers involved in note taking) are explained with good suggestions. No summation of his own principal points is given. Last paragraph is childish in tone. For example, abstracting is described as "an important first step on the road" which leads "to discovering the joy of learning." The "joy of learning"! Ugh!

Examine the article abstract sample that follows. It was written from the notes recorded here on Albert Colombo's article, which is actually a chapter from his book Scholastic Skills.

ABSTRACT of ARTICLE

Colombo, Albert, "How to Write an Abstract of an Article," Scholastic Skills. Dalton Press, Chicago, 1962. pp. 33–35.

Summary of Article

Albert Colombo divides the abstract of an article into two parts: the summary in which the author's major arguments are presented "in a straightforward and objective manner," and the personal commentary where the reader evaluates the article. Abstracting articles is a useful exercise in identifying the main arguments of a writer and in learning how to take notes. Colombo warns that quoting sources in one's notes can lead to excessive direct quotation, or plagiarism, and advises "taking notes in the lousiest, most ungrammatical English possible," to avoid both problems. Colombo explains how notes should be recorded, including when the source should be quoted and listing the "two principal reasons for quoting a writer." Colombo also urges the use of page numbers in notes, and argues for notes so thorough that "you can compose your abstract entirely from them."

Comment and Evaluation

Colombo is both clear and explicit in his directions for abstracting an article. He carefully explains

the difficulties involved in identifying an author's
main ideas and the hazards of note taking, and offers
useful suggestions. His own article could probably
benefit from a summation of its major points at the
conclusion. At times he seems to be talking down to his
readers, especially in the final paragraph when he
calls learning to abstract "an important first step on
the road" which will lead students "to discovering the
joy of learning." Despite such lapses into childish
prose, Colombo has made clear the concept of an abstract of an article.

THE LINDBERGH KIDNAPPING

The most sensational murder trial of the 1930's was that of Bruno
Richard Hauptmann in Flemington, New Jersey, for the kidnap-
murder of the infant son of Charles Augustus Lindbergh. Following his solo flight across the Atlantic in 1927, Lindbergh had
received an incredible hero's welcome in New York, and he continued for several years to bask in the adulation of a nation which
saw him as an example of individual initiative and courage, as the
living symbol of the qualities which had made America great.
When his son was first kidnapped and then found murdered in
1932, America mourned, and seethed with a desire to see the killers brought to justice.

The man eventually charged with the crime, Bruno Hauptmann, was a German veteran of World War I with a criminal
record in his own country who had entered the United States
illegally. Hauptmann's trial, viewed by the American public
against the rising specter of Nazism in Germany, seemed to some
a contest between American "good" and German "evil." Others
abhorred this treatment of a capital trial as a morality play.

After his conviction Hauptmann became, for a time, a pawn
in a political tug-of-war between New Jersey's Democratic attor-

ney-general, David Wilentz, who had prosecuted the German as the only man involved in the crime, and Harold Hoffman, the Republican governor who pinned his hopes for a vice-presidential nomination on proving that Hauptmann was completely innocent. To the end, Hauptmann maintained his innocence but, in the eyes of many, the weight of circumstantial evidence against him was conclusive. After several delays he was executed in the electric chair on April 3, 1936.

Read the following article in preparation for abstracting it. First record all the information needed for a bibliographical entry. To be sure your entry is complete, copy in your notebook the form for periodicals which appears on page 135. Then take careful notes on the author's main points as you read. Follow the techniques for note taking demonstrated in the preceding sample. When you have finished reading the article and your notes are complete, follow the directions at the conclusion of the article.

Hauptmann Was Innocent
by Augustus L. Harrison

Atlantis Monthly, vol. 10, October, 1968, pp. 122–127.*

On the evening of Tuesday, March 1, 1932, while American flying ace and national hero Charles Lindbergh and his wife, Anne, were relaxing in their home outside the village of Hopewell, New Jersey, their infant son, Charles Jr., was kidnapped from his second-floor bedroom. The kidnapper entered through a window which, because of a broken latch, could not be locked. He used a crude, homemade ladder, which was abandoned at the scene. He took the baby from its crib, left a ransom note written in ungrammatical English which suggested the writer was either German or Dutch, and escaped unnoticed from the Lindbergh estate. Attempts to recover the child proved futile although $50,000 in ransom money was paid through an intermediary, Dr. John Condon, to a man with a heavy German accent who called

To the student: To simplify your later work in making cross-references to the articles, the page numbers for this and all subsequent articles in Section IV will coincide with the page numbers in the text.

himself "John." On May 12 the body of the baby was discovered in the woods not far from the Lindbergh lands. It had been murdered on the night of the kidnapping, perhaps before the killer left the house.

Because Lindbergh, "The Lone Eagle," was an American legend, sympathy for the bereaved parents ran extremely high, and the investigation of the crime became perhaps the most extensive and widely publicized in United States history. At last one of the bills of ransom money turned up at the Irving Trust Company. The bill had been passed at a filling station, and the attendent had penciled a New York license plate number, 4U-1341, in the margin. The bill was traced through the station to the owner of the car bearing that license, Bruno Richard Hauptmann, a Bronx carpenter and a German immigrant who had entered this country illegally. On September 19, 1934, nearly two and one-half years after the crime, Hauptmann was arrested and charged with the kidnap-murder of Charles Lindbergh, Jr. Though he steadfastly refused to admit the crime, Hauptmann was extradited to New Jersey, tried as the sole perpetrator of the brutal killing, found guilty, and executed at Trenton in the electric chair at forty-seven and one-half minutes past eight on the evening of Friday, April 3, 1936.

From the moment of his arrest Hauptmann's guilt was assumed, not merely by the authorities, but by the press and public throughout the United States. Although there was ample evidence that the crime had been planned and carried out by more than one person, the prosecution insisted during the trial that Hauptmann had worked alone. A strange quirk in New Jersey law made it impossible to give the accused man the death penalty if the jury determined he had acted as part of a conspiracy, and outrage over the crime was at such a fever pitch that it was clear the public would be satisfied with nothing less than Hauptmann's death. For this reason it is difficult not to believe that the state may have deliberately suppressed evidence that the Lindbergh kidnapping was the work of a gang.

Consider the fact that on May 1, 1933, $2,980 of Lindbergh ransom money, all gold notes, had been exchanged at the Federal Reserve Bank in New York by a man who signed his name J. J. Faulkner. All the handwriting experts consulted agreed the signature on the exchange slip was definitely not Hauptmann's handwriting. Obviously someone other than Hauptmann was in possession of nearly $3,000 of the ransom, yet how was this possible unless Faulkner was part of the gang to which the money was paid? Even more intriguing is the fact that, after Hauptmann's conviction, New Jersey Governor Harold Hoffman received a letter proclaiming the German's innocence and signed J. J. Faulkner. Despite this, the police made little or no effort to locate the elusive Mr. Faulkner.

Consider the strange case of Violet Sharpe, a servant in the Englewood, N.J., home of the Dwight Morrows, Mrs. Anne Lindbergh's parents. From the outset of the investigation, the authorities considered the kidnapping an inside job since the murderer knew things about the Lindberghs' Hopewell house that no outsider could have known. He knew exactly where the baby's bedroom was located and just which window was broken so it could not be locked. Further, it is obvious that the night of the crime, a Tuesday, would not have been chosen without inside knowledge. The Lindberghs always spent their week nights at the Morrow home but had decided to stay in Hopewell on March 1 because the baby had a slight cold. And on March 1 Lindbergh was not expected to be home. He was scheduled to speak at a dinner in New York, which would have left his wife and child unprotected. In fact he was at home, but only because he had absent-mindedly forgotten his speaking engagement.

Neither Hauptmann nor anyone else outside the Lindbergh-Morrow household could have known these special facts, but Violet Sharpe knew them and must have communicated them to the kidnapper. When she was questioned she became extremely nervous and angry and lied about her whereabouts on the murder night. When she learned she was to be questioned again, she committed suicide rather than face another police interrogation. Obviously this was very suspicious, yet the police did not follow up on this evidence.

Finally, consider the testimony of Dr. John Condon that when he was on the telephone with the kidnapper he heard voices speaking with Italian accents in background, and that he was once approached by a mysterious Italian woman who claimed to have knowledge of the crime. Once again the authorities did little to check these clues.

So it is clear that the murder of Charles Lindbergh, Jr., was the result of a conspiracy and that the Hauptmann prosecution ignored this fact in order to obtain the death sentence for the Bronx carpenter. But was Bruno Hauptmann a part of that conspiracy? Was he actually involved in the crime in any way at all, or was he a scapegoat, an innocent victim of the state's thirst for glory and revenge? When he was executed in 1936, the whole world believed in his guilt, and it still does. In the latest book on the subject, *The Lindbergh Case,* Rexford West calmly asserts, "It is a moral certainty that the killer of Charles Lindbergh, Jr., was Bruno Richard Hauptmann." And yet a dispassionate, objective evaluation of the evidence presented against Hauptmann proves conclusively that there is nothing of any importance whatever to link the man with the crime for which he was convicted.

Two witnesses placed Hauptmann near Hopewell on the day of the murder, Amandus Hochmuth and Millard Whited. But Hochmuth saw, or thought he saw, only Hauptmann's face and that *only for a split second in a speeding car!* How can we rely on such testimony, particularly when we know that old Amandus Hochmuth was all of eighty years of age. As for Whited, a suspected thief and an illiterate hillbilly, he told three different stories at different times, and though he picked Hauptmann out of a lineup, he did so only after being offered a bribe in the form of a "reward" from the police for his cooperation. Simply compare the statements of these state witnesses with those of Christian and Katie Fredericksen, a respected baker and his wife for whom Hauptmann's wife worked, that Hauptmann had come to their store to pick up his wife at the very moment the prosecutor claimed he was breaking into the Lindbergh home! Whose testimony would you believe?

The ladder used by the kidnapper had been homemade. The state emphasized the fact that Hauptmann was a carpenter and produced Arthur Koehler, a so-called "wood detective," who claimed by some pseudoscientific mumbo jumbo to prove that one of the rungs was actually sawed from a floor board in Hauptmann's attic. This claim was disputed by a wood expert from Washington, Arch Loney. Loney was unable to testify for the defense because the state would not give him sufficient opportunity during the trial to examine the ladder, but, after the verdict was in, he was able to demonstrate that the nail holes in the ladder rung did not match the holes in the attic joist to which it had supposedly been nailed. Obviously there was no connection between the controversial rung and Hauptmann.

The most damaging evidence against Hauptmann were the facts that shortly after the kidnapping his financial situation had taken a sudden turn for the better, and that some of the ransom money had been found in his garage. At first this might appear very suspicious, but in fact it is nothing of the kind. As Hauptmann acknowledged, he had been close friends with another German immigrant, Isidor Fisch, who fled back to the old country after the murder. Hauptmann had loaned Fisch a great deal of money and, just before he left, Fisch gave

The Lindbergh Kidnapping

his friend a box to hold for him. Finding that the box contained money and believing it to be a repayment of his loans to Fisch, Hauptmann spent some of it, though naturally with no idea that it was a part of the Lindbergh ransom (and a very small part at that). For this innocent mistake, Richard Hauptmann was railroaded to his undeserved death. It is tragic that Fisch had died in Germany before Hauptmann's arrest and therefore was unavailable to testify in his defense.

There was other evidence against the accused. Writers like Rexford West make much of the fact that a leading handwriting expert, Albert S. Osborne, identified Hauptmann as the writer of the ransom notes, but somehow neglected to mention that several equally prestigious experts testified to the contrary. West also mentions, in fact devotes an entire chapter of his book, to Dr. John Condon's identification of Hauptmann as the mysterious "John" to whom he had turned over the ransom money. It is true that Condon identified Hauptmann at the trial as "John," but it is also true that Condon was a man in his seventies, never saw "John" except at night, and refused at first to identify Hauptmann at all.

The reader is invited to examine this evidence. Where is the "proof" that Bruno Richard Hauptmann was anything more than a tragic victim of chance, circumstance, and the desperation of police officials who, under pressure from the public and the press to solve a crime they had bungled for more than two years, chose to sacrifice an innocent man to the nation's lust for vengeance and blood?

There is one more aspect to this case, stranger than all the rest, yet one which self-styled "historians" of the Lindbergh case like Rexford West always ignore. At the time of Hauptmann's execution (I hesitate to call it murder), another man, one Paul Wendel, had *signed a confession* to the murder of the Lindbergh child. Wendel was *under indictment* and in prison. There can exist no more eloquent testimony against capital punishment than this. It is perhaps the only time in history when one man was executed for the same crime for which another man was under indictment and to which that same man had confessed. With the death of Hauptmann, the state, of course, had to drop murder charges against Wendel. Any other course of action might have proved far too embarrassing. Still, any intelligent, objective student of the Lindbergh murder must surely wonder whether the conviction and "murder" of Bruno Richard Hauptmann served the cause of either justice or truth.

Was Hauptmann innocent? I believe he was, and I believe too that history will prove me right.

INSTRUCTIONS

1. *When you have read the article by Harrison and compiled your notes, prepare an abstract of "Hauptmann Was Innocent." Your Summary section should include only information describing the content of the article. The Summary should tell the reader what Harrison has to say, not what you think about what Harrison has to say.*

2. *In your Comment and Evaluation, give your opinion of the validity of Harrison's arguments and the effectiveness with which he expresses them. Are his points logical? Are they supported with sufficient factual evidence? Be sure to include your opinion of whether Bruno Hauptmann was guilty or innocent.*

3. *The final draft of your abstract should follow the form shown on page 120. If you plan to type your report, set margins 1¼ inches in from each edge of your paper. If more than one page, the report should be stapled in the upper left corner. Sign your name at the end of your abstract.*

Note below the proper form for a bibliographical entry for the Harrison article. Most periodicals, such as *Atlantis Monthly,* group their issues in volumes, usually by year. It is preferred practice to give the volume number as well as the date of publication in bibliographies. In the following bibliographical entry, "10: 122–127" indicates volume 10, pages 122–127. However, the volume number for newspapers may be omitted, but the complete date must be given. In footnotes the volume number may be omitted for all periodicals.

Harrison, Augustus L. "Hauptmann Was Innocent,"
    <u>Atlantis Monthly</u>, 10:122–127, October, 1968.

Read the following article, "The Guilt of Richard Hauptmann," in preparation for abstracting it. Record all the information needed for a bibliographical entry, and take careful notes on the author's main points. Copy the form for periodicals in your notebook from page 135, and follow the same note-taking techniques you used for the Harrison article. When your notes are complete, follow the directions at the conclusion of the article.

The Guilt of Richard Hauptmann
by Rexford West

Saturday Preview, vol. 23, February 18, 1970, pp. 128–131.

In 1932 the newspapers called the Lindbergh kidnap-murder case the "Crime of the Century," perhaps an example of journalistic over-statement since the century was not quite one-third over at the time. Yet today, with only thirty years remaining of the 1900's, the brutal crime for which Bruno Richard Hauptmann was convicted bodes well to live up to its initial title. At least nine book-length studies of the in-famous affair have already been published, including my own (*The Lindbergh Case,* New York, Stodd-Bead Inc., 1968). Countless articles have also appeared, many of them more imaginative than factual, I'm sorry to say. And now comes, alas, the most speculative and absurd theory of the case ever to appear in print. Writing in the *Atlantis Monthly* for October, 1968, Augustus L. Harrison has attempted to inflict upon his readers the notion that Richard Hauptmann was a poor, innocent lamb led to the slaughter by the police and the prosecution who, it seems, deliberately framed a guiltless man to cover up their failure to unearth the real conspirators. And the kidnapping was a conspiracy, Mr. Harrison hastens to assure us: a conspiracy involving a man named Faulkner, a servant in the Dwight Morrow household, Isidor Fisch, and a few assorted Italians. The press was wrong, the public was wrong, the jury was wrong, but now we can all relax. Thanks to Mr. Harrison, the truth is out at last.

In real life Mr. Harrison earns his daily bread as a professor of his-tory. He is one of those historians who subscribe to the paranoiac theory that everything that has ever happened was the result of a con-spiracy. Man is presented by them as forever banding together in nasty little knots to plot against his fellow creatures. A baby is kidnapped and murdered. It must have been a conspiracy. An illegal alien is caught red-handed with the blood money stashed in his garage. That too, must have been a conspiracy. Said alien is tried and convicted on a veritable mountain of evidence. "Aha!" cries Mr. Harrison. "Yet another con-spiracy!" Nonsense!

If Professor Harrison's only offense was his stubborn clinging to a ridiculous historical theory, however, it would hardly be worth the time and trouble to answer him. Unfortunately this is the least serious of the accusations which can be made against him. His article is shot through with inconsistancies of logic, half-truths and, though it pains me to say it, deliberate falsifications. For a "scholar" who is pretending to provide a "dispassionate, objective evaluation of the evidence," this kind of dishonesty is simply inexcusable.

Let me begin with the most obvious and most insidious of Professor Harrison's fabrications, the matter of Paul Wendel. Harrison states quite accurately that, at the time of Hauptmann's execution, Wendel was in jail under indictment for the Lindberg murder, to which he had confessed in writing. What Harrison conveniently fails to mention is that Wendel had been, himself, kidnapped by agents of the chief of detectives of Burlington County, New Jersey. For one week he was beaten and tortured in the basement of a Brooklyn tenement until he finally agreed to sign a "confession" which was dictated to him by one of his captors. Although the "confession" contained numerous contradictions, and Wendel, once in police custody, denied it completely, a grand jury did indict him; but the charge was so obviously groundless that he was never tried. The Burlington County chief of detectives was tried, however, found guilty of kidnapping, and sentenced to six years in prison, where he died of a brain tumor.

You now have an idea of Mr. Harrison's method of propaganda. It is simply this: those facts which he cannot misrepresent, he suppresses. Observe his discussion of the testimony brought against Richard Hauptmann. He admits that two strange circumstances constituted "the most damaging evidence" against the defendant: first, Hauptmann's sudden rise from rags to riches right after the ransom was paid; second, the fact that "some of the ransom money" was discovered in his garage. "Some" money was no less than $14,600 in Lindbergh gold notes. And proof of Hauptmann's sudden financial windfall dated from *shortly after April 2, 1932,* when the ransom was paid, although Hauptmann himself did not claim to have received any money from Isidor Fisch until *December 5, 1933*! His wealth before that date was the result, he said, of profits taken from the stock market, though an agent of the Treasury Department testified that Hauptmann's records showed he had not made money on the market but lost!

Harrison also notes that wood from the ladder used by the kidnapper was identified as coming from Hauptmann's attic by Arthur Koehler whom he dismisses as "a so-called 'wood detective'" using "pseudoscientific mumbo jumbo." In addition, the professor argues that following the trial a government "wood expert," Arch Loney, proved "that the nail holes in the ladder rung did not match the holes in the attic joist to which it had supposedly been nailed." Thus, concludes the professor, "obviously there was no connection between the controversial rung and Hauptmann."

Once again it is more enlightening to study the facts which Mr. Harrison chooses to omit than those which he includes. Among these are the following: (1) Koehler's credentials as a "wood detective" were admitted even by the defense attorneys. (2) Loney, though disagreeing with Koehler, refused to do so under oath for the defense. (3) Although it is true that originally it appeared the nail holes did not match those in the joist from which it had been pried loose, tests at Columbia University proved that small wooden plugs had been inserted into the joist holes; when these were removed, the nails fit perfectly. Thus there can be no question that part of the wood used to build the ladder came from Hauptmann's attic. (4) Most of the wood in the ladder was traced from a Southern lumberyard to a lumberyard in the Bronx where a salesman positively identified Hauptmann as the purchaser. (5) The marks of a plane blade are as distinctive as fingerprints. During the trial, Koehler was able to demonstrate that plane marks made on boards used in the ladder were made by a blade found in Hauptmann's workshop.

In addition, Harrison implies that Hauptmann produced an alibi for the murder night. Mrs. Hauptmann did work for a baker named Christian Fredericksen. Normally on Tuesday evenings Fredericksen's wife, Katie, was off. Mrs. Hauptmann replaced her and was regularly picked up from work by her husband. At the trial the Fredericksens testified to this and nothing more, *for neither of them could swear under oath that Hauptmann had been at their shop on the night of the crime.* However, Hauptmann had no alibi for April 2, the evening when Dr. Condon was passing the ransom money to the kidnapper, a man with a German accent who called himself "John." It should also be kept in mind that Condon, the Lindberghs' contact with the kidnapper, positively identified Hauptmann as the elusive "John," and that handwriting experts who compared the defendant's writing with the writing on fourteen separate ransom notes testified that Hauptmann was clearly the author of the incriminating documents.

Finally Professor Harrison infers, not merely that the Lindbergh crime was the work of a conspiracy, not merely that Hauptmann was not involved, but that the German man who stole and murdered the baby, and who wrote the ransom notes in broken English, was Isidor Fisch. To support his allegation he cites Hauptmann's unbelievable and unsubstantiated story that Fisch, supposedly to repay a loan, had left him over $15,000 in a shoe box without explaining what the box contained. Harrison admits Hauptmann passed some of the kidnap cash (he calls it an "innocent mistake") and says the fact that Fisch died before Hauptmann's arrest was "tragic," though it should be obvious that Fisch's death, and thus his inability to deny Hauptmann's lies, was far more opportune for the accused man than it was "tragic."

If there is any doubt remaining in the reader's mind of the guilt of Bruno Richard Hauptmann, let him consider this fact, also conveniently ignored by Professor Harrison. On the wall inside Hauptmann's closet, written in pencil, the police found the address and phone number of Lindbergh's contact, Dr. John Condon. For what reason would Hauptmann keep so unique a record of Condon if he were not the kidnapper?

Look at the circumstances any way you wish, gentle reader. There can be no doubt of two facts. Professor Augustus L. Harrison has twisted the evidence at will in his attempt to clear Richard Hauptmann of guilt in the murder of Charles Lindbergh, Jr. Nevertheless it is obvious that Hauptmann, and Hauptmann alone, planned and carried out this incredible and horrible "Crime of the Century."

Bibliographical entry

West, Rexford. "The Guilt of Richard Hauptmann,"
    <u>Saturday</u> <u>Preview</u>, 23:128–131, February 18, 1970.

INSTRUCTIONS

1. *When you have read the article by West and compiled your notes, prepare an abstract of "The Guilt of Richard Hauptmann." As before, your Summary should include only information describing the content of the article. Remember that, although West criticizes the article by Harrison which you have just read, you must not assume that your reader is as familiar with Harrison's arguments as you are. Explain Harrison's points, when necessary, as if your reader had never read Harrison's article. Make no direct references to the abstract you have written of Harrison's article.*

2. *In your Comment and Evaluation, give your opinion of the va-lidity of West's arguments and the effectiveness with which he expresses them. Are his points logical? Are they supported with sufficient factual evidence? Are his criticisms of Harrison fair and accurate or not? Do you now believe that Hauptmann was guilty or innocent?*

3. *In preparing the final draft of your abstract follow the form shown on page 120 and the additional instructions given under number 3 on page 127.*

4. *Attach to your abstract of West's article a brief statement of your reactions to the two articles on the Hauptmann case. Do you feel you were deceived at all by Augustus Harrison? Do you feel Harrison was* **deliberately** *trying to deceive you? Before reading West, what was your opinion of Hauptmann's guilt or innocence? Has West's article changed your opinion? Do you feel West's argu-ments can be trusted? What now is your opinion of Bruno Richard Hauptmann's connection with the Lindbergh kidnap-murder, if any? What additional information would you like to know before you formed a final opinion on Hauptmann's guilt or innocence?*

FOLLOW-UP

An important purpose of the preceding section was to demon-strate again the need for distinguishing between a fact, an opinion and a deliberate deception. In all your reading, and particularly when you are reading in source material for the purposes of re-search, you need to be able to recognize and draw these distinc-tions. This requires close reading, objectivity and, above all, a healthy skepticism toward the writer, his motives, his arguments and his conclusions.

Review the following definitions.

☐ *Fact: a statement which is proved, indisputable, or at least un-disputed and uncontroversial.*

☐ *Opinion: a statement made with complete confidence but not definitely proved; a statement based on incomplete evidence or evidence which could be questioned.*

☐ *Deception: a statement made with apparent confidence and sincerity but based on a deliberate misrepresentation of the truth, or an intentional suppression of facts which would tend to disprove the statement.*

When you feel you understand these terms, identify each of the following statements as fact, opinion, or deception.

1. Two witnesses placed Hauptmann near Hopewell on the day of the murder, Amandus Hochmuth and Millard Whited.

2. Neither Hauptmann nor anyone else outside the Lindbergh-Morrow household could have known these special facts, but Violet Sharpe knew them and must have communicated them to the kidnapper.

3. On September 19, 1934, nearly two and one-half years after the crime, Hauptmann was arrested and charged with the kidnap-murder of Charles Lindbergh, Jr.

4. The ladder used by the kidnapper had been homemade.

5. From the moment of his arrest, Hauptmann's guilt was assumed, not merely by the authorities, but by the press and the public throughout the United States.

6. With the death of Hauptmann, the state, of course, had to drop murder charges against Wendel. Any other course of action might have proved far too embarrassing.

7. So it is clear that the murder of Charles Lindbergh, Jr., was the result of a conspiracy.

8. [Loney] was able to demonstrate that the nail holes in the ladder rung did not match the holes in the attic joist to which it had supposedly been nailed. Obviously there was no connection between the controversial rung and Hauptmann.

9. On May 12 the body of the baby was discovered in the woods not far from the Lindbergh lands.

10. At last one of the bills of ransom money turned up at the Irving Trust Company.

11. It is true that Condon identified Hauptmann at the trial as "John," but it is also true that Condon was a man in his seventies, never saw "John" except at night, and refused at first to identify Hauptmann at all.

12. Was Hauptmann innocent? I believe he was, and I believe too that history will prove me right.

The Lindbergh Kidnapping

13. If Professor Harrison's only offense was his stubborn clinging to a ridiculous historical theory, however, it would hardly be worth the time and trouble to answer him.

14. What Harrison conveniently fails to mention is that Wendel had been, himself, kidnapped by agents of the chief of detectives of Burlington County, New Jersey.

15. It should also be kept in mind that Condon, the Lindberghs' contact with the kidnapper, positively identified Hauptmann as the elusive "John."

16. On the wall inside Hauptmann's closet, written in pencil, the police found the address and phone number of Lindbergh's contact, Dr. John Condon.

17. Countless articles have also appeared, many of them more imaginative than factual I'm sorry to say. And now comes, alas, the most speculative and absurd theory of the case ever to appear in print.

18. [Mr. Harrison] is one of those historians who subscribe to the paranoiac theory that everything that has ever happened was the result of a conspiracy.

19. "Some of the ransom money" was discovered in [Hauptmann's] garage. "Some" money was no less than $14,600 in Lindbergh gold notes.

20. Nevertheless, it is obvious that Hauptmann, and Hauptmann alone, planned and carried out this incredible and horrible "Crime of the Century."

In researching any topic you must be able to feel the tensions created by disputes between the writers of sources. Reread the articles by Harrison and West and compile a list of areas of principal disagreement between the two authors. As we will see, the most effective research papers begin by identifying a question about a topic, a question usually raised by the conflicting assertions and arguments of the authors of source materials.

In listing the major areas of dispute between Harrison and West, consider the following questions:

1. What is each author's opinion about the guilt or innocence of Bruno Richard Hauptmann in the Lindbergh case?

2. What is each author's opinion of the possibility that the crime

could have been committed by one man alone? If a conspiracy, who might have been involved?

3. How conclusive is the circumstantial evidence in the case? (Consider especially the ransom money, the kidnap ladder board, the testimony of handwriting experts.)

4. How legitimate are West's accusations against Harrison's scholarship and basic honesty? Does West at any point appear to leave himself open to similar accusations?

LIBRARY FORMS FOR ABSTRACTS
(*see also page 136*)

LIBRARY FORM (Periodical Article)

Author —————————————————————————

Title —————————————————————————

Periodical —————————————————————————

Publishing Organization (professional organization or

government agency, if any)—————————————————

—————————————————————————————

Volume —————————————————————————

Month and Year of Publication —————————————

Pages Article Occupies in Periodical —————————

Pages Used —————————————————————————

MAIN POINTS OF ARTICLE FOR SUMMARY:

[*Allow one-third of page for space.*]

IMPRESSIONS OF ARTICLE FOR COMMENT AND EVALUATION:

[*Allow one-third of page for space.*]

LIBRARY FORMS FOR ABSTRACTS
(continued from page 135)

LIBRARY FORM (Newspaper Article)

Author _____

Title or Headline _____

Newspaper _____

Section of Newspaper _____

Page Numbers and Columns _____

Date (complete) _____

MAIN POINTS OF ARTICLE FOR SUMMARY:

[Allow one-third of page for space.]

IMPRESSIONS OF ARTICLE FOR COMMENT AND EVALUATION:

[Allow one-third of page for space.]

LIBRARY FORM (Book)

Author _____

Title _____

Edition _____

Place of Publication _____

Publisher _____

Year of Publication _____

Pages of Importance _____

MAIN POINTS FOR SUMMARY:

[Allow one-third of page for space.]

IMPRESSIONS FOR COMMENT AND EVALUATION:

[Allow one-third of page for space.]

Introduction to Research

You are ready to tackle a project in research writing. It is time to pull together the skills of critical reading, analytical thinking and persuasive writing you have been working to develop. This part offers you source materials in two areas, the outbreak of witchcraft in Puritan Salem in 1692, and the 1893 trial of Lizzie Borden for the ax murders of her parents.

Unless you and your instructor decide otherwise, at this point you will limit your investigation to the materials provided in this book. Your instructor may wish to supervise the separate stages of this initial project fairly closely until both you and he are sure you have grasped the concepts and techniques of research writing and penetrated the mysteries of footnoting and correct paper form. Later on you will have an opportunity to test your skill on an independent project.

The sources in this section have been designed to create for you the experience of sensing the tensions within a topic, recognizing the existence of a question resulting from conflicting assertions and arguments, determining those issues which must be decided before the question can be answered, and reading defensively to distinguish between fact, opinion and deception. These are all skills which you have already practiced.

Before beginning to read in the sources, look at the essay "What a Research Paper Is Not." Many misconceptions are held by students regarding research writing, and this brief essay aims hopefully at dispelling the most insidious of them.

The discussion titled "The Most Commonly Asked Questions About Writing a Research Paper" presents a chronological procedure to carry you from the initial selection of a topic to the submission of your final draft. It includes sample worksheets, notes and outlines, many based on the Lindbergh kidnapping case with which you have just dealt. Read through it before delving into Salem witchcraft or the Lizzie Borden murders. It will help you to understand the direction in which you are heading when you begin your investigation of one of those areas. Later you can refer back to this section as you move through the process of preparing your research project.

That discussion and the one which follows it, "The Most Commonly Asked Questions About Footnotes," are obviously structured around those questions most likely to bother students struggling for the first time with research writing. This organization permits you to use them for reference purposes while putting your paper together. As soon as a question about footnoting crosses your mind, look it up. Of course, whenever you are in doubt about a requirement your wisest move is to ask your instructor.

What A Research Paper Is Not

A great many words have been written about what a research paper is and very few about what it is not, which is strange because to know what a research paper is not is much more important. For example, a research paper is not a particular number of pages in length. Some students think it is when they are assigned a paper of three pages, or five, or ten, or whatever. The problem is how to make the paper stretch until it fills the assigned number of pages. You need a typewriter with big type, of course, and then you have to sneak the margins in a bit on the sides, top and bottom of the page. And if you must, you can always triple space the thing. Then, too, you only need to type two or three lines on the last page. After all, a five-page paper only means you have to get to the fifth page. It doesn't mean you have to fill it!

However a research paper is not a particular number of pages in length.

Sometimes the required length of an assignment is given in words. The problem now becomes how to say what you have to say in as many words as possible. Remember that "an," "that" and "and" are as good as long words. Writing "very big" is twice as good as "enormous," and "until the end of time" is five times as good as "eternally." Keep a count at the bottom of each page of the number of words you have used on that page, and when you get within about two hundred words of the required number begin writing your conclusion. It is probably wise to go five or ten words past the assignment just to be safe.

But a research paper is not a specific number of words.

Nor does a research paper need a particular number of sources. But sometimes an assignment requires a minimum number of sources. This leads students to believe that when they have found at least one scrap of information on the topic in the required minimum number of sources, they have finished their research. With this kind of assignment the first rule to follow is: never read more sources than are required. Almost all your footnotes will come from only one source anyway. The problem is to find one fact in each of the other sources, never mind how obscure or irrelevant, which can be footnoted. Cite these facts as early as you can and get the footnotes out of the way. Remember the encyclopedia is always good for one citation and usually the dictionary can be used for another, so if the assignment calls for four sources you will only have to read two more, and only one carefully.

Except that a research paper is not based on a specific number of sources.

Nor is a research paper a series of direct quotations from outside sources glued together by a few sentences in your own words. But some students think it is and even believe it is necessary to quote a source before it can be footnoted, which, of course, it is not.

Research writing is a self-defining term which simply means research + writing, implying that research is one process and writing is another. Research is the collection and organization of facts and informed opinions relevant to a particular question raised by the paper. Writing is the presentation of that information *in the student's own words* in a way that will lead the reader to a conclusion or resolution of the question. This does not mean that it is never permissible to quote a source directly. Direct quotation is necessary to avoid misrepresenting a source, or when primary sources are being presented. The articles on the Sacco-

Vanzetti case, to which we will come soon, offer ample illustration of this. What should be remembered is that the ideas and information found in outside sources can usually be adequately expressed in the student's original words without the necessity of quoting the language of the source.

A research paper is not a bunch of facts lumped together in the same essay because they have some vague relationship and because they were all found in some sort of outside source. For example, the following is not a satisfactory outline of a research paper: Herman Melville was born in 1819, *and then* he went to sea and served on merchant, whaling and naval vessels, *and then* he wrote several books based on his experience at sea, *and then* failing to achieve success as a writer, he worked as a customs inspector in New York, *and then* he died in 1892. This is simply one of those "and then" papers which give a chronological outline of events without making a point or proving an argument. To be certain that your paper makes a point, you must establish a question which your paper is going to attempt to answer.

Having covered what a research paper is not, we have come around to the question of what it is. *A research paper is one which asks a question, reflects a sufficient amount of research to venture an answer to the question, and presents enough documentation to render that answer reasonable and plausible.*

How many sources are necessary? Enough to support a rational answer to the question raised by your paper. How long, in pages or in words, should your paper be? The best answer is that given by Lewis Carroll's King of Hearts: "Begin at the beginning, and go on till you come to the end: then stop."

The Most Commonly Asked Questions About Writing a Research Paper

1. How do I find a topic to write about?

The simplest way to come up with a topic is to formulate a *question* which you intend to answer in your paper. The formulation of a question to be answered gives direction to your research and should guarantee that your paper will have a clear purpose (answering the question) and will accomplish that purpose.

2. **How do I formulate a *question?***

By discovering an area of basic disagreement between two sources. For example, Harrison and West obviously disagree on the question of whether Bruno Richard Hauptmann was innocent or guilty of the kidnap-murder of Charles Lindbergh, Jr. Once you are aware of this disagreement you can formulate a question to be answered in your paper: *Was Hauptmann innocent or guilty of the Lindbergh kidnap-murder?* This question becomes your *working title,* the title you will use while you are writing your paper. Remember that your working title need not be the title you will finally use on your report.

After you have decided on a question to be answered you will determine the issues raised by that question.

3. **What are *issues?***

The *issues* are the smaller questions which must be answered before your *question* can be answered. The answers to the issues provide the information which must be known before any attempt is made to resolve the question.

Here is a typical example similar to ones you saw earlier in the course. The question is: Is Ricky a better basketball player than Jim? Before you can answer, you must have additional information. To get that information, you would ask questions like the following.

Q. Which boy is taller?
A. Ricky.
Q. Which boy is faster?
A. Ricky.
Q. Which boy is older?
A. Jim is a senior, two years older.
Q. What are the scoring averages of each boy?
A. Ricky's is 16 points per game. Jim's is 7 points per game.
Q. Which boy is the team captain?
A. Jim.
Q. Which boy plays better defense?
A. Ricky.

Although you might feel you still need more information before answering the *question,* you can probably support a conclusion that Ricky is the better basketball player on the basis of the information you now have. The only facts in Jim's favor are that he is two years older and team captain. Since the first fact may explain the second, and all the other facts are in Ricky's favor, you can conclude that Ricky is better.

Study the questions asked to gain information about the two boys. Each is designed to learn facts which must be known before the original question can be answered. Each is, therefore, an *issue* raised by the original *question.*

Now consider this question: Was Hauptmann innocent or guilty of the Lindbergh kidnap-murder? What issues must be answered before the question can be resolved?

Study the sample worksheet on page 149. Also refer to the worksheet on page 147 for another model dealing with a simpler question.

After you have determined your *question* and defined your *issues,* decide the possible *conclusions,* or answers to your question, which your paper may reach. Do not assume in advance what your conclusion will be. Instead, let your conclusion be determined by your research.

Study the sample conclusions on the worksheets.

4. **How do I organize my notes?**

Once your issues are defined and before you begin to take notes, prepare to organize your notes according to the issue or issues to which they refer. To make this organization possible, assign a letter or other symbol to each issue and code each note you take according to the issue it discusses. Choose a letter or symbol you can easily identify with each issue; this is easier to remember than a number. Such coded symbols are called *slugs.* Keep a record of your slugs and the issues they symbolize on your worksheet.

Study the samples on pages 147 and 149.

Also prepare a *bibliography worksheet* on which you will record all bibliographical information for every source you consult.

5. How do I take notes?

Most students prefer recording their notes either on file cards or in a notebook.

If you use file cards, record each note on a separate card. If the note continues onto a second card, use a paper clip to fasten the cards together. Keep the cards in a box and separate them by the issues to which they refer, using dividers marked with different slugs.

If you use a notebook, separate the pages into sections corresponding to the different issues of your research, using dividers coded with the appropriate slugs.

Here are other suggestions on how to take notes:

Each note card or notebook entry you make *must* include the following information: (a) One or more slugs to indicate the issue or issues to which the note refers. (b) The name of the author of the source from which the note is taken; if the author is unknown (as is sometimes the case in a newspaper article or pamphlet), give the title. (c) The exact page number or numbers of the source on which the information in your note appears. You will need this data when you are composing the footnotes for your final paper.

In some of your notes you may also wish to include *cross-references* to other notes you have already taken. A cross-reference indicates that there is information in another note which is closely related to the information in the note you have just taken. Cross-references are extremely useful and time-saving when you are arranging your notes to begin writing your paper.

See the sample notes on pages 147 and 150.

Take notes on all facts, information and opinions which seem related to your topic and its issues in any conceivable way, even if you are not sure you will eventually use the information. *Do not expect to use all your notes in the final paper.* A good researcher always takes more notes than he will eventually need or use. Though this may seem like unnecessary extra work, it will actually save you time by guaranteeing you will not have to return later to a source to get information you failed to note the first time and later discovered you would need.

In taking notes, avoid direct quotation of your sources. Take notes in your own words. Avoid taking notes in complete sentences: instead write in intelligible phrases. Students who quote their sources while taking notes often find it very difficult to write a paper based on those notes in their own words. The student may be tempted to overload his paper with quotations or, worse, to plagiarize his sources.

Taking notes in intelligible phrases rather than complete sentences makes it easier to translate the information in your notes into your own words, and it further reduces the chance of copying, even unconsciously, the wording of your sources.

6. **What is the best way to organize my notes into an outline of my paper?**

Before beginning to write, be certain you have a clear concept of your entire paper in your mind. To accomplish this, organize your notes into units according to the issues with which they deal. This will be easy if you have coded your notes carefully with slugs.

Working from your notes, compose a rough outline of your materials in the order in which you wish to present them. The form of this outline need not be formal, but it must be clear to you. Do not use one- or two-word entries in your outline. To be of any use to you in organizing and writing your paper, an outline must be composed of complete sentences. Each entry in the outline should be either a question to be answered in a section of your paper or a direct statement to be proved.

The more time and effort spent in organizing your material before you begin writing, the easier your writing, and the clearer your paper will be.

Study the sample outlines on page 148.

7. **How do I write the paper? How many drafts must I write?**

An inexperienced writer should compose his paper in at least two drafts. If writing the first draft in longhand, skip lines on the pages. If composing on a typewriter, triple space. This leaves plenty of space to make changes and corrections between the lines on the first draft before typing the final paper.

While writing your first draft, do not be concerned with mechanical errors such as spelling and punctuation. The time to correct these is when you are editing your paper in preparation for typing the final draft. The fear of making mechanical errors in a first draft leads many students to write in a style which is either very simple and immature or excessively formal and unnatural. It also spoils whatever pleasure you might find in discovering facts, forming opinions, and communicating both to someone else.

If you have trouble finding the right words to express an idea, write it down any way at all. Your wording can be changed when you edit the paper. It is much easier to rephrase an idea than it is to phrase it correctly the first time. Do not get bogged down in your first draft by worrying your sentences to death. Get *something* on paper and go on writing.

As you write, keep a separate page nearby to record your footnotes as soon as you use them in your paper. This is much less trouble than having to search through your notes to locate and record your footnotes after the draft is finished.

See the samples on pages 148 and 149.

Edit your first draft carefully. Check the spelling of any word you are uncertain of. It is very helpful to read your work aloud. If you have access to a tape recorder, read portions of your paper into the machine and listen to determine whether or not your writing makes sense, whether or not it "sounds funny." Let someone whose judgment you trust read your paper and make suggestions. Make all necessary changes on the first draft and be sure you are satisfied with your paper before typing the final draft, because it is very difficult to make changes after the final draft is begun.

"Edit your first draft carefully." Of all the suggestions offered in these pages this is the most likely to be ignored. The odds that many who read this now will also ignore this suggestion are, conservatively estimated, ten to one. Nevertheless, before you ignore it, before you let yourself be satisfied with a fast rereading of your paper, before you proceed to type your final draft complete with all the mistakes you would have discovered if you *had* edited your first draft carefully, please consider the following.

The editing of the first draft is the single most important step you will take in writing your paper. During this step you will find and correct the little mistakes which, in past papers, may have made the difference of a full grade or more in your mark. During this step, rework and reword the paper until you know the satisfaction of communicating your ideas to someone else exactly as they exist in your mind. (If you doubt the reality of this satisfaction, try to recall the frustration you felt the last time you had an idea clearly in mind and could not make someone else understand it as you did.) Perhaps you will feel the even greater satisfaction of having an opinion and convincing someone else of the truth of that opinion.

Edit the first draft carefully.

8. How do I type the final draft?

It is strongly advised that you type the final draft on erasable bond typing paper, particularly if you are not an experienced typist, since this paper permits easy correction with an ordinary eraser. Make a carbon copy for your own files. Never turn in a final draft typed on onionskin.

The final draft should include a title page, a footnote page (unless footnotes are typed at the bottom of each page) and a bibliography. The correct forms for these pages are to be found in Appendix B.

When your final draft is finished, proofread it carefully and correct all typographical errors. These corrections may be made on the final copy if they are done carefully and in ink.

The packaging of your paper is very important. Charts, photographs, and other illustrations should be mounted with care above clearly worded explanations or captions. The paper should be bound. Bindings with see-through covers, which may be used again and again, are available at a low price at any stationery store.

SAMPLE WORKSHEET (*written in notebook*)

WORKING TITLE: Did Edgar Allan Poe use opium?

ISSUES: SLUG: **O** Is there evidence that Poe did use opium?

SLUG: **⊗** Is there evidence that Poe did not use opium?

SLUG: **U** If he was a user, was Poe addicted?

• • • • • • • •

BIBLIOGRAPHY SHEET

Allen, Hervey. *Israfel.* New York: George Doran and Company, 1927.

Paul, Raymond. *Who Murdered Mary Rogers?* Englewood Cliffs, N.J.: Prentice-Hall, Inc., 1971.

Wagenknecht, Edward. *Edgar Allan Poe, The Man Behind the Legend.* New York: Oxford University Press, 1963.

• • • • • • • •

SAMPLE NOTES (*written on separate cards*)

Code: **O**	Allen, pp. 592–593.

Poe used opium according to his friend William Wallace. Hard to say if an addict. Rosalie Poe (sister) says Poe used morphine (1846).

Code: **⊗**	Wagenknecht, pp. 42–43.

Thomas Lane and Thomas Dunn English knew Poe well (1846) but "saw no signs" of drug habit. Poe tried suicide (Boston, 1848), took too little of drug (laudanum). Author says if Poe a user he would know enough to take a deadly dose.

SAMPLE NOTES (*continued from page 147*)

(*continued from page 147*)

Code: **U**	Paul, p. 205.

Poe's attempted suicide: Author says probably it was "gesture."
Poe deliberately took too small a dose. Author says that shows
Poe did know about drugs.

Cross-reference: Wagenknecht, pp. 42–43.

GOOD OUTLINE

WORKING TITLE: Do Effective Cures for Drug Addiction Exist?

1. "Halfway House" projects are successful.

2. Methadone is sometimes successful and always controversial.

3. Imprisoning addicts is never an effective deterrent to drug use.

4. Finding social work for former addicts is usually helpful.

5. Most addicts who are labeled "cured" do not stay straight.

CONCLUSION: There are some proven cures for drug addiction, but we have a long way to go for a final solution to the problem.

POOR OUTLINE

WORKING TITLE: Do Effective Cures for Drug Addiction Exist?

1. "Halfway House" projects.

2. Use of Methadone.

3. Effect of imprisonment.

4. Reformed addicts who go into social work.

5. Proportion of "cured" addicts who stay straight.

CONCLUSION: Cures, if any, for drug addiction.

SAMPLE FIRST DRAFT (*based on note cards on pages 147–148*)

There is disagreement over the significance of
Poe's attempted suicide in Boston as a measure of his

knowledge of drugs. Some see the author's failure to take a lethal dose of laudanum as proof that he could not calculate a lethal dose.[4] Others, contending Poe never intended to kill himself, argue that the small dose demonstrates he knew exactly what he was doing.[5]

FOOTNOTE RECORD FOR SAMPLE FIRST DRAFT

[4]Wagenknecht, pp. 42–43.

[5]Paul, p. 205.

SAMPLE WORKSHEET FOR THE LINDBERGH CASE

WORKING TITLE (QUESTION):

Was Bruno Richard Hauptmann guilty or innocent of the kidnap-murder of Charles Lindbergh, Jr.?

ISSUES:

A (1) Did Hauptmann have an alibi for the night of the kidnapping?

$ (2) Was Hauptmann's explanation for possessing marked ransom money satisfactory?

C (3) Could Dr. Condon's word be accepted as true?

W (4) Was Paul Wendel's confession believable?

B (5) Was the testimony which connected a board from Hauptmann's attic with the kidnap ladder conclusive or not?

I (6) Was it possible for someone to kidnap the Lindbergh baby without information from the inside (i.e., from one of the servants)?

VS (7) Why did Violet Sharpe commit suicide?

JJ (8) How did J. J. Faulkner get hold of part of the ransom money?

F (9) Is there any evidence to connect Isidor Fisch to the crime?

POSSIBLE CONCLUSIONS:

(1) Hauptmann was completely innocent of the crime.

(2) Hauptmann alone was guilty of the crime.

(3) Hauptmann was guilty as one of a number who conspired to commit the crime.

NOTES FOR LINDBERGH CASE (*on separate cards*)

F $ Harrison, p. 126.
Hauptmann said ransom money left with him by friend, Isidor Fisch. Hauptmann discovered money in box and thought it was intended as repayment of loan. Spending it was "innocent mistake"—Fisch died in Germany.

F $ West, p. 131.
Hauptmann's "Fisch story" called "unbelievable and unsubstantiated"—West says it was lucky for Hauptmann that Fisch not alive to deny the story. Compare with Harrison, p. 126.

SAMPLE BIBLIOGRAPHY

Harrison, Augustus L. "Hauptmann Was Innocent," *Atlantis Monthly*, 10:122–127, October, 1968.

West, Rexford. "The Guilt of Richard Hauptmann," *Saturday Preview*, 23:128–131, February 18, 1970.

The Most Commonly Asked Questions About Footnotes

1. When must I use a footnote?

When you quote a source directly, and when you present facts, opinions, or any information which is not your own but has been taken from outside sources.

2. Since I need not footnote a fact which is common knowledge, how can I tell whether a fact is common knowledge or not?

The most sensible rule for determining common knowledge is this: If you did not know the fact yourself before you found it in your source, it is not common knowledge and must be footnoted.

In defining common knowledge, common sense must be used. If you are working in an area in which you have special knowledge (if, for example, you are writing a paper about the automobile engine and have worked as a mechanic), then you may consider yourself something of an expert on the subject. In this kind of situation you may be able to state facts without the necessity of footnoting. This situation is extremely rare. In almost all cases, the above rule is the best one to follow.

3. Why is it necessary to use footnotes?

There are several possible reasons, although each does not always apply.

a. To validate the facts, opinions and information given in your paper. In most cases your source will be someone widely considered an expert in his field. As an expert, his statement of facts and expression of opinions carries the weight of his reputation and authority.

b. To make clear that the facts or opinions expressed are not your own but belong to someone else. Sometimes you will have to include opinions in your paper with which you do not agree. You will want to make it clear to the reader that the opinion is that of the author of your source.

c. To avoid academic dishonesty or plagiarism.

4. What is plagiarism?

According to the *American College Dictionary* it is "the copying or imitating the language, ideas, and thoughts of another author and passing off the same as one's original work." Study the following rules carefully.

a. All direct quotations must be footnoted. A direct quotation may be a word, a phrase, a sentence, a series of sentences, a paragraph, or a series of paragraphs. In addition to a footnote, it is set within quotation marks or it is indented and typed single spaced.

b. Paraphrased writing in which the wording of another author is changed but the ideas of that author are presented must be footnoted.

5. Must I quote a source in order to footnote it?

No. Quotation marks and footnotes indicate different things. Quotation marks indicate that the specific word or words used in your paper are not your own but those of your source. A footnote indicates that the ideas, information and opinions expressed are not your own but those of your source.

Obviously you will frequently be expressing ideas and information from your sources without quoting the sources' words. When you do so, a footnote will be necessary. Failure to footnote at such times is plagiarism.

6. If I find the same fact in two or more different sources, which source should I put in the footnote?

All of them. The more sources you cite to validate your facts, the more valid your facts will appear to the reader. This is also true of opinions. The more experts you can cite who hold the same opinion, the more true the opinion will seem to your reader.

7. If I have used information from two or more sources in a single paragraph, how should that be indicated?

Normally it is acceptable form to list all sources used in one paragraph in a single footnote. Place the footnote number at the end of the paragraph. Common sense must be used in determining footnoting. The basic rule in footnoting is: never mislead or confuse the reader. Study the following rules carefully.

☐ *a. If a direct quotation from one particular source is used within the paragraph, it should be footnoted separately.*

☐ *b. If contradictory assertions or opinions have been expressed by two or more sources, they should be footnoted separately.*

8. **If several consecutive paragraphs in my paper all come from a single source, must I footnote each paragraph, or is one footnote at the end of the sequence of paragraphs sufficient?**

For the sake of clarity, if the sequence of paragraphs is three or more you should footnote each paragraph separately.

9. **How accurate do I have to be in giving the page numbers of my sources in a footnote?**

You must be precise. If information in your paper does not actually appear on the specific page or pages cited in your footnote, you are guilty of academic dishonesty. Never fake a footnote.

10. **How should I number my footnotes?**

Consecutively. Never repeat a number (such as returning to the number 1 because you have begun a new page, or numbering 1 to 9 and then beginning again with 1). If your paper contains twenty footnotes, the last should be numbered 20.

11. **When is it not necessary for me to use a footnote?**

You need not footnote a fact which is common knowledge (see question 2). Nor is it necessary to footnote any statement based on your own experience or specific knowledge, or any opinion or conclusion which you have yourself reached based on your research.

12. **I have read many sources where the author stated facts and information which were obviously not his own ideas, yet he did not footnote them. Why do I have to footnote everything?**

Professional scholars and writers know that whatever they write will be read and reviewed by other experts in their subject. If they give false information, fake their evidence, or draw ridiculous conclusions, they will be subject to public attack and exposure, much as Rexford West attacked Augustus Harrison's article on the Lindbergh case. They also know that if they plagiarize, it is extremely likely they will be caught and exposed, in which case their careers will be ruined. Students normally present their papers to a one-man audience, the instructor, and no matter how well-read he is, the instructor may not be an expert in the field dealt with in your paper. Your footnotes help him judge and evaluate your research and scholarship. When you become a recognized, published expert in your field, you will not have to "footnote everything" either.

13. What should I do if I am not sure whether I need a footnote or not?

When in doubt, footnote. You will never lose points for having too many footnotes, but you can lose points for having too few. Remember that different instructors may have different requirements. Whenever you are in doubt about a requirement, ask your instructor.

THE SALEM WITCH TRIALS

In 1692 the only significant outbreak of witchcraft in American history was recorded at Salem, Massachusetts. Before it was over, twenty of those accused had lost their lives, a small number perhaps when compared with the thousands executed in Europe, and yet Salem has lived in our national memory as a symbol of the havoc which can result from governmental repression and public paranoia.

What really happened at Salem? Were the accused denied even the most fundamental protections of common law? Were they innocent martyrs sacrificed to religious superstition and mass terror? Or was witchcraft actually practiced at Salem, and were the convicted, or at least some of them, really guilty of performing black magic?

1. *Read closely through all three sources on Salem witchcraft. Make no attempt to take complete notes on your first reading, but keep*

a notebook handy to jot down each author's major points and to note any areas of dispute or contradiction between authors. It is vital, even in this most preliminary stage of researching, that every note you take be identified in the margin of your notebook by author and the page number of the source.

2. *As you read, identify possible* questions *you might attempt to answer in your research paper. Keep a record of these questions on a special page in your notebook, leaving space under each to note relevant issues as they occur to you. After each entry, jot down related sources and page numbers as you find them in your reading.*

   During this initial reading of your sources, keep your mind as free and active as possible. Do not worry yet about distinguishing fact from opinion from deception. The time for that is later. Now concentrate on each writer's principal arguments and where they contradict each other. Try to become interested in which of them is right. From such curiosity on your part, your paper's question *will arise.*

3. *When you have completed the first reading of your sources follow the directions at the conclusion of the materials.*

   While you research and write on Salem witchcraft, stop thinking of yourself as a student. Instead, think of yourself as a social historian, an authority on evidence and the law, an expert in black magic and witchcraft.

The Witches of Salem
by Peter Oakes

Odyssey Magazine, vol. 14, April, 1970, pp. 155–160.

Imagine for the next few minutes that you and I are seated with some old friends before a crackling fire in an ancient country house. Outside, a violent wind whips the pouring rain in sheets against the window panes. The room is warm but dark except for the soft glow from the hearth, and grotesque shadows glide in eerie patterns along the walls and dance in the blackened corners. From somewhere upstairs comes the sound of a shutter clattering in the gale against the house, a sound now and then lost in the crashes of thunder and the howl of the storm. It is a good night to tell each other stories of ghosts and witches, of souls sold to the devil and strange, unholy terrors, and black magic.

Of course all such tales are fiction. Things like witchcraft and black magic don't really happen. Or do they?

Before you answer, think a moment, and listen to the stories I am about to tell. They happened in Massachusetts during the infamous outbreak of witchcraft at Salem Village in 1692, and each story can be fully documented. Every one of them is true.

Salem's epidemic of witchcraft began in the dead of winter when several young girls from the village began to be afflicted with strange, horrible tortures which could only have been caused by supernatural forces. These "afflicted girls," as they came to be called, would go into crazed fits of hysterical screaming during which they experienced severe pain, and then lapse suddenly into trances of stony silence. At such times these unfortunate children might lose their powers of speech, sight, hearing, and even memory, though these losses were always temporary. It was not unknown for "witch wounds" to appear on the bodies of the afflicted. Their bellies might swell rapidly to twice normal size, or the girl might cry that burning brimstone was being poured over her, and immediately *blisters would actually appear on her skin.* There is no possible physical cause for such symptoms. Obviously, then, they were the result of black magic.

The identity of the witches remained at first unknown, since only the afflicted children could reveal them and the power of the fiends was so great that their victims' eyes and mouths were sealed. Finally a woman named Mary Sibley gave directions for a "witch cake" to be made according to an ancient formula by mixing meal with the children's urine. By this means *the spell of silence was, in fact, broken,* and the girls were suddenly able to name their tormentors.

Before the Salem witch trials were over, twenty-seven people had been condemned to death, of which nineteen were hanged, and over fifty more had confessed to crimes of witchcraft. In our modern and supposedly enlightened age it is popularly believed that all those convicted were innocent martyrs, while those who confessed must simply have been psychotic mental cases. This explanation is at best only partially true, and at worst it is merely simple-minded. For there were things that happened at Salem for which no natural explanation is conceivable.

One of those who was hung was Sarah Good, an ugly, pipe-smoking hag whose witchcraft had been known for years by her neighbors.

Her own daughter admitted her mother had betrayed her into evil and testified against her at her trial. During that trial one of the afflicted cried out that Sarah Good had sent an evil spirit to attack her with a knife. The judges were suspicious of this story, but when the child was searched, *not only was a knife wound found in her body, but the tip of the blade was discovered where it had broken off* during her struggle with the demon. Yet even this is not the strangest proof of Sarah Good's evil powers.

On the day of her execution, when the Reverend Nicholas Noyes, a Salem minister, stepped up to the scaffold and urged her to confess her wickedness, Sarah instead put a curse on him. With her dying breath she shrieked, "If you take my life away, God will give you blood to drink!" It is *known, historical fact* that Nicholas Noyes died of a pulmonary seizure, a heart attack in which blood is forced up into the victim's throat. Thus *Nicholas Noyes died while choking on his own blood.*

Nor is this the only known case of murder committed by black magic. A wizard named Roger Toothaker freely admitted, in fact bragged, that he and his daughter had bewitched a woman to death by one of the most ancient of spells. Toothaker believed this woman was tormenting a child with witchcraft. Obtaining a specimen of the child's urine, he put it into a clay pot and sealed the pot in an oven. The following morning the curse was lifted from the afflicted child, *and the witch herself was dead.*

Small dolls or puppets were often used by witches to torture their victims by what is called "image magic." The doll is used as an "image" or symbol of the victim, and whatever pain is inflicted on the doll will be felt by the victim. Many examples of successful image magic have been documented in countries where voodoo is practiced, but these hellish tricks also occurred at Salem, where a female slave from Barbados named Candy not only confessed her guilt *but actually demonstrated her powers* in the courtroom before the judges and dozens of witnesses. Her "puppets" were nothing more than rags with knots tied in them, yet when she pinched them the girls were horribly afflicted and *real pinch marks appeared on their arms and faces.* When one of the rags was set on fire an afflicted child was burned on her hand, and two others immediately began to gasp helplessly for air when other rags were immersed in water.

These are things not easily explained by natural causes, nor are the following, all recorded and verified as true by the Reverend Cotton

The Salem Witch Trials

Mather in his contemporary account of the witchcraft, *Wonders of the Invisible World*. From the many supernatural events described by Mather, I will select only four. The first involved a young man named Bishop who was aiding in the branding of cattle seized by the sheriff from the farm of a witch. As the brand was burned into the fourth of these cattle the youth simultaneously felt a fiery pain in his thigh, and when his leg was examined, the lasting marks were *actually to be seen in his flesh*.

Secondly, one of the afflicted girls complained that an evil spirit was attempting to stab her with a spindle, though both the spirit and the spindle were at first invisible to others present. But when the girl snatched the spindle away, *it suddenly became visible in her hand* and was found to be, as Mather says, "indeed a real, proper, iron spindle."

Thirdly, another child, being haunted by an evil specter in a sheet, grabbed at the sheet, and immediately the corner of the sheet she had torn off became visible and was examined and touched by a roomful of witnesses.

The last event is the strangest of all. The phenomenon of levitation, in which a person rises into the air and floats without visible support in defiance of gravity, is almost unheard of today except on the magician's stage. Yet levitation was recorded in Massachusetts. This form of torture, though rare, was practiced by witches on one of the afflicted and *we have the sworn testimony of witnesses who saw it happen:*

> I do testify that I have seen Margaret Rule in her afflictions from the invisible world lifted up from her bed, wholly by an invisible force, a great way towards the top of the room where she lay. In her being so lifted she had no assistance from any use of her own arms or hands or any other part of her body, not so much as her heels touching her bed or resting on any support whatsoever. And I have seen her thus lifted when not only a strong person hath thrown his whole weight across her to pull her down, but several other persons have endeavored with all their might to hinder her from being so raised up, which I suppose that several others will testify as well as myself when called unto it.

This statement was signed by an eyewitness, Samuel Ames, and his assumption that others would confirm his story was correct. *No less than five others* pledged their solemn oaths that Margaret Rule had levitated in their presence. The modern skeptic may scoff at this evidence, but let him keep something in mind if he does. Lying, even under oath, is fairly common in our century, but to the seventeenth-century Puritan swearing false witness was not only a crime but a serious sin which could damn his immortal soul. Is it reasonable that these six God-fearing Puritans would perjure themselves under these circumstances? Let the reader decide.

I have left until last the most convincing proof that black magic and witchcraft were actually performed in Salem: the numerous confessions of the guilty witches. Although incidents such as the curse of Sarah Good and the levitation of Margaret Rule are more spectacular, the fact that over fifty persons actually admitted being witches, actually admitted selling their souls to the devil, must be considered the most important evidence of unholy, supernatural practices in Massachusetts.

Let it be acknowledged at the outset that a few of these confessions were fanciful and imaginary, that a few of the confessors were undoubtedly mentally deranged and therefore untrustworthy. Nevertheless, it is incredible that more than fifty different people all deliberately endangered their lives and their souls by making false confessions to the most vicious and evil of crimes.

Typical of these many confessions is that of William Barker who admitted he had "been in the snare of the Devil three years," and that Satan's "design was to destroy Salem Village, and to begin at the minister's house, and to destroy the Church of God, and to set up Satan's kingdom, and then all will be well." Others followed Barker's example. Samuel Wardwell stated he had "covenanted with the Devil until I should arrive to the age of sixty years." Wardwell's confession was corroborated by his wife, nor was this an isolated example of one member of a family testifying to the guilt of another. George Jacobs was convicted on the evidence of his granddaughter, Margaret, that he was a wizard. Martha Carrier, who was promised by Satan that she would reign as "Queen of Hell," was convicted after two of her sons not only admitted practicing black magic but charged their mother had initiated them in these wicked activities.

Perhaps the most damning, and certainly the most important, of the confessions was made by old Tituba, the Indian slave woman of Salem minister Samuel Parris, who, like Candy, had come from Barbados. It was in Tituba's kitchen that the afflicted children first experienced the sensation of watching witchcraft performed, and it was Tituba who made the first confession, so vivid and convincing in detail that the judges could not help but accept it, which led to the full revelation of the truth.

The Salem Witch Trials

Was there witchcraft in Salem? If you wish to appear wise and sophisticated you will probably answer no. It was all merely superstition, not supernatural. No one in these enlightened days sells his soul in return for the evil powers of black magic. There are no such things as spells, no such things as ghosts, no such things as witches. These are all just weird tales from an earlier, more credulous age.

Of course they are. Tell yourself that the next time you avoid crossing the path of a black cat or walking under a ladder. Say it out loud the next time you hear strange noises in the night. Tell it, if you dare, to the ghost of Nicholas Noyes, who, it is whispered by some, still walks the streets of Salem, choking on his blood.

Bibliographical entry

Oakes, Peter. "The Witches of Salem," Odyssey Magazine, 14:155–160, April, 1970.

Footnote entries

[1]Peter Oakes, "The Witches of Salem," Odyssey Magazine, April, 1970, p. 159.

Often in a research paper there is opportunity for the writer to show the reader how thorough his research actually is. It is wise to take opportunities like this as they come to you. One such way is with the use of compound footnotes, or footnotes that include more than one source. The following is an example of how a compound footnote might appear:

[4]Peter Oakes, "The Witches of Salem," Odyssey Magazine, April, 1970, p. 159. Christopher Ross, "The Salem Tragedy," Truth Magazine, September 27, 1969, p. 162.

Footnote 4 tells us that supporting evidence can be found in each of the sources cited. This adds weight to research.

It is often possible to show the depth of your research by indicating that more than one source was consulted before selecting the information that you eventually wrote into your paper. You can tell the reader that he should compare (cf.) the cited source with a contrasting source, or he should consult for additional information (see) another source which agrees with the cited source. The following is an example of a compare notation:

[5]Peter Oakes, "The Witches of Salem," Odyssey Magazine, April, 1970, p. 159.; cf. Christopher Ross, "The Salem Tragedy," Truth Magazine, September 27, 1969, p. 162.

Or if Oakes has already been cited:

[5]Oakes, p. 159.; cf. Christopher Ross, "The Salem Tragedy," Truth Magazine, September 27, 1969, p. 162.

Or if both were previously cited:

[5]Oakes, p. 159.; cf. Ross, p. 162.

See Appendix B, pages 283–302, for a complete discussion of footnotes.

The Salem Tragedy
by Christopher Ross

Truth Magazine, vol. 81, September 27, 1969, pp. 161–165.

It is now almost three centuries since the tragic witchcraft trials at Salem, Massachusetts, yet the passage of time cannot erase the grim memory of that sad and horrible era, and perhaps we should not be allowed to forget. For the witch-hunts stand as an awesome reminder of the terrors which can result from uncontrolled fanaticism and widespread public panic. By the time the official prosecutions were finally halted, a staggering price in human lives and human misery had been paid by the people of the Massachusetts Bay Colony. Nineteen innocent men and women had been hanged, one had been pressed to death, and still more had died in the vermin-infested prisons. Another eight had been sentenced to death, over one hundred and fifty more awaited trial after their arrests, and an additional two hundred had been accused of witchcraft and were being sought by the authorities.

How could such a tragedy have happened? It would be vain hypocrisy for us to condemn these seventeenth-century Puritans for their superstitious belief in witches. In their time even the most enlightened men were convinced of the existence of an "invisible world" of spirits, both good and evil, who struggled for possession of human souls. Witches were mentioned in the Bible and a belief in them was an important part of a Puritan's religious faith. Yet witch scares had occurred before in New England without assuming the huge proportions of the outbreak at Salem. Usually no more than one or two unfortunate old women would be accused, and acquittals were as common as convictions. Why, then, was it different at Salem?

To answer this question we must look briefly at the history of the

p. 162.

The Salem Witch Trials

witch-hunts. They began early in 1692 in the kitchen of the Reverend Samuel Parris where old Tituba, the minister's slave, entertained a small circle of young girls with harmless spells and tricks learned in her native Barbados. Innocent as this might seem to us, to the seventeenth century such things were thought the work of Satan himself. The girls, fascinated with Tituba yet torn apart by their deep sense of guilt, began to exhibit symptoms of hysteria. Their fits and trances are easily explained by modern psychiatry. Even the more horrible effects, such as a swelling of the belly or the raising of skin blisters, are known today to be merely psychosomatic. But in 1692 these things seemed certain signs that the girls were being afflicted by witches.

Hysterics are extremely suggestive, as any psychologist can tell you. The girls were told that the baking of a "witchcake" would enable them to name their tormentors and, once the cake had been prepared, they were of course able to do so. The three they accused were likely enough candidates: a pipe-smoking old tramp, Sarah Good; a woman of immoral reputation, Sarah Osbourn; and poor Tituba. The others denied all charges, but Tituba told wild stories of midnight broomstick rides to unholy "witches' Sabbaths" where the devil, not God, was worshipped. Later, in prison, the old slave retracted her "confession," saying it had been beaten out of her by her master, the Reverend Parris, and she stuck to her denials even though it meant long months in jail, since Parris refused to pay for her release until she once again admitted to witchcraft. She never did and was eventually sold to pay her prison expenses, but the damage done by her original testimony could not be undone. The judges believed her tales of devil worship and became convinced that a whole nest of witches was operating in Salem.

One factor which seemed to confirm this was the large number of accused witches who confessed their guilt, over fifty before the trials were halted. Many of these were children, some too young to realize what they were saying, like little Dorcas Good, a mere six years old, who charged her mother, Sarah, with betraying her to Satan. Many others were tortured into confessing, like the teen-aged sons of Martha Carrier, whose heels were chained to their heads until they vomited blood. Some, less hardy, were simply bullied into their admissions, although a few, like Margaret Jacobs, had immediate attacks of conscience and tried desperately to withdraw their statements of guilt. Some others, like William Barker who made numerous confessions, appear simply to have been psychotic.

One rugged individualist refused to enter any plea at all. Giles Corey, though nearly eighty, endured two days of "pressing," a torture in which the accused was spread-eagled on the ground and rocks piled on his chest. At last he died without pleading to the charge. The only words he ever spoke were "more weight."

The principal explanation for the confessions seems to be that those who admitted their guilt were not hanged; this was about the only way an accused witch's life could be spared. During the height of the trials in Salem only one defendant, an elderly woman named Rebecca Nurse, was acquitted. The jury was ordered to reconsider their verdict and they changed it to guilty. In spite of a petition from her neighbors testifying to her excellent character and begging compassion for her ill health and her age. Rebecca Nurse, too, was hanged.

We have said that the Puritans should not be condemned for their superstitions. Nevertheless, the ready willingness of even the most learned of them to believe fantastic tales of black magic must be considered a prime cause for what happened at Salem. For example, it was credited that a doctor named Roger Toothaker had cast a fatal spell over a witch not because Toothaker said so, but merely because someone else said that Toothaker said that he had done so. In a modern court of law such "evidence" would be clearly inadmissible as the worst kind of hearsay.

Even the Reverend Cotton Mather, though probably the best educated man in the colonies at the time, found no miracle too improbable to accept and repeat. Robert Calef, a Boston merchant and skeptic who openly ridiculed Mather for his support of the trials, undertook to explode the minister's accounts of supernatural events. Mather wrote of a youth named Bishop who had been burned by an invisible branding iron. The boy "has exposed the lasting marks of it," Mather noted, "unto such as asked to see them." Absurd, snorted Calef. The so-called brand was only a boil on the lad's thigh which broke as he strained to hold down a cow that was being branded. The corner of a ghostly sheet which Mather claimed had appeared suddenly in the hand of an afflicted girl was, said Calef, actually smuggled in to the child the day before.

Stung by Calef's sarcasm, Mather sent him the affidavits of six men who swore they had seen another afflicted girl, Margaret Rule, levitate to the "garret floor" (i.e., the ceiling of her room). Calef's response was sardonic:

The Salem Witch Trials

> You were pleased to send me another paper containing several testimonies of the possessed being lifted up, and held a space of several minutes to the garret floor, etc., but they omit giving the account, whether after she was down they bound her down: or kept holding her: and relate not how many were to pull her down, which hinders the knowledge what number they must be to be stronger than an Invisible Force. Upon the whole, I suppose you expect I should believe it . . . and that the Devil can work such miracles.

Elsewhere Calef had noted that Margaret Rule had a fondness for rum and much preferred the company of men to that of her own sex, particularly when they spent the night. If Mather's six male witnesses were alone with Margaret in her room, there were other activities Robert Calef could imagine them engaged in besides trying to pull her down from the ceiling.

As noted earlier, the afflicted children, at least most of them, seem to have been suffering from hysteria, a form of neurosis marked by hallucination and amnesia, in which they would be abnormally susceptible to suggestion. In other words, if it were suggested to them that a person were a witch and that this witch was about to torment them, they would believe it and would actually feel the pain. This pain, though rooted in psychological rather than physical or supernatural causes, would be real enough to both the sufferer and those who witnessed the suffering. This fact explains much of the torture felt by these girls. When an accused witch was brought into court it was expected by both the judges and the girls that the latter would be afflicted by her. This *expectation* alone led the judges to suggest, and the girls to experience, these afflictions.

But hysteria by itself is not sufficient to account for the physical marks of torment which sometimes appeared on the girls' bodies. It is unfortunately apparent that a few of the children, having come to realize the great power they held over their superstitious elders (for a word of accusation from any one of them could cause the arrest of almost any adult), sought to maintain that power by faking the symptoms of affliction. It is not difficult to pretend the temporary loss of speech, appetite or memory, nor is it hard to pinch oneself while in the throes of an apparent fit or fainting spell. On at least one occasion a girl was detected in such a pretense. During the trial of Sarah Good one of the afflicted (unfortunately the records do not indicate her name) claimed to have been attacked with a knife by Sarah's demon and produced a part of the blade as proof. But a youth in the courtroom recognized the blade as having broken off his own knife the previous day and been picked up by the same girl. He even produced the broken knife, but the judges merely warned the girl to be truthful and allowed her to continue to sit as one of the accusers.

When the trials finally were halted in October of 1692 it was for a number of reasons. So many had been accused of witchcraft that it seemed the whole population might be wiped out. The afflicted, over-estimating their power, had cried out against several of the most prominent citizens of Massachusetts, including the governor's wife. Opposition to the trials was mounted by merchants like Calef and Thomas Brattle, and by moderate ministers like Samuel Willard and Joshua Moody. At last the governor, Sir William Phips, put an end to the pitiful charade. When it was over, nineteen people (and two dogs!) had been hanged, another had been pressed to death, others had died in prison, or had their health broken, their fortunes destroyed, their reputations ruined, their relatives murdered, their sanity impaired.

It is easy enough, of course, to attack these Puritans of Salem for their religious fanaticism and intolerance, but it would be a waste of time, for they are long dead and far beyond the sound of our sputtering moral indignation. It is more difficult to recognize that *fanaticism,* the conviction that we have truth, and *intolerance,* the conviction that those who disagree with us are devoted to falsehood and must be con-verted or removed, are but two faces of extremism. And extremism may be religious, or political, or racial, or economic.

One of the earliest witch-hunters, the Reverend John Hale, ex-perienced a change of heart after the ghost of Mary Esty, a convicted witch, accused his own wife, through a medium, of consorting with the devil. But Hale had the courage to speak against the persecutions be-fore it was quite fashionable, or quite safe, to do so. "We walked in clouds and could not see our way," Hale would write. "And we have most cause to be humbled for error . . . which cannot be retrieved."

Bibliographical entry

Ross, Christopher. "The Salem Tragedy," Truth Mag-
    azine, 81:161–165, September 27, 1969.

Original footnote entry

[1]Christopher Ross, "The Salem Tragedy," Truth Magazine, September 27, 1969, p. 163.

The Salem Witch Trials:
A Travesty of Justice

by Max Arnold

Excerpt from a lecture at Colbridge College, Gloucester, Mass.,
November 19, 1970.

The most fundamental protections of the law were denied to those
accused of witchcraft at Salem. They were refused the advice of counsel and forced to defend themselves alone as best they could, although
many were ignorant and some were obviously demented. They were
not permitted to confront their accusers or to know the nature of the
testimony against them before their trials. They were forced to testify
against themselves. The judges, far from being impartial, actually
prosecuted the defendants, asking leading and argumentative questions. The examination of Sarah Good by the magistrate, John Hathorne, is typical.

> Q. Sarah Good, what evil spirit have you familiarity with?
> A. None.
> Q. Have you made no contract with the devil?
> A. No.
> Q. Why do you hurt these children?
> A. I do not hurt them. I scorn it.
> Q. Who do you employ then to do it?
> A. I employ nobody.
> Q. What creature do you employ then?
> A. No creature, but I am falsely accused.

Not only did the judges act as prosecutors; they assumed automatically that anyone brought before them was guilty. This is evident
in all the examinations but nowhere more clear than in the questioning
of Deliverance Hobbs:

> Q. Why do you hurt these persons?
> A. It is unknown to me.
> Q. How come you to commit acts of witchcraft?
> A. I know nothing of it.
> Q. It is you or your appearance, how comes this about? Tell us
> the truth.
> A. I cannot tell.
> Q. Tell us what you know in this case. Who hurts them if you do
> not?
> A. There are a great many persons hurts us all.
> Q. But it is your appearance.

A. I do not know it.

Q. Have you not consented to it, that they should be hurt?

A. No in the sight of God, and man, as I shall answer another day.

Examine these questions closely. There is an assumption of guilt behind every one of them. The afflicted girls have accused Deliverance Hobbs of tormenting them. Hathorne does not ask her *whether* she hurts them; he asks her *why* she hurts them. He has no doubt of her guilt; he merely asks her motive. He states flatly that mischief has been done by Deliverance or her "appearance," by which he means her "shape," a ghostly demon in the witch's own form which she commanded. And, despite her brave denial, only moments later his bullying and the shouted accusations of the afflicted destroy her courage and she confesses.

Q. Is it not a solemn [true] thing, that last Lord's day you were tormented, and now you are become a tormentor, so that you have changed sides? How comes this to pass? (At this point the girls cried out that the defendant's shape was in the court, sitting on a beam under the roof.)

Q. What do you say to this, that though you are at the bar in person, yet they see your appearance upon the beam, and whereas a few days past you were tormented, now you are become a tormentor? Tell us how this change comes. Tell true.

A. I have done nothing.

Q. What! Have you resolved you will not confess? Hath anybody threatened you if you do confess? You can tell how this change comes. [The accused here looked at some of the afflicted and they immediately began having fits.] Tell us the reason of this change: tell us the truth. What have you done?

A. I cannot speak.

Q. What do you say? What have you done?

A. I cannot tell.

Q. Have you signed to any book?

A. It is very lately then.

Q. When was it?

A. The night before the last.

The question "Have you signed to any book?" referred to the belief that witches wrote their names in a book carried by Satan as a pledge of their souls. When Deliverance, cowed by the magistrate's aggressive interrogation and frightened by the howling of the afflicted, admitted signing the book, she was acknowledging herself a witch.

Scenes like this occurred constantly in Salem. Because the judges always presumed the guilt of the accused, they naturally felt great sympathy for the afflicted children. Any outburst from the girls was not only permitted but encouraged and used as proof of the defendant's wickedness. Since it was taken for granted that the accused was in league with the devil, it was thought that Satan stood beside her during the trial, an invisible defense counsel, whispering evasive answers and diabolical lies to her. The magistrates, therefore, were particularly aggressive in their cross-examinations. They considered each examination to be a battle of wits with the "Prince of Lies" himself.

The most vile cruelties were committed against the accused from the most humane motives. Those who refused to confess were tortured until they did, not for the sadistic pleasure of it, but because the authorities, convinced of their guilt, were equally certain that their souls would be damned unless they confessed and repented. Still, it must be said that official concern for the souls of sinners is not sufficient to explain the terrible suffering undergone by the prisoners. Once indicted, they were herded in open carts to stinking prisons where they lay for months under heavy chains, since it was believed a chained witch could not cast spells. They were actually required to pay the government room and board for these charming accommodations. Miserably undernourished, forced to lie in their own filth, exhibited to the public like creatures in a zoo, many of them died before ever coming to trial.

Those who survived to stand trial had no chance of acquittal. The imaginations of the afflicted and the superstitious minds of the judges and jurymen combined to produce all the "proofs" of witchcraft necessary for conviction. Among these proofs was the test of touch. Witches were thought to possess the "evil eye," the power to strike their victims down simply by looking at them. (This, you will recall, is just what happened to some of the afflicted when Deliverance Hobbs cast her eye upon them.) When the girls were in the throes of their agony the witch was led from the witness stand and forced to touch each of them in turn with her hand. As each child was touched, it was thought, an evil spirit flowed out of the victim's body into the witch. Immediately the girl's painful fits would cease and she would drop in a dead faint. Such highly dramatic scenes seemed convincing evidence of black magic to those who witnessed them.

Even more common than the test of touch was spectral evidence. It was believed that a witch had the power to transform herself into any shape she chose, and to command demons who also could assume any form, natural or monstrous. (Again, recall the afflicted girls' claim that they could see Deliverance Hobbs' "shape" in the courtroom.) From literally scores of spectral testimonies we might select as typical the deposition of Jack Louder in the trial of Bridget Bishop.

> [I] did see a black thing jump into the window and came and stood just before my face . . . the body of it looked like a monkey only the feet were like a cock's feet with claws and the face somewhat more like a man's than a monkey and I being greatly affrighted, not being able to speak or help myself by reason of fear I suppose, so the thing spoke to me and said, "I am a messenger sent to you for I understand you are troubled in mind and [if] you will be ruled by me you shall want for nothing in this world." Upon which I endeavored to clap my hands upon it, and said, "you devil, I will kill you," but could feel no substance and it jumped out of the window again, and immediately came in by the porch although the doors were shut, and said, "you had better take my counsel." Whereupon I struck at it with a stick but struck the ground-sill and broke the stick, but felt no substance and that arm with which I struck was presently disenabled. Then it vanished away, and I opened the back door and went out, and going towards the house end, I espied said Bridget Bishop in her orchard going towards her house, and seeing her had no power to set one foot forward but returned in again . . . going to shut the door, I again did see that . . . creature . . . in such a posture as it seemed to be agoing to fly at me, upon which I cried out, "The whole armor of God be between me and you." So it sprang back and flew over the apple tree, flinging the dust with its feet against my stomach, upon which I was struck dumb and so continued for about three days' time.

Louder assumed that this hybrid monkey-monster was either Bridget Bishop or one of her demons, and the judges and jury agreed. To convince the Salem court of the truth of spectral visions one need only claim to have seen them. To us several possible explanations of Louder's testimony may occur: he was lying; he was hallucinating; he was drunk. But only one explanation appeared plausible to Bridget Bishop's judges, and the lady became the first of nineteen convicted witches to make the trip to the Salem gallows.

The prosecution in the witch trials made great use of the testimony of confessed witches like Deliverance Hobbs to implicate those who protested their innocence. It was particularly helpful if close relatives of the "witch" could be persuaded to give evidence against her, even if the methods of persuasion sometimes became rather crude. In his petition to five moderate Boston ministers, accused wizard John Proctor complained that the children of suspected witches were tortured into leveling charges against their parents:

The Salem Witch Trials

> Here are five persons who have lately confessed themselves to be witches, and do accuse some of us of being along with them at a sacrament [a witches' Sabbath] since we were committed into close prison, which we know to be lies. Two of the five are (Carrier's sons) young men who would not confess anything till they tied them neck and heels till the blood was ready to come out of their noses, and 'tis credibly believed and reported this was the occasion of making them confess that [which] they never did, by reason they said one had been made a witch a month, and another five weeks, and that their mother had made them so, who has been confined here this nine weeks. My son, William Proctor, when he was examined, because he would not confess that he was guilty when he was innocent, they tied him neck and heels till the blood gushed out at his nose, and would have kept him so twenty-four hours if one more merciful than the rest had not taken pity on him and caused him to be unbound.

The principal purpose of Proctor's petition was to plead that his own trial and those of four others be held in Boston rather than Salem where, he charged, "the magistrates, ministers, juries, and all the people in general" were "so much enraged and incensed against us by the delusion of the devil" that he feared their "innocent bloods" would be shed. His request was ignored. All five were tried at Salem, including Proctor's wife, Elizabeth, and Martha Carrier whose teen-aged sons had accused her under torture. All five were convicted and only Elizabeth Proctor escaped hanging when she was found to be pregnant.

Equally tragic was Proctor's neighbor, Rebecca Nurse, the aging, infirm matriarch of one of Salem's largest families, who was originally indicted on the evidence of an eleven-year-old girl that she had been tormented by Rebecca's shape. At her trial Rebecca's poor health and excellent former reputation raised both pity and doubt in the minds of the jury who found her not guilty. At the verdict the afflicted girls set off such a howl of protest that the chief judge, William Stoughton, instructed the jury to *reconsider* their decision. Stoughton pointed out a bit of evidence he thought they might have overlooked. When Deliverance Hobbs and her daughter were called to bear witness against Rebecca, the old woman had expressed surprise: "What! Do these persons give in evidence against me now? They used to come among us." Since Deliverance was accusing Rebecca of attending witches' Sabbaths with her, the unfortunate phrase, "they used to come among us," was interpreted as a confession. By the time the defendant explained her real meaning, that Deliverance and her child were also prisoners and thus presumably unable to testify, it was too late. The jury now declared her guilty.

In a last-ditch effort to save her from the rope, Rebecca's family obtained a reprieve from the royal governor, Sir William Phips. But when the afflicted learned of this they again began to accuse her of tormenting them and Phips withdrew the reprieve. Rebecca Nurse was hanged by the neck until she was dead.

I cannot avoid observing here, before continuing our discussion of the events at Salem, that of all the follies committed by the authorities during the trials the most unforgivable was their presumption of the guilt of the accused, a clear violation of the most important principle of law, that a defendant must always be presumed innocent until proven guilty. Placed beside this monumental error, their cruelties and absurd superstitions seem almost insignificant.

Bibliographical entry

Arnold, Max. "The Salem Witch Trials: A Travesty of Justice." An excerpt from a lecture delivered by Professor Max Arnold at Colbridge College, Gloucester, Massachusetts, November 15, 1970.

Note: Usually, lectures are not listed in a bibliography, but in a case where a printed excerpt is referred to, it is wise to allow the reader recourse if he challenges your material.

Footnote entry

[1]Information obtained from a lecture delivered by Professor Max Arnold at Colbridge College, Gloucester, Massachusetts, entitled "The Salem Witch Trials: A Travesty of Justice," on November 15, 1970.

Note: Since it is usual to list just the lecture footnote without a bibliographical notation, it is necessary to have as complete a footnote as is possible.

There may be at your campus several persons who are authorities on the subject of witchcraft. If it is at all possible, an attempt should be made to interview one of these people. Often the interview or conversation will give you direction or greater insight into the subject. Here is an example of what an interview footnote might look like:

[3]An interview with Max Arnold, Professor of English

The Salem Witch Trials

at Colbridge College, on December 5, 1971, to discuss
the subject of "Imported Superstition" and what bearing
it might have had on the Salem witchcraft trials.

Footnote 3 is adequate as it is, but there are times when it would be proper to give a little more of the interviewee's background. An example of this might be:

[1]An interview with Max Arnold, Professor of English
at Colbridge College, on December 5, 1971, to discuss
the subject of "Imported Superstition" and what bearing
it might have had on the Salem witchcraft trials. Dr.
Arnold is presently investigating the Salem trials in
preparation for a major novel. He has spent many years
investigating published materials.

INSTRUCTIONS

1. *Having finished your first reading of the sources, check through the notes you have taken and, as you did with the articles on Hauptmann, make a list of areas of significant disagreement or contradiction. The introduction on page 154 may be helpful in suggesting areas of tension. Select the controversy in which you feel the greatest interest. It should be obvious that your own genuine curiosity is an essential ingredient in research. If you really do not care what the truth is, your work is merely drudgery.*

2. *Phrase the controversy you will investigate as a question to be answered by your paper. This question is your working title. Review the section called "The Most Commonly Asked Questions About Writing a Research Paper," (pages 140–150). Return to this section as often as necessary for guidance and reference in developing your paper.*

3. *Prepare a worksheet for your project, following the form illustrated on page 149. Determine the issues which you must settle before your major question can be answered. Review the suggestions on note taking (pages 142–144) and then reread the sources, taking careful notes on all material relevant to your topic. Use the jottings from your preliminary reading to guide you to the most pertinent parts of the articles.*

4. *Review the instruction on organizing your notes (page 142). Plan your paper carefully and be certain its organization is clear in*

your mind before beginning to write. Suggestions for writing and revising your paper are on pages 144–146.

5. *Take particular care with the form, placement and accuracy of your footnotes. The proper form for both footnotes and bibliography entry follow each article, and additional instructions appear in Appendix B, pages 283–302. Remember, footnote numbers should be placed in the text of your first draft as you write, and the footnote itself recorded immediately on a separate page. Study the sample on pp. 148–149. This practice simplifies the footnoting procedure for you and insures that your annotation will be accurate. Review also "The Most Commonly Asked Questions About Footnotes" (pages 151–154), and refer to it when needed.*

    Remember you are re-searching, searching again, through facts, opinions and arguments first presented by other people. You must use footnotes to give credit (or place blame) for these ideas to the people who first advanced them. This does not mean that there is nothing original, nothing of your own, in your paper. Of course you may express opinions and conclusions "of your own" directly to your reader, but, beyond that, it is your originality which determines how your sources' ideas will be organized and phrased for your reader, how they will be made to complement each other or be pitted against one another. Your sources are only the servants of you as researcher: in a very real sense they are at your mercy. And to research means not just to rummage through old ideas but to rethink them, to analyze them, and then to uphold them or to expose them as stupidity or fraud.

6. *Even better, rethinking their old ideas may lead you to a new idea which never occurred to your sources at all. Should this happen, you will have reached a level of research writing seldom required or expected below graduate school.*

THE LIZZIE BORDEN CASE

Whether because of its savage brutality or its unnaturalness, the double murder of Andrew Jackson Borden and his wife, Abby, in 1892 in Fall River, Massachusetts, has a permanent place in American folklore. The barbaric violence of the killings was enough to bring them to national attention, but when authorities accused the couple's younger daughter, Lizzie, the case took on the aspects of a Greek tragedy.

For the amateur detective who enjoys sifting the dust of old crimes, the Borden case offers a challenge to the powers of logic and deductive reasoning. Did Miss Lizzie alone have the opportunity to commit the murders, as was charged at her trial, or could her parents have been killed by an outsider or by the maid, Bridget Sullivan, as her defenders have claimed?

As with most celebrated capital trials, the trial of Lizzie Borden provides valuable insights into the social attitudes and prejudices of its time. The defendant was an active Congregationalist in a period when Protestant Christianity was still the dominant religious force in America. She was a woman at a time when the feminist movement was both powerful and influential. She received the public support of numerous church and feminist organizations, support which contributed heavily to her eventual acquittal. Those interested in the current feminine liberation should find interesting parallels with the suffragette movement of the 1890's.

1. *Read closely through all four sources on Lizzie Borden. Make no attempt to take complete notes on your first reading, but keep a notebook handy to jot down each author's major points and to note any areas of disagreement or contradiction between authors. It is vital, even in this most preliminary stage of researching, that every note you take be identified in the margin of your notebook by author and the page number of the source.*

2. *As you read, identify possible questions which you might attempt to answer in your research paper. Keep a record of these questions on a special page in your notebook, leaving space under each to note relevant issues as they occur to you. After each entry jot down related sources with page numbers as you find them in your reading.*

  During this initial reading of your sources, keep your mind as free and active as possible. Do not worry yet about distinguishing fact from opinion from deception. The time for that is later. Now concentrate on each writer's principal arguments and where they contradict each other. Try to become interested in which of them is right. From such curiosity on your part your paper's question will arise.

3. *When you have completed the first reading of your sources, follow the directions at the conclusion of the materials.*

Excerpts from *The Legend of Lizzie Borden*
by F. Lincoln Hall

New York: Hall, Simon and Schwartz, 1934. Pp. 175–188.

The rhyme has perhaps faded from memory now, but in 1893 every schoolchild in America was singing it:

Lizzie Borden took an ax
And gave her mother forty whacks.
When she saw what she had done,
She gave her father forty-one.

The poet exaggerated slightly: Abby Borden was not struck forty blows but a mere nineteen, while her husband, Andrew, received only ten wounds. And, though the vicious little rhyme reflects the eventual, wide-spread belief in the guilt of their daughter Lizzie, we must not forget that that lady was acquitted at her trial and that she still finds many spirited defenders today.

•　　•　　•　　•　　•

Abby was Andrew Borden's second wife, a friendless, vapid, grossly overweight frump whom Andrew had married when Lizzie was four and her older sister, Emma, fourteen. As for Andrew, the tall, gaunt, grim-faced son of a fishmonger, he had begun life as an undertaker and built a considerable fortune on his talents as a usurer and slumlord. His mania for frugality was proverbial. His cramped little house on Second Street had neither gas nor hot water: the Bordens burned coal for heat and kerosene for light. His sole concession to modern convenience was a tiny water-closet in the basement beside which a stack of old newspapers were kept for "sanitary purposes." Andrew's miserly reputation dated back to his undertaking days when, it was whispered, he bought abbreviated coffins at abbreviated prices and chopped the feet off the corpses to assure a good fit.

When her parents were killed Emma Borden was forty-two, timid,

The Salem Witch Trials

straitlaced and extremely single. Lizzie, at thirty-two, was much more outgoing, active in church and charitable organizations, and had made the grand tour of Europe with a circle of spinsters who called themselves "the girls." Both daughters felt a keen rivalry with their stepmother which amounted, at least in Lizzie's case, to a dislike bordering on hatred which she took no pains to hide. They measured their father's love for them as opposed to his love for Abby by old Andrew's only way of demonstrating love: his gifts of cash and property. Generosity was not one of the old skinflint's faults, yet he did periodically sign over stocks and deeds to the sisters. For Abby there was nothing, nothing that is until 1887.

Five years before the murders, with the connivance of his first wife's brother, John Morse, and without the knowledge of his daughters, Andrew purchased a small piece of property and put it in his wife's name. The girls blamed poor Abby for this perfidy and they never forgave her. All pretense of domestic bliss vanished from the unhappy household. The little house on Second Street became an armed camp.

•   •   •   •   •

Emma was away visiting friends at Fairhaven during the week of August 1, 1892, when the murders took place. The household thus consisted of four: the old man; his second wife; Lizzie; and the Irish maid-servant, Bridget Sullivan, then in her third year of service with the Bordens. To this cozy group a fifth was added when, on the afternoon of Wednesday, August 3, "Uncle John" Morse arrived unexpectedly to spend the night in the Borden guest room. The day before, Tuesday the second, both elder Bordens had been extremely ill, spending much of the night vomiting into their slop-pails. Miss Lizzie later claimed she had also felt queasy though she had not vomited. On Wednesday morning, much to Andrew's annoyance, Abby had complained to their neighbor, Dr. Bowen, that she and her husband were being poisoned. Bowen brushed it off.

Also on Wednesday morning, Miss Lizzie attempted to purchase prussic acid, a deadly poison, from a local pharmacy, ostensibly to kill moths in a sealskin collar. Apparently she was unaware that moths never breed in sealskin. In any case, she was refused and stamped out in a huff.

On Wednesday evening Miss Lizzie confided to her sister's friend Alice Russell her fear that her father had an "enemy" who was trying to poison their milk. Andrew had argued with a man (whose identity was unknown to Lizzie) and had thrown him out of the house. Furthermore, the house had been robbed by a daring daylight burglar. Miss Russell expressed surprise at the robbery since she had never heard Emma mention it. She thought Lizzie was being overly melodramatic and she said so, but nothing could shake Lizzie's sense of impending doom. "I feel," she said, "as if something was hanging over me that I cannot throw off."

Her parents and Uncle John were talking in the sitting room when Lizzie returned from Miss Russell's, but she did not go in to speak with them. Instead she went to her room. Shortly afterwards Abby also retired. Andrew and Uncle John continued talking until late, sitting in the dark to conserve kerosene.

In order to understand what happened on Thursday, August 4, the murder day, you must grasp fully both the layout of the Borden house and the sequence of events.

Study the floor plans on pages 178–179 of the first and second floors of the murder house. The plans are virtually identical except that two small rooms on the first floor were made into one long, narrow dining room. This was done by Andrew Borden when he purchased the house and remodeled it from a two-family into a one-family dwelling. At the same time he transformed the upstairs kitchen into a master bedroom. At first Emma slept in the larger of the remaining bedrooms (No. 4 in Fig. 2) and Lizzie in the smaller (No. 3 in Fig. 2). This arrangement lasted from the purchase of the house in 1874 until shortly before the murders, when the sisters suddenly switched rooms. The guest room (No. 5 in Fig. 2) was used by the girls to entertain their friends. The dressing room (No. 2 in Fig. 2) served as a clothes closet for the elder Bordens and contained Andrew's desk and safe. For some reason it was known as "Mrs. Borden's room." Lizzie and Emma kept their dresses in the large closet which opened off the second-floor landing (No. 7 in Fig. 2).

Besides the front and rear entries and a small sink room and pantry, there were four rooms on the first floor, all considerably more cramped than they may appear on the diagram. The parlor, following the custom of the Victorian period, was reserved only for special occasions and virtually never used. Even after the murders, the bodies were laid out not in the parlor, but on the dining-room table. The family gathered in the sitting room, which served the purpose of a modern living room.

The Lizzie Borden Case

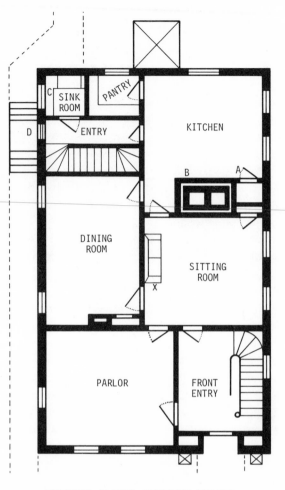

GROUND FLOOR, BORDEN HOUSE

Mr. Borden's head rested on the sofa arm by the door—see X—as he took his nap.

A. Lizzie stood here, in angle of coal-closet door, as she burned the dress she had placed on the closet shelf some hours before.

B. Stove in which she burned it.

C. Where Emma was washing the dishes when Lizzie began to burn the dress.

Note that upstairs guest room (5, next floor plan) can be reached from kitchen entry (D) only by way of the kitchen and sitting room. There are shelves at the left side of the sink room and at two sides of the pantry; the sitting-room closet is also filled with shelves. An extremely small broom closet facing stairs at right side of front door is not indicated on this floor plan.

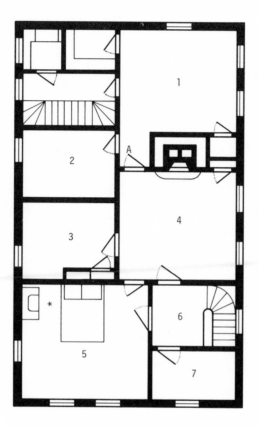

SECOND FLOOR, BORDEN HOUSE

1. Mr. and Mrs. Borden's room. 2. Mrs. Borden's dressing room. 3. Emma's room. 4. Lizzie's room. 5. Guest room, in which Mrs. Borden was killed. 6. Landing at head of stairs. 7. Dress closet.

Asterisk (*) marks Mrs. Borden's body, between the bed and the bureau.

A indicates the door that was kept locked and fastened on both sides from the time of the robbery until the murders, thus making it impossible to get from 5 to 1 without going down the front stairs, through the sitting room and kitchen, and up the back stairs.

The Lizzie Borden Case

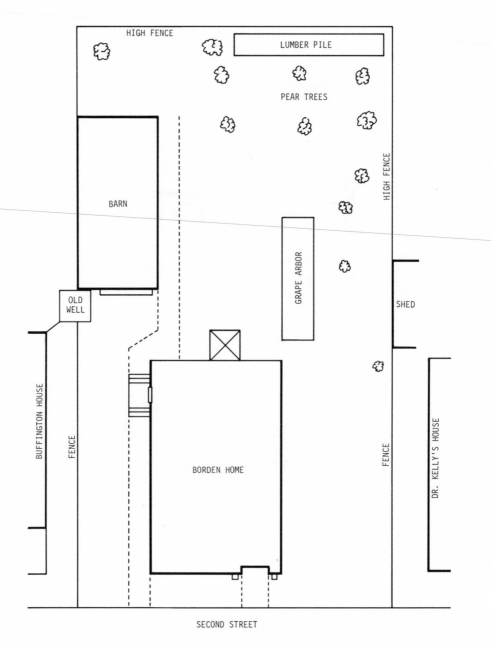

PLAN OF BORDEN HOUSE AND YARD

Meals were served in the dining room, though for the past five years Lizzie and Emma had avoided eating at the same time as their parents whenever possible. On the morning of the murders, Lizzie waited for breakfast until the elder Bordens and Uncle John were finished.

The maid, Bridget Sullivan, slept in a small attic room at the head of the back stairs. She was under orders, and this is extremely important, never to set foot in any of the second-floor rooms.

Look closely at the diagrams. There are no hallways to connect the rooms. One could move through the house only by passing through certain rooms to get to others, thus the placement of the doors becomes very important. On the ground floor the only way to get from the kitchen entry to the front hall lies through the kitchen and sitting room. Note in the plan of the second floor that the Bordens' bedroom is just above the kitchen and Lizzie's just above the sitting room. The only route from the back of the house to the front on the second floor lies through door A (Fig. 2) but *on the day of the murders, and for some time before, this door had been kept locked and bolted on both sides.* It was therefore impossible to go from the Borden bedroom to the guest room without walking through the kitchen and sitting room. The significance of this will become apparent when we attempt to reconstruct the movements of the household on the fatal day.

A few more points. Entrance to the house was possible only through the rear door. The windows were high off the ground and, despite the intense August heat, all the first-floor windows were closed when the murders were committed because Abby had ordered Bridget Sullivan to wash them on the outside. The front door, locked and double-bolted on the inside, was opened only briefly at about 10:40 by the maid to admit Andrew and then relocked. Only the rear door ever stood unlocked and unattended for any period of time, and then apparently only when Bridget was in the yard since she habitually latched the screen door on the inside when she entered the house.

The murders occurred in broad daylight in a busy, residential neighborhood in which the houses were crowded so close together that neighbors could speak to one another from their windows without raising their voices. The Borden house (see Fig. 3) was protected on both sides and at the rear by fences. The rear fence and that on the south side were six feet high and reinforced by barbed wire, both top and bottom, to discourage the theft of pears from a tiny orchard in the backyard. On the north, behind the house and just a few steps from the kitchen door, stood a small stable which the Bordens called "the barn."

The Lizzie Borden Case

The barn contained a vise, a few heavy hammers and a water faucet. Until recently it had also housed a horse and some pet pigeons that belonged to Lizzie, who was extremely fond of animals. But Andrew had sold the horse and, irritated by the attempts of neighborhood boys to steal Lizzie's pet birds, he had recently slaughtered the pigeons—with an ax.

It is the morning of Thursday, August 4, 1892. (The times given are approximate, but they are not more than a very few minutes off.)

6:00: John Morse, who has spent the night in the guest room, descends to the first floor and waits for the rest of the family in the sitting room.

6:15: Bridget Sullivan comes down, starts a fire in the kitchen stove, and begins to prepare breakfast.

6:30: Abby comes down the rear stairs and gives orders for the breakfast menu. It is, incredibly, mutton, mutton-soup, johnny-cakes and bananas.

6:45: Andrew comes down. He goes out the rear door to gather the pears which have fallen from his trees during the night.

7:25: Abby, Andrew and Uncle John sit down to breakfast in the dining room.

8:15–
8:30: They finish the meal and go into the sitting room.

8:40: Andrew lets Uncle John out through the latched screen door at the rear. Then he latches the door again.

8:50: Lizzie comes down the front stairs. She is wearing a light-blue and navy figured dress. (Note: she owns two such dresses, very similar in appearance. One is cotton, one is silk.) She passes Abby in the dining room and the maid hears them exchange greetings.

8:52: Bridget, who had escaped the general illness of the family on Tuesday night, this morning feels sick to her stomach. She goes out into the backyard and vomits her breakfast.

8:57: Bridget returns. She is in the sink room when Andrew leaves by the kitchen door on his way downtown.

9:00: Abby repeats orders, first given to Bridget during breakfast, to wash the ground-floor windows.

9:00–

9:15: Abby goes up the front stairs to make up the bed in the guest room. Bridget goes through the first floor, closing windows. Not seeing Lizzie, she assumes Lizzie has returned to her bedroom. She goes out to the barn to get the bucket, mop and stepladder. Entering at the rear door, she is surprised to see Lizzie in the back entry. (According to the maid's later testimony, Lizzie "appeared in the back entry and says, 'Maggie, are you going to wash the windows?' I says, 'Yes,' I said, 'you needn't lock the door, but you can lock it if you want. I can get the water in the barn.'" Bridget [Lizzie's pet name for the maid was 'Maggie'] assumed that Lizzie did latch the screen door and got all the water she needed from the barn.)

Let's suspend our chronological account of the murder day here, at about 9:15. Bridget has just gone out into the yard to begin washing windows. Shortly she will get into a gossipy session with the maid next door, chattering over the fence on the south side of the house. Then she will return to the windows, using the stepladder to reach the upper panes. She will finish at approximately 10:30. *At no time between 9:15 and 10:30 will she notice anyone on the first floor.* (Study the placement of the windows in Fig. 1. There are three windows in the kitchen and parlor, two in the dining room and sitting room, one each in the sink room and pantry. It is possible that someone moved through the ground floor without Bridget's noticing. But Miss Lizzie was inside the house. *Could a stranger have moved about without either woman seeing him?*)

At 9:15 Lizzie has been seen by Bridget in the back entry. The back stairs lead down into the cellar, where several hatchets are stored in a large box.

At 9:15 Abby is making up the bed in the guest room. She has less than fifteen minutes to live.

Between 9:15 and 9:30 neighbors suddenly notice that the shutters on the windows of the Borden guest room have been closed. This seems unusual, especially on such a hot day.

10:30: Bridget finishes the windows and enters the house for the first time since 9:15. To her surprise the screen door is unlocked. She latches it behind her.

The Lizzie Borden Case

10:35–
10:40: Andrew Borden returns and attempts to enter the rear door. Finding it latched, he goes around to the front door, also locked and double-bolted. With some anger he knocks until the maid admits him. As she does she hears Miss Lizzie laugh at the top of the stairs. For the first time since 9:15 Bridget sees Lizzie. She is descending the front stairs, dressed to go out in a light-blue and navy figured dress (the silk one, not the cotton one). Bridget again locks and bolts the front door.

10:40–
10:45: Andrew goes into the dining room. Lizzie, changing her mind about going out, follows him, taking off her hat. The old man asks for his wife. (Bridget's memory reconstructed the scene as follows: "They had some talk between them that I didn't understand, but I heard her say that Mrs. Borden had a note and had gone out." Lizzie's story was that a note had been delivered by hand calling Abby to the bedside of a sick friend. Neither the note nor anyone admitting to having sent or delivered it ever appeared, even though a $5,000 reward was offered.)

10:45–
10:50: Andrew goes up the rear stairs to his room. He returns shortly and goes into the sitting room. Bridget finishes washing the inside of the sitting-room windows and goes into the dining room where Lizzie, who moments before was prepared to go out, has suddenly decided to iron handkerchiefs instead.

10:50: Lizzie informs Bridget that Abby "has gone out on a sick call" after having "had a note this morning." She also suggests that the maid go out to a "cheap sale of dress goods" at a local store. But Bridget feels too sick to go out.

10:55: Bridget goes up to her room to lie down. Minutes later she hears the city hall bell ring eleven o'clock. Then she dozes off while, at perhaps the same moment, her employer, Andrew Borden, is napping on the settee in the sitting room. Ten, perhaps fifteen minutes pass. Bridget tells what happened next: "The next thing was that Miss Lizzie hollered, 'Maggie, come down quick. Father's dead. Somebody came in and killed him.'"

It is approximately 11:15 a.m. Andrew Jackson Borden, age seventy, lies in his gore in his brightly lit sitting room, killed while he slept, by ten blows from a hatchet delivered by an unsteady hand (some will say by a woman's hand). Upstairs in the guest room, felled like a redwood tree, lies the 200-pound corpse of his second wife, the gluttonous Abby. Although medical evidence will show that she predeceased her husband by at least an hour and a half, her body will not be discovered until Bridget and a neighbor creep fearfully up the front stairs at 11:45. She has been struck nineteen times by a blade of the exact size that killed her husband. Neither victim's face shows any sign of expecting the attack, although Abby, struck from behind while standing between the bed and the bureau, was clearly not asleep when she was killed. In both cases the first blow caused death. The additional wounds were delivered gratis.

Neither the "murder weapon" nor the "blood-stained dress" allegedly worn by the murderer will ever be officially found. The police *will* find a box of dust-covered hatchets in the cellar. One of the blades will have obviously been recently washed clean and, after being covered with white coal ash, perhaps to simulate dust, replaced in the box. This blade will have had its wooden handle knocked off (possibly with a hammer while the blade was held in a vise) and it will occur to some that blood stains which can be rinsed from a blade cannot be removed from wood. It will be demonstrated in court that this blade is the exact size as that which murdered the Bordens, but a jury will not believe that this handleless ax is the death weapon.

Miss Lizzie now sits, stonily calm in that house of death, while neighbors offer her the comfort she does not appear to need. She is wearing the light-blue and navy silk dress (not the cotton one which looks so much like it), and there is not a drop of blood on her. This will be the most significant circumstance in her defense, both at her trial and forever after. Had she murdered her parents, her defenders will say, she could not fail to have gotten blood stains on her dress, yet there were none.

Of course the possibility of a second dress does occur, even to the police. They will conduct an extensive but sloppy search for it without success. No blood-stained dress will ever be found.

On Sunday, August 7, Lizzie will be observed by two witnesses burning her light-blue and navy *cotton* dress in the kitchen stove. She will say she burned it because it had become stained with brown paint when the house was painted three months before. One of the witnesses, Alice Russell, will reluctantly testify to this dress burning in court, but her evidence will not sway the jury.

•   •   •   •   •

The Lizzie Borden Case

The easiest way to reconstruct the crime is to use the floor plans of the house as if they were a chessboard and move the characters around like chess pieces. Let the white king and queen represent Andrew and Abby, and a white pawn stand for Bridget. For Miss Lizzie the red queen will do.

Lizzie told so many conflicting stories about her own movements that her testimony is virtually useless. On two points, however, she insisted. She had gone to the water-closet in the basement early in the morning and she had been out in the barn when her father was killed. For both these stories we have corroboration: Bridget saw her in the kitchen entry at 9:00 or shortly thereafter. And she was seen returning from the barn to the house between 11:00 and 11:15 by an ice-cream vendor named Hyman Lubinsky who testified for her defense. We know that the box of hatchets was in the basement. Lizzie's admission that she went into the basement before the murders proves that she had the *opportunity* to acquire a hatchet. We know that the barn contained a vise, a heavy hammer and running water. Lizzie's admission that she went to the barn after the murders proves her *opportunity* to wash the blade clean, discover that the blood could not be washed from the wooden handle, secure the blade in the vise and use the hammer to knock the handle off. (There was a fire in the kitchen stove and Lizzie confessed to having thrown "a stick" on the fire during the morning. It is not hard to imagine what happened to the handle.)

Now for the reconstruction. We begin at 8:45. Uncle John has been gone for about five minutes. The kitchen screen door is latched on the inside. Andrew is in his room preparing to go out: place the white king on No. 1, Fig. 2. Bridget is in the kitchen. Lizzie, having just come down for the first time, speaks briefly to Abby in the dining room. (Place the red and white queens on the proper space.) Now Bridget, feeling ill, goes out into the yard. Lizzie continues into the kitchen. Bridget returns and goes to the sink room. Andrew comes down the back stairs and leaves. Bridget speaks to Abby in the kitchen. Abby goes up the front stairs to the guest room. It is shortly after 9:00.

Move the pieces in sequence; the effort will pay dividends. Notice that Lizzie must have gone to the basement during the minutes when Bridget was in the yard. She is not in the kitchen when the maid returns, nor does Bridget see her as she moves through the first floor closing windows. She is still in the cellar when the Irish girl goes out to the barn. When Bridget returns through the back door, her entrance nearly coincides with Lizzie's appearance in the rear entry.

> [Lizzie] appeared in the back entry and says, "Maggie, are you going to wash the windows?" I says, "Yes," I said, "you needn't lock the door, but you can lock it if you want. I can get the water in the barn."

Lizzie has learned that Bridget has a task which will keep her outside for at least an hour. Bridget goes back into the yard. Lizzie is left in the kitchen. Abby is in the guest room. It is a few minutes after 9:00.

Lizzie and Abby are alone in the house. Move the red queen slowly through the sitting room, up the front stairs and into the guest room. Imagine the ax being raised and then striking again . . . again . . . again . . . .

Between 9:15 and 9:30 the guest room shutters are suddenly closed.

During the time between 9:15 and 10:30 Lizzie later claimed to be sitting in the kitchen near the stove waiting for the fire to heat up so she could iron. No one saw her. If she had been in the kitchen no one could have gone from the kitchen door to the front stairs (and thus up to murder Abby) without being seen by her, yet Lizzie said she saw no one. This rules Bridget out as a suspect, though Lizzie's defenders have tried to cast suspicion on the maid. Bridget could not have reached the guest room through the front door, which was locked and double bolted from the inside.

It is about 9:35. Abby Borden is dead. Lizzie goes into her own room and washes off the blood. (There is cold water in the basin. Lizzie is in the middle of her menstrual period. Blood-stained linen will not raise many questions.) She conceals the hatchet and the stained cotton dress, changing to a silk dress almost identical in appearance. (Downstairs, Bridget finishes her work and reenters the house at about 10:30. Then she hears Andrew pounding at the front door, at about 10:35, and unlocks it to admit Andrew. From the second-floor landing Miss Lizzie laughs.)

Place the white king and pawn near the front door and the red queen on the second-floor landing. It is 10:40. No one except Bridget and Andrew will ever be able to testify that, when she first dressed that morning, Miss Lizzie wore cotton. Soon there will be no one but Bridget. (Before the trial, Bridget will apparently come into sudden, unexplained wealth. The rumor will always persist that the maid was bribed to conceal that Lizzie changed her dress from cotton to silk on the murder day.)

Now, between 10:45 and 10:50 move the pieces quickly. Andrew and Lizzie to the dining room. Bridget to the sitting room. Andrew to his bedroom. Lizzie to the kitchen. Lizzie to the dining room with iron-ing implements. Andrew downstairs and to the sitting room. Bridget to the dining room, where Lizzie attempts to talk her into a trip downtown for a sale on dress goods.

10:55. Bridget goes to her room in the attic. Andrew is lying on the settee in the sitting room. In less than ten minutes he will be dead.

Lizzie will always claim that during the time her father was being murdered she was out in the barn. Her reason for going will change as she rethinks her alibi, but she will insist on spending the time in the barn. At first she will state that she was looking for a piece of tin to mend a screen. When none of the screens are found to need mending, she will change her story to one of searching the barn for lead sinkers with which to go fishing. Even after it is proved that she owns no hooks or line and has not fished in years she will hold to this story, while amending it to say that most of the time she spent in the barn was whiled away in the loft eating pears. Though the police will observe that the dust in the loft is undisturbed and the heat unbearable, she will stick to this story until her attorneys, mercifully, advise her to give no further statements.

10:57. Bridget is in her room. Andrew is near sleep in the sitting room. Lizzie goes up the front stairs to her room and changes back into the cotton dress. Carrying the ax, she descends and walks into the sitting room where her father has dozed off. Slowly, waveringly, she raises the hatchet . . . .

Her father dead, Lizzie returns to her room. Again she washes the blood from her hands and conceals the blood-stained dress. (The hid-ing place is probably the slop-pail in her room.) Again she puts on the silk dress and, having tried to rinse the ax-handle clean without suc-cess, she goes downstairs and out to the barn. She fastens the blade in the vise and uses a hammer to knock the handle off. (The wood re-maining in the blade was, said one policeman, a former carpenter, "very bright," evidence of a very recent break.)

With blade and handle Lizzie returns to the house. The handle is thrown into the kitchen stove. The blade is taken to the cellar, covered with coal dust from a bin (so it will appear as dusty as the others in the box from which it was taken) and replaced in the box.

Weapon disposed of, Miss Lizzie, dressed in unstained silk, rushes up the back stairs from the cellar to the second floor and calls up to the attic: "Father's dead. Somebody came in and killed him."

It is about 11:15. The most incredible murders in American history have just occurred. . . .

Excerpts from "Lizzie Didn't Do It!"
by Grady Sprague

Mystery Magazine, November, 1968, pp. 189–192.

Anyone who attempts to defend Lizzie Borden immediately finds himself bombarded with angry questions: who else could have killed the Bordens? Didn't Lizzie hate her stepmother and say so to everybody in Fall River? Didn't the Borden sisters inherit the old miser's considerable fortune? Didn't Lizzie, as soon as she was acquitted, leave the old Second Street house for a mansion on "the hill" and begin living in the style to which she had always wanted to become accustomed?

•　　•　　•　　•　　•

There was evidence that attempts had been made to poison old Andrew and his wife before they were murdered with an ax. They were so ill after supper on Tuesday night that they vomited up their meal. Lizzie was also sick on Tuesday night. On Thursday morning Bridget, the maid, was equally sick. Much is always made of all this to demonstrate that *Lizzie* sought to poison her father and stepmother. It is pointed out that Lizzie tried to buy prussic acid on Wednesday, August 3, and that, after having failed to do so, she told Alice Russell that she feared a poisoning plot against her father by one of his "enemies." Further, we are always reminded, Abby Borden had confessed a fear of being poisoned to her doctor on Wednesday morning. Somehow this is all supposed to prove that Lizzie was attempting to poison Abby and Andrew.

Though those who condemn Lizzie never admit it, this evidence points to a far more obvious conclusion than the one they reach: someone *was* trying to poison the Bordens. And that someone was *not* Lizzie.

The Bordens were sick on Tuesday night. If they had been fed prussic acid they would have died on Tuesday night. The very fumes of prussic acid are lethal. According to some of her detractors, Lizzie had been trying to buy prussic acid for two weeks; yet clearly, even if this were true, she had failed. If Lizzie had bought prussic acid before

The Lizzie Borden Case

Wednesday, August 3, her parents would have been dead on Tuesday, August 2. There is no such thing as a little prussic acid.

If Lizzie had been trying to buy prussic acid to kill her parents, she was still trying on Wednesday. *She had not yet succeeded.* Yet Abby was certain that someone was attempting to poison her and her husband. She said as much to the doctor, Bowen, on Wednesday morning. She never mentioned Lizzie's name to Bowen, or anyone else. She did tell Bowen that Andrew had received an unsigned note threatening poison. (It is typical of the logic practiced by Lizzie's detractors that they find Abby's failure to accuse Lizzie of poisoning and her claim that her husband had received an anonymous threat as proof that Abby was lying to Bowen. Since Abby accused an unknown enemy of her husband and did not accuse Lizzie, it apparently means that she was really accusing Lizzie and *not* an unknown enemy of her husband's.)

All that was ever proven was that Lizzie had tried to buy prussic acid to kill moths in sealskin. Lizzie's detractors note that, not only did moths not grow in sealskin, but had Lizzie (poor, stupid murderess) only known, she could have bought arsenic poison without prescription or question. The possibility never occurs to these characters that Lizzie was simply ignorant of the habits of moths and prussic acid.

What are the facts? That on Wednesday morning Abby told Dr. Bowen she feared someone was trying to murder her husband. That on Wednesday evening Lizzie told Alice Russell she feared someone was trying to murder her father. That on Tuesday, before Lizzie could have purchased poison, her parents were poisoned. That on Thursday morning in broad daylight someone slaughtered both Bordens with an ax.

•　　•　　•　　•　　•

There were no eyewitnesses to the Borden murders. The entire case against the younger daughter was built solely on circumstantial evidence. And even the circumstantial evidence was flimsy. The murder weapon was never found. A hatchet head, claimed as the weapon, had been wrapped and rewrapped by the police until the original amount of dust on it could only be guessed at. Lizzie had worn a light-blue and navy dress, silk with a figured pattern, and there was no blood whatsoever on that dress. With their usual inverse logic, those who attack Lizzie reason that the absence of blood on her dress proves that she must have committed these bloody murders. By the same reasoning we may assume that a man standing with a bloody ax in his hand and dripping with gore must be innocent of murder since his appearance is so suggestive of guilt. . . .

The blood-stained dress, so-called, was never found, in spite of the fact that a police team of five men went over the Borden home searching for it. The note, supposedly sent to Abby from a "sick person" in town, was also never found, and has generally been assumed to be the invention of Lizzie. Yet, as soon as we assume the plot to have been designed to murder Andrew, the story of the note makes sense. The murderer sent Abby a fake note in order to decoy her away from her husband's murder. When this failed, Abby had to be killed too.

• • • • •

Certainly Andrew Borden, money-lender, skinflint and slumlord, made money and enemies. If his daughter Lizzie or his wife Abby feared the attack of an enemy, they had excellent reason to do so. There were dozens of people in Fall River whom Andrew Borden had antagonized enough to inspire murderous feelings. . . .

Lizzie's attackers usually overlook events of the murder morning which, viewed from the possibility of an outside killer, assume tremendous importance. At about 9:00 a buggy containing two men stopped in front of the house next door to the Bordens. One of the men, described by witnesses as youthful, rang the Bordens' front doorbell. The door was opened and immediately slammed. The buggy remained at the curb, the young man pacing nervously around it, from 9:00 until about 10:30 when it disappeared. The second man, of whom no good description was ever obtained, was not seen at all from 9:00 on. It is not unreasonable to assume that the young man was the deliverer of the "sick note" designed to lure Abby away from the house, and that while Abby was at the front door receiving the note the second man slipped in through the side door unobserved. (Bridget was in the barn at this time and Lizzie in the cellar, you will remember.)

The killer assumed that Andrew was still in the house. The old man had left by the side door only moments before the buggy arrived. The plan had been to wait until Abby went out and then kill Andrew and escape in the buggy. But Abby did not go out. She had to be removed in another, bloodier way. The murderer now faced the dangerous but necessary ninety-minute wait beside his victim while his accomplice hovered anxiously outside. (During this time Lizzie noticed that the door to the guest room was closed. But when Bridget and a neighbor found Abby's body at 11:45 the door stood open, as the killer had left it when he went down to slaughter Andrew.)

Andrew returned at about 10:30. Around the same time Mark Chase, proprietor of a livery stable across from the Borden house who had been watching the buggy, got up from his chair and went into the stable.

The killer waited until the house was still and then, ax in hand, crept down the front stairs. He benefited from an incredible series of circumstances. He found his victim asleep and helpless in the sitting room. Bridget was in her attic room at the farthest possible distance from the crime. Lizzie was in the barn. He killed Andrew and escaped through the side door moments before Lizzie returned. His partner still waited with the buggy and they sped away unseen because Mark Chase had chosen that moment to go into his stable. When Chase returned to the street the first thing he noticed was that the buggy was gone.*

Lizzie Revisited

Book Review by Arthur Coopersmith

New York Herald, Sunday, September 16, 1967, section 5, p. 11.
A PRIVATE DISGRACE: LIZZIE BORDEN BY DAYLIGHT.
By Victoria Lincoln. 317 pages. G. P. Putnam's Sons. $6.95.

Victoria Lincoln considers herself preeminently qualified to study the grisly, timeless Borden parricides both because she is a woman and because she is an "insider," a member of the elite social class of Fall

---

To the student: It is a useful exercise in the logic of possibilities and probabilities to test this theory by adding another chess piece representing this alleged outside killer and attempting to reconstruct his movements. In doing so, keep in mind that Lizzie's story of her own movements as it slowly evolved during the inquest was that she spent the entire morning between about 9:00 and her father's return sitting by the kitchen stove waiting for the fire to heat some flats so she could iron some handkerchiefs. Only once, for about five minutes, did she leave the kitchen to carry some clean laundry to her bedroom. It was then she noticed that the guest-room door was locked. At first she claimed to have gone upstairs shortly after 9:00 but changed the time to 10:30 when reminded that Bridget had seen her come down the front staircase as she let old Andrew in. No one could have passed from the side entry to the front stairs unnoticed by someone seated in the kitchen.

River, Massachusetts, which lived in Victorian pomp up on "the hill," and to which Lizzie Borden herself belonged. She wastes no time debating with those of her predecessors who have sought to pin the guilt on an outside killer or the family's Irish maid. Lizzie was plainly guilty, asserts Miss Lincoln. Everybody who was *anybody* in Fall River knew that perfectly well, yet the upper crust rallied around her as one of their own, their "private disgrace."

Considering the reams of material, much of it sheer nonsense, which has been written about this infamous case, it is difficult to imagine anyone bringing a truly fresh, original approach to the crime, yet this is exactly what Miss Lincoln does. Writing in a lucid, extremely readable style, she throws new light on several significant aspects of the Borden tragedy.

The legendary Lizzie, coldly hewing down her parents for the family fortune, Miss Lincoln dismisses as a baseless myth. The real motive was much more subtle and, on the surface, trivial. Lizzie and her sister Emma had broken with their stepmother, Abby, five years before the murders, when their father put a $1,500 property in his wife's name. The rift continued even though old Andrew Borden tried to pacify his daughters with property of equal value. The murders were precipitated by the simple fact that Andrew was once again scheming to put land in Abby's name behind his daughters' backs.

The property involved was Andrew's farm in Swansea which he intended to lease to his first wife's brother, John Morse. Since "Uncle John" had also been involved in the original deal, his sudden arrival at the Borden house on the day before the murders was not mere coincidence, Miss Lincoln contends, but the catalyst which set Lizzie off on her murderous binge.

It has long been known that Lizzie spent two weeks before the crime in a fruitless attempt to purchase prussic acid. Miss Lincoln believes she planned to murder only Abby, whom she had always viewed as a hated rival for her father's love. But on the morning of August 4, 1892, several unfortunate factors coincided which ignited the tense situation and led to the murders. Emma, calmer and far more stable than her sister, was away. Morse had arrived and Lizzie realized that the treacherous land transfer was imminent. And then Lizzie had one of her "spells."

The Fall River "in crowd" knew about Lizzie's spells. Miss Lincoln diagnoses them as temporal epilepsy, a rare form of the disease in which the victim blacks out and spends a period of time, in effect, "sleepwalking" in a kind of trance. These spells, says Miss Lincoln, occurred only when Lizzie was menstruating, which she was at the time of the murders.

Miss Lincoln theorizes that during this seizure Lizzie crept up the front stairs to the guest room, concealing the hatchet in a pile of clean laundry, and felled her hapless stepmother in a blind rage. Coming to, she changed her dress and prepared to go out and establish an alibi, but her father came home an hour and a half before his habitual time and, knowing that he would be certain of her guilt, she was forced to kill him as well.

Among the author's other theories, she surmises that the daring, daylight robbery committed on the Borden house prior to the murders (and oddly aimed only at Abby's poor trinkets), was the work of Lizzie herself. When Andrew realized this he hushed up the police investigation and began the practice of locking his room but leaving the key on the sitting-room mantle as a constant reproof to his daughter. She also believes that a note *was* brought to Abby, not from a sick friend, but by an agent of Andrew and Uncle John to give Abby an excuse to leave the house and sign the papers transferring the Swansea farm to her name without arousing Lizzie's suspicions. Unfortunately Lizzie intercepted the note and guessed its real purpose.

Miss Lincoln even comes up with an explanation for the failure of the police to find the blood-stained dress before Lizzie burned it on Sunday morning. They examined every dress in the closet except "two or three in the corner . . . which were heavy or silk dresses." Since they were looking for a cotton dress they passed over the silk, but Lizzie had concealed the cotton garment simply by hanging a silk dress over it on the same hanger. A woman's trick, observes Miss Lincoln, and only a woman could have figured it out. She also notes that only Bridget Sullivan had seen the dress worn by Lizzie when she first came down to breakfast and repeats the common gossip of the time, fostered by Bridget's sudden affluence just before the trial, that the Borden sisters bribed the maid to withhold the evidence that Lizzie changed that morning from cotton to silk.

A Private Disgrace is a literate and thought-provoking analysis of the Borden case. It is certain to attract the admiration of those who believe Lizzie guilty and the anger of her supporters, and to fuel once again the flames of controversy which occasionally burn as hotly as they did when Lizzie dominated the headlines in 1892.

Excerpt from "Lizzie Borden Took an Ax"

by Margaret Macready

in *Tales of Murder,* edited by George Altick. New Brunswick, N.J.: Hall-Mills & Co., 1972. Pp. 195–197.

People are always surprised to learn that Lizzie Borden was acquitted. Her guilt has been generally accepted for so many years that it amazes us she was able to beat the rap so easily. Of course part of the reason lies in the consummate skills of her chief attorney, ex-Governor George Robinson, and the fortunate fact that Robinson, when governor, had raised to the bench the very man who was to conduct Lizzie's trial, Justin Dewey. Strongly influenced by Dewey, the three-man court made several rulings crucially favorable to the defense, notably the exclusion of Lizzie's terribly damaging inquest testimony and of the evidence that she had tried to buy poison.

But the main reason for Lizzie's acquittal was that she had really been tried before her trial, in the newspapers and by public opinion, and the overwhelming verdict was "Not Guilty." It's not difficult to see why, in the Victorian 1890's, a period obsessed with self-righteousness, respectability and "conscious virtue," the Fall River spinster was the recipient of an outpouring of public good will. Lizzie was a long-time member of the Fall River Central Congregationalist Church. She was the secretary of Christian Endeavor and had formerly taught Sunday school. America in the '90s was still predominately a small town or rural population, white–Anglo-Saxon–Protestant, distrustful of Catholics and foreigners. The attitude is exemplified in one letter to the authorities urging that the Irish maid "and her confessor" be thrown into jail until they admitted her guilt.

From her arrest through her trial Lizzie was never seen in public except leaning for support on the arm of one of her two ministers, the Reverend Mr. Buck and the Reverend Mr. Jubb. To all "right-thinking people" in the 1890's it was obvious that no good, church-going, Sunday-school-teaching Congregationalist could be guilty of slaughtering her parents with an ax. Didn't the Bible say "Honor thy father and thy mother"?

But Lizzie was more than a Congregationalist: she was a woman, and every leading feminist and every suffragette organization in the busy "Woman's Rights" movement sprang to her defense. Mrs. Mary A.

The Lizzie Borden Case

Livermore, Mrs. Susan Fessenden and Miss Lucy Stone (nowadays we should refer to all of them as Ms.) each issued statements on Ms. Borden's behalf. The woman's auxiliary of the Y.M.C.A. held meetings to offer up prayers for her deliverance. The Woman's Christian Temperance Union, in which Lizzie had been active, supported her with spirited ignorance. Could a teetotaler commit murder? Clearly it was a drinking man's crime.

Daily, from pulpit and editorial page, the public were assured that the Deity was watching and would make all come right in the end. Didn't the Bible say that not a sparrow fell but the Lord's eye saw? "God is with the poor, storm-tossed girl," thundered a typical sermon of the time. "He will vindicate and He will glorify!"

In her classic study of the Borden case, Victoria Lincoln has observed: "The human race has a remarkable ability to select and interpret facts according to its emotional needs." She might have added that it also has a remarkable ability to *ignore* facts which threaten its emotional needs. The fact of a recently scrubbed hatchet blade in the basement, the fact of a brown-stained dress burned in the kitchen stove, the facts of demonstrable lies, absurd alibis, and missing notes, were all ignored by a society whose moral and social foundations would have been profoundly shaken had it, even for an instant, permitted itself to believe that a female, teetotaling Protestant had murdered her parents with an ax.

When the verdict was announced the newspapers were jubilant, particularly the New York *Times* which called the decision "a certain relief to every right-minded man and woman." The key word is "right-minded." To be right-minded in 1893 was to *know* that Christian ladies are by definition incapable of parricide.

It is easy to laugh at this narrow-minded, simplistic attitude of our great-grandparents. Don't laugh too quickly. Their assumptions, their "emotional need to believe" if you will, was based on religious and social prejudice. Ours is based on political prejudice. That is the only difference. As they did, we transform the major figures in our great, public trials into symbols which stand for the absolute "good" and "evil" we imagine perpetually at war in the world. From the right or the left side of the political spectrum we divide the characters into the good guys and the bad guys and prejudge on the sole ground of rooting interest. Our self-righteousness is exceeded only by our ignorance. We have no more knowledge of the facts than we have need of them.

"Don't bother us with facts!" we shout. "What's needed now is opinions!"

Our trials are not trials; they are morality plays. We view and judge William Calley, the Berrigan brothers, Angela Davis, as our predecessors viewed and judged the Rosenbergs, Alger Hiss, Bruno Richard Hauptmann, Sacco and Vanzetti, and even Lizzie Borden, whose case is surely one of the most extreme examples of a generation gap on record.

INSTRUCTIONS

1. *Having finished your first reading of the sources, check through the notes you have taken and, as you did with the articles on Hauptmann, make a list of areas of significant disagreement or contradiction. The introduction (pages 173–174) may be helpful in suggesting areas of tension. Select the controversy in which you feel the greatest interest. It should be obvious that your own genuine curiosity is an essential ingredient in research. If you really do not care what the truth is, your work is merely drudgery.*

2. *Phrase the controversy you will investigate as a question to be answered by your paper. This question is your working title. Review the section called "The Most Commonly Asked Questions About Writing a Research Paper," (pages 140–150). Return to this section as often as necessary for guidance and reference in developing your paper.*

3. *Prepare a worksheet for your project, following the form illustrated on page 149. Determine the issues which you must settle before your major question can be answered. Review the suggestions on note taking (pages 142–144) and then reread the sources, taking careful notes on all material relevant to your topic. Use the jottings from your preliminary reading to guide you to the most pertinent parts of the articles.*

4. *Review the instruction on organizing your notes (page 142). Plan your paper carefully and be certain its organization is clear in your mind before beginning to write. Suggestions for writing and revising your paper are on pages 144–146.*

5. *Take particular care with the form, placement and accuracy of your footnotes. The proper form for both footnotes and bibliography entry follow each article, and additional instructions ap-*

pear in Appendix B, pages 283–302. Remember, footnote numbers should be placed in the text of your first draft as you write, and the footnote itself recorded immediately on a separate page. Study the sample on page 149. This practice simplifies the footnoting procedure for you and insures that your annotation will be accurate. Review also "The Most Commonly Asked Questions About Footnotes" (pages 151–154), and refer to it when needed.

6. *Remember you are re-searching, searching again, through facts, opinions and arguments first presented by other people. You must use footnotes to give credit (or place blame) for these ideas to the people who first advanced them. This does not mean that there is nothing original, nothing of your own, in your paper. Of course you may express opinions and conclusions "of your own" directly to your reader, but, beyond that, it is your originality which determines how your sources' ideas will be organized and phrased for your reader, how they will be made to complement each other or be pitted against one another. Your sources are only the servants of you as researcher: in a very real sense they are at your mercy. And to research means not just to rummage through old ideas but to rethink them, to analyze them, and then to uphold them or to expose them as stupidity or fraud.*

The Independent Research Project

You are now ready for a completely independent project in investigative writing. In this section four sources probe different aspects of the case against Nicola Sacco and Bartolomeo Vanzetti. For some, the Sacco-Vanzetti affair is an intriguing mystery; for others it represents an important legal episode or a significant milestone of social history. The opportunities it offers for research topics are endless because of its highly controversial nature. Even fifty years later there is little general agreement about any area of the case, and the questions it raised about the American way of life are being asked even more vociferously today.

If your earlier research has not already led you into the library, your instructor may now expect you to expand your investigation beyond the sources provided within these covers. Appendix C, "Using the Library," offers helpful information, including instruction on the use of several fruitful indexes often overlooked by students. Read through Appendix C before going to the library, and keep it handy for reference.

A brief introduction sketches the Sacco-Vanzetti case in broad outline and suggests possible questions to bear in mind as you read. After that, there are only the sources and you, the researcher. You are on your own.

THE SACCO-VANZETTI CASE

The Sacco-Vanzetti case, which began with a payroll robbery and double murder in 1920 and ended in 1927 with the executions of Nicola Sacco and Bartolomeo Vanzetti amid a storm of international protest, raises questions about the United States' image of itself which are at least as vital today as they were fifty years ago. Unlike the Lizzie Borden affair it was not the uniqueness and enormity of the crime but the character of the defendants which brought this case to national and eventually worldwide attention.

Sacco and Vanzetti were Italian immigrants, confessed anarchists, and suspected Communists. They were tried during a period when America's fear of radicalism was at a fever pitch, in a state, Massachusetts, which many considered one of the most reactionary in the nation. In the years between their conviction and execution they came to be viewed as innocent martyrs by the American liberal-intellectual community and a *cause célèbre* by leftists in Europe, Africa and South America.

Were Sacco and Vanzetti innocent or guilty of the crimes of which they were convicted? Did they receive a fair trial, or were the judge and jury prejudiced against them because of their admitted leftist leanings? Is there any meaningful connection between these first two questions, or is it sometimes possible for a guilty man to receive an unfair trial?

Was the Morelli gang responsible for the crimes, as the liberal-intellectuals insisted? To what extent did the American public's fear of left-wing terrorism influence the Sacco-Vanzetti trial and its aftermath? Was it possible for members of a minority to receive a fair trial in the United States of fifty years ago? Is it possible today?

What parallels can be drawn between the Sacco-Vanzetti case and recent trials? How objective was the view of the Sacco-Vanzetti case taken by American liberals at the time and since? How objective is the view expressed by either the extreme left or the extreme right on such recent trials as those of Angela Davis, the Berrigan brothers or William Calley?

In a celebrated trial, does the public tend to draw conclusions about the guilt or innocence of a defendant on the basis of political considerations rather than a knowledge of the evidence? To what extent is the public informed on the evidence? To what extent does the public need, or want, to be informed? Were Sacco and Vanzetti ultimately more important as individual men or as political symbols? Have recent defendants been more important as individuals or as political symbols?

These are some of the questions to keep in mind while reading the four articles which follow.

The Sacco-Vanzetti Case

by Mark Winston

in *Famous American Trials,* edited by George Hodnovich and Wendell Banks. Boston: Small, Brown & Co., 1959. Pp. 201–212.

Thursday, April 15, 1920. The 9:18 train arrives in South Braintree, Massachusetts, carrying the payrolls for the town's two Slater & Morrill shoe factories, $30,000 in cash. At the small railroad station, American Railway Express agent Shelley A. Neal receives the money and prepares to return to his office in the upper Slater & Morrill plant just across Railroad Avenue, a few steps from the corner of Pearl Street. Crossing Railroad Avenue, Neal notices a large Buick parked nearby, occupied by grim-faced men, strangers. A vague, undefined suspicion brushes his mind. Neal shakes it off and enters his office. Outside, the Buick starts up and moves away. Shelley Neal begins sorting out the bills. It is 9:23.

The year 1920 marked the height of the "big Red scare" which rocked the United States in the wake of World War I. In April, 1919, dozens of bombs were mailed to the homes and offices of American leaders such as financier J. P. Morgan, Supreme Court Justice Oliver Wendell Holmes, and U.S. Attorney General A. Mitchell Palmer. Another thirteen bombs exploded in unison at midnight, June 3, at the residences of prominent officials in Washington, New York, Boston, Paterson, Cleveland, Pittsburgh, Philadelphia, and Newtonville, Massachusetts. Again Palmer was a target, part of his home destroyed, and the two men who brought the bomb blown up with it. The bombings were interpreted as part of a Communist plot to bring the American government to its knees. The attorney general estimated this plot involved 60,000 alien radicals and anarchists. The *New York Times* demanded that the government "employ every resource at its command to find out who these venomous miscreants are, to trace them to their hiding places, to destroy them."

Shortly after 10:00 a.m. piano tuner Harry Dolbeare watches a large Buick driving through South Braintree. The auto contained, he would say later, a "tough-looking bunch." From 11:00 on, the Buick is parked in front of the lower Slater & Morrill factory on Pearl Street. One man, sallow and sickly in appearance, lingers nervously nearby. Another, dark and swarthy, tinkers with the motor. Two other men,

The Sacco-Vanzetti Case

dressed in dark clothes, one wearing a cap, loiter by a fence before the Rice & Hutchins building on Pearl Street between Railroad Avenue and the lower Slater & Morrill plant. In her office in the upper S & M factory, assistant paymaster Margaret Mahoney finishes separating the payroll for the lower plant's workers. She places the pay envelopes in two metal boxes, each weighing, when full, about five pounds. Together they contain $15,775.51. Her work completed, Margaret Mahoney waits for the arrival of her boss, Frederick A. Parmenter, Slater & Morrill's paymaster and chief bookkeeper, and the plant guard, Alessandro Berardelli, who will deliver the boxes to the lower S & M building. Outside the sun is shining and a light breeze is blowing. It is 2:55.

In late 1919 the federal government launched raids against leftist organizations on November 7 and December 29 in an attempt to quiet criticism from the press and stymie further bombings. This flurry of Justice Department activity, however, failed to camouflage the government's failure to uncover even one culprit in the earlier bombing attacks. On the night of January 2, 1920, a massive raid conducted in thirty-three cities netted between 2,500 and 3,000 suspected radicals. Many of them, it developed, were seized and searched without regard for their constitutional rights. Sixteen such raids were carried out in Massachusetts alone, under what federal judge George W. Anderson was to call "terrorizing conditions." In granting the release of twenty accused radicals on writs of habeas corpus on June 23, 1920, Anderson observed that "a mob is a mob, whether made up of government officials acting under instructions from the Department of Justice, or of criminals, loafers, and the vicious classes." It is estimated that between July, 1919, and June, 1920, approximately 4,000 radical aliens were arrested, though less than one-fourth of those were actually deported.

2:58 p.m. Frederick Parmenter and Alessandro Berardelli arrive at the upper Slater & Morrill factory to pick up the payroll for the lower plant. Their route is south a few paces on Railroad Avenue to Pearl Street. From there they will turn left and proceed west on Pearl toward the lower factory, crossing the railroad tracks and continuing past the Rice & Hutchins building on their right, where two men in dark clothing still linger near the fence. Their destination is the lower plant, some hundred and twenty feet beyond Rice & Hutchins. They will never reach it. It is 3:04. Parmenter has thirteen hours and forty-four minutes to live. Berardelli will be dead in less than half an hour.

3:05. One of the two strangers in front of Rice & Hutchins approaches Berardelli and appears to engage him in conversation. In almost the same moment, pistol shots ring out. Berardelli drops into a partial crouch. Parmenter releases the money box, which clatters to the pavement. He begins to run across Pearl Street. James P. Bostock, an S & M millwright with whom Parmenter has spoken moments earlier, turns and starts running toward the holdup. Louis Pelsor, a worker in Rice & Hutchins, runs to a window seven feet from the crime and throws it open. The gunman with the cap stands over the crouching guard and fires at Bostock. The millwright retreats rapidly. Parmenter is staggered by a shot in the back. Another gunman appears suddenly with a rifle. The Buick, still parked in front of the lower S & M factory, begins to move slowly up Pearl Street toward the holdup. The capped gunman shoots down at Berardelli's fallen body. His partner pursues Parmenter, still firing. The Buick arrives and the capped thug (his cap having now fallen to the ground) hoists one money box into the car. The second box is thrown aboard, and the trio of gunmen scramble into the vehicle. A train is approaching across the escape route. The gate-tender, Michael Levangie, begins lowering the gate which will block Pearl Street. "Up! Up!" is shouted from the moving car. Yielding less to the cries than to the volley of bullets whistling past his skull, Levangie raises the gate. The Buick crosses the tracks, headed east.

Retracing his steps, the millwright, Bostock, reaches the dying Berardelli. He will later recall, "I wiped his mouth out [of blood], and he lay in my arm, and as he lay in my arm, I thought he died." Peering from his window at Rice & Hutchins, Louis Pelser notes the license number of the Buick. Others kneel beside the fallen paymaster, Parmenter. He will be carried to a house on Pearl Street and from there to Quincy Hospital. At 4:45 the following morning he will die.

"So far as the crime is concerned," wrote law professor Felix Frankfurter in 1927, "we are dealing with a conventional case of payroll robbery resulting in murder." Conventional? At first it must have seemed so. The Buick was found on April 17, abandoned a mere eight miles from South Braintree after a circular flight of thirty to forty miles. The tracks of a smaller car in which the criminals had apparently completed their getaway led from the deserted vehicle.

The Sacco-Vanzetti Case

Bridgewater Police Chief Michael E. Stewart suspected that the South Braintree gang was the same bunch that had attempted an unsuccessful payroll heist in his community in December, 1919. There had then been three gunmen, two packing pistols, the third carrying a rifle or shotgun; and witnesses to both crimes thought the holdup men had the appearance of foreigners, probably Italians. Stewart's attention focused on one Mike Boda, an Italian alien, and on Boda's 1914 Oakland automobile as the possible "second car" used in the robberies. The Oakland had been left for repairs at Simon Johnson's garage in West Bridgewater. On the evening of Wednesday, May 5, Boda and three other Italians arrived to reclaim the car, but Johnson talked them out of driving it until license plates for it had been obtained. While her husband kept the four occupied, Mrs. Johnson slipped away to a neighbor's and called the police. When the quartet left his garage, Johnson tailed two of them to the Bridgewater-Brockton streetcar. Minutes later, acting on a call from Stewart, Patrolman Michael J. Connolly boarded the car and arrested the pair, Nicola Sacco, a shoe factory workman, and a sometime fish peddler named Bartolomeo Vanzetti. "They wanted to know what they were arrested for," Connolly later testified, "I says, 'Suspicous characters.'"

Sacco produced an alibi for the attempted holdup in Bridgewater. From June 22 to July 1 Vanzetti stood trial alone on the charge of assault with intent to rob. Convicted, he was given a sentence of twelve to fifteen years by the judge, Webster B. Thayer. Boda, meanwhile, had vanished. He would not surface until 1928 in Italy. The fourth man, Ricardo Orciani, was arrested but released after he, too, proved an alibi for the Bridgewater crime. Throughout the summer of 1920, the police and District Attorney Frederick G. Katzmann labored to build a case against Sacco and Vanzetti for the South Braintree job. On September 11 the two immigrants were indicted for the murders of Frederick Parmenter and Alessandro Berardelli.

The trial opened on May 31, 1921, in the picturesque little courthouse in Dedham, Massachusetts. Webster Thayer presided. The burden of the prosecution was carried by Frederick Katzmann and Assistant D. A. Harold P. Williams. The chief defense attorney was Fred Moore, a Midwesterner with the courtroom instincts of a street fighter and a long history of defending leftist and radical causes. In Massachusetts, Fred Moore was an outlander.

It was a long trial. The Commonwealth paraded fifty-nine witnesses to the stand. Ninety-nine more testified for the defense. Katzmann's thesis was that Sacco was the capped gunman who had fired the fatal bullet into Berardelli, while Vanzetti, though not participating actively in the robbery, had been in the Buick and was thus guilty of conspiracy to murder. The case against Sacco was the stronger of the two. More than half a dozen witnesses placed the factory worker in South Braintree on April 15. Two ballistics experts testified that the bullet which killed Berardelli had been fired from a .32 Colt pistol found on Sacco at the time of his arrest (although one, State Police Captain William Proctor, gave ambiguous evidence and later retracted it). In addition, the Commonwealth produced the cap, lost at the scene by the murderer and retrieved by millwright Bostock, and claimed it belonged to Sacco. This resulted in an almost comic episode with Sacco, on the stand, insisting the cap was too small for him while Katzmann urged him to "try and pull it down in back." "Oh," cried the defendant, jamming the cap on his head, "but it is too tight."

Sacco's story was that on the day of the murders he was in Boston trying to arrange for passports which would enable him and his family to return to Italy and visit his father. The defense presented witnesses to that effect. Fred Moore had his own pair of ballistics experts, but their value to Sacco's cause was severely weakened by their contradictions of each other and by the inability of one, James E. Burns, to withstand Katzmann's badgering. At one point Burns refused to respond to the D. A.'s cross-examination, shouting, "You fooled me yesterday, and I don't want you to do it again."

Against Vanzetti, the prosecution had only four eyewitnesses, and one of them, railroad gatekeeper Michael Levangie, insisted that Vanzetti was the driver of the Buick in the teeth of overwhelming testimony that the driver was pale, sickly and clean-shaven, a description which hardly fit the swarthy and magnificently moustachioed fish peddler. The defense countered with thirty-one eyewitnesses who testified that they had seen no one in the Buick resembling Vanzetti and thirteen more who claimed that on April 15 the fish peddler was in the town of Plymouth peddling, naturally enough, fish. It was, perhaps, a problem for the defense that all thirteen alibi witnesses were friends and associates of the accused.

The only hard, circumstantial evidence against Vanzetti was the .38 Harrington & Richardson revolver taken from him when he was arrested. The dead guard, Berardelli, had owned a .38 H. & R., and the gun was not found on his body, leading to speculation that it was carried from the scene by the killers. This was the Commonwealth's contention. Against it, the defense argued that Vanzetti had purchased the gun legitimately and attempted to trace it back through a series of owners. These witnesses, however, had a tendency to contradict one another, and Vanzetti himself seemed unsure of the price he had paid for the revolver. On the other hand, though it was clear Berardelli had his gun repaired shortly before the holdup, it was unclear whether he had ever reclaimed the weapon and equally unclear whether the repairs acknowledged to have been made on the dead man's pistol matched those made on the gun found in Vanzetti's possession. The evidence on this part of the affair seemed hopelessly confused.

To the jury of "representative" and "substantial" citizens (according to their recollections of the case twenty-nine years later for the New Bedford *Standard-Times*) the most conclusive evidence against the defendants came from ballistics expert Earl J. Vaughn, (who invited them to compare the Berardelli death bullet [under a magnifying glass] with bullets fired from Sacco's pistol), and from certain eyewitnesses who placed Sacco and Vanzetti at the scene. Perhaps so. But Judge Thayer's view, expressed little less than a year after the trial, was that "the evidence that convicted these defendants was . . . known in law as 'consciousness of guilt.' " In other words, Sacco and Vanzetti, at the time of their arrest, had behaved as guilty men.

This last statement remains undisputed. When they were arrested, both men were carrying guns. Sacco, the defense claimed, had acquired the habit of toting a pistol while working as a night watchman. Vanzetti explained that when he "went to Boston for fish, I can carry eighty, one hundred dollars, one hundred and twenty dollars." It was, he said, "a very bad time, and I like to have a revolver for self-defense." In addition, both men told lies about things easily proved, lies which they later admitted under oath. Sacco said he was unaware of the South Braintree crime and claimed to be at work on the day it took place. Vanzetti lied about how long he had known Sacco, how he had come to possess his revolver, how long before he was arrested he had left his home. Both denied knowing Mike Boda, whom they later admitted accompanying to the Johnson garage. Obviously both men had displayed "consciousness of guilt" when taken into custody; the question was: guilt of what crime? Robbery and murder said the prosecution. Nonsense! answered the defense. Sacco and Vanzetti were consciously guilty of only one thing, radical activism. Both men were anarchists, leftist agitators. Their reason for trying to deceive the police was perfectly natural and understandable in that violent period when the authorities were pursuing radical aliens so ardently and indiscriminantly: they feared deportation.

Thus the issue of the defendants' unpopular political beliefs, which had been carefully kept out of Vanzetti's trial for the Bridgewater crime from a fear of alienating the jury, was deliberately introduced by Fred Moore at Dedham to counter the prosecution's evidence of "consciousness of guilt." For Moore it was a calculated risk. If the jury believed Sacco and Vanzetti had lied to protect themselves from a charge of radicalism, not of murder, they would vote for acquittal. Yet a knowledge of the defendants' radical activism might poison the jurors' minds with a fatal prejudice.

Moore's gamble failed. The jury found Sacco and Vanzetti guilty of murder in the first degree.

> The trial was almost completely ignored by the public and the press outside Massachusetts. The papers were filled with accounts of a disastrous tornado which had roared through Texas and Arkansas killing sixty-one and with stories on the upcoming heavyweight fight between Jack Dempsey and Georges Carpentier in Jersey City. No one took much notice when Judge Thayer sentenced the two Italians to death. America was too busy playing the latest game to sweep the country, Mah-Jongg, and singing the newest song hit, based on the comical cry of an immigrant Italian fruit vendor, "Yes, We Have No Bananas."

The issue of "consciousness of guilt," like all the other issues of this strange case, remained confused. Defense partisans pointed out that after their arrest Sacco and Vanzetti had been questioned heavily concerning possible radical activity while no direct references had been made to the South Braintree murders. Therefore, it was argued, the defendants could only conclude they were under suspicion of radicalism, of which, of course, they were guilty. Innocent of murder, they would hardly have anticipated such a charge. On the other hand, both men were aware that the police had found (in Sacco's pocket) a notice handwritten by Vanzetti which announced an anarchist meeting at which Vanzetti would speak. Thus, said the prosecution, they must have realized it was useless to deny that they were radicals. Furthermore, it seemed odd for Sacco to be so terrified of deportation when he was in fact preparing to return to Italy anyway. And, since both men were avowed pacifists, why were they carrying loaded guns?

Between the conviction and November, 1924, when he left the

The Sacco-Vanzetti Case

case, Fred Moore made six motions in a desperate attempt to win a new trial. He went after the three most vulnerable of the prosecution's witnesses: Lola Andrews, a woman with a past; a convicted thief named Carlos Goodridge; and a shoe worker, Louis Pelser. Pelser repudiated his testimony but later claimed he had done so only after Moore got him drunk and attempted to bribe him. Lola Andrews, a former prostitute, also repudiated her testimony after Moore threatened to drench her and her son in scandal. Later she reaffirmed her trial evidence. As for Goodridge, he refused to change his story even when threatened by Moore with arrest on an eleven-year-old larceny charge. In addition, Moore produced two affidavits accusing the jury foreman, Walter H. Ripley, of prejudice, and dug up a new witness, a traveling salesman named Roy Gould, who swore that the gunman he had seen in South Braintree was not Sacco. However, the facts that Gould was a known leftist and a close friend of one of Moore's investigators cast some doubt over his testimony.

Moore's most serious charge against the prosecution involved State Police Captain William H. Proctor, a ballistics expert who had testified that in his opinion the bullet which killed Berardelli was "consistent with being fired by" Sacco's Colt automatic. More than two years after the trial, Proctor now denied he had ever believed that the bullet was actually fired by Sacco's gun, but only that it had been shot from *some* Colt automatic. Furthermore, said Proctor, the prosecutors knew this and arranged with him in advance to frame their questions so as to obtain ambiguous answers which could be interpreted by the jury as indicating that Sacco's pistol was the fatal weapon. Moore pointed out that the judge had made this interpretation of Proctor's evidence and said as much in his charge to the jury.

The defense, in short, was accusing the prosecution of deliberately rigging testimony in an effort to mislead the jury. Both District Attorney Katzmann and his assistant, Harold Williams, issued denials, but the denials themselves were ambiguous and avoided answering Proctor's principal charge. Nevertheless, Judge Thayer considered their statements "clear and convincing" and denied this last defense motion as he had denied all the others.

The Proctor affidavit had been obtained, not by Moore, but by William G. Thompson, a prominent Boston attorney who, in late 1924, took over from Moore as chief defense counsel. It was Thompson who directed the next motion for retrial, the so-called Medeiros motion of May 26, 1926.

Phase III: The Independent Research Project

Celestino Medeiros, a young, epileptic Portuguese, had been con-victed on his own confession of the holdup-murder of an eighty-year-old bank teller in Wrentham, Massachusetts. In 1925 he was in Dedham prison (where Sacco was also confined) awaiting a new trial awarded him on a legal technicality. On November 18 he sent the following mes-sage to Sacco's cell: "I hereby confess to being in the South Braintree shoe company crime, and Sacco and Vanzetti was not in said crime." Medeiros' story was that he had been persuaded by four members of an Italian gang from Providence to go along on the South Braintree job. The young hoodlum, only eighteen at the time, claimed he was "scared to death" when the shooting began. "I sat on the back seat of the automobile. I had a Colt .38 calibre automatic but did not use it. I was told that I was there to help hold back the crowd in case they made a rush." He had been promised a $5,000 payoff, but the gang double crossed him. Medeiros refused to name the other gangsters, except to insist that Sacco and Vanzetti were not among them, but his partner in the Wrentham robbery, James F. Weeks, deposed Medeiros had told him it was the Morelli mob, a Providence pack headed by the five Morelli brothers and including such colorful underworld charac-ters as Bibber Barone and Gyp the Blood. According to Weeks, the quartet involved with Medeiros in South Braintree were Mike, Joe, and Butsy Morelli and a shadowy figure known only as "Bill."

Defense lawyers interviewed the gang's leader, Joe Morelli, at Leavenworth where he was residing at the federal government's ex-pense. Shouting frame-up, the gangster adamantly and at times tear-fully denied everything, calling on a "just God" to avenge him and accusing the defense of "trying to spoil my record with the warden." To a man, the members of the Morelli mob, at least those who could be found, swore they had never heard of Medeiros. On October 22, 1926, Webster Thayer denied the "Medeiros motion," noting inaccu-racies and contradictions in the Portuguese's various confessions. The judge was unprepared to accept the word of a man he character-ized as "a crook, a thief, a robber, a liar, a rum-runner, a 'bouncer' in a house of ill fame, a smuggler, and a man who has been convicted and sentenced to death for . . . murder."

His decision on the Medeiros matter having been upheld by the State Supreme Judicial Court, Thayer sentenced Sacco and Vanzetti to death on April 9, 1927. The defendants petitioned Massachusetts Governor Alvan T. Fuller for clemency. In response, the governor ap-pointed a blue-ribbon panel, comprising an eminent judge and the presidents of Harvard University and the Massachusetts Institute of Technology, to review the entire case. This committee advised against clemency and, on August 3, the governor denied the appeal. This latest defeat left the defense with only one card in their hand. Three days later they played it.

The final motion for a new trial was based on the alleged prejudice against the defendants of Judge Thayer himself. William Thompson had resigned in despair, and the argument was made by his successor, Arthur D. Hill. Hill's brief cited Thayer's persistent denial of defense motions; his original refusal to permit Sacco and Vanzetti separate trials or to allow them to call character witnesses; his "prejudicial cross-examination" of defense witnesses from the bench; his emphasis in his charge to the jury on the subject of consciousness of guilt; his numerous references to patriotism in the same charge, with the jury well aware that both defendants had been draft dodgers. There were affidavits alleging that outside the courtroom Thayer had called Sacco and Vanzetti "anarchistic bastards" and said of his charge to the jury, "I think that will hold them."

To the horror of the defense, Thayer himself was assigned to hear the motion and, predictably, he refused to consider it on the ground that state law forbade any motion for a new trial once sentence had been passed. In fact, the law was very clear on this point and the Supreme Judicial Court proclaimed its support of Thayer on August 19. Sacco and Vanzetti had four days to live.

Almost from the moment of their conviction, thanks to the efforts of the defense to publicize their case, Sacco and Vanzetti had attracted sympathy from left-wing organizations throughout the world. The radical press of Europe and South America, eventually supported by large numbers of American liberal-intellectuals, assumed the innocence of the accused and portrayed them as Christ-like martyrs being crucified by an entrenched, conservative establishment inspired by narrow bigotry and mindless terror. The reaction abroad was unfailingly violent. A bomb exploded in the home of the American ambassador to France. A second Paris bombing obliterated twenty people. An attempt to blow up the home of the American consul-general in Lisbon was narrowly avoided. A mob attacked the American embassy in Montevideo, and riots occurred in such diverse places as Mexico City and Algiers.

As the time for the executions drew closer, American liberals became increasingly active and angry. What was at stake, they cried, was not simply the lives of two Italian immigrants, but the question of whether members of minority groups had any rights in America at all. It was not two obscure anarchists who were on trial, it was the American judicial system, the American sense of justice, the American way of life.

Writing to a friend in 1926, Supreme Court Justice Oliver Wendell Holmes, himself a liberal-intellectual (as well as a target for radical threats and bombs), expressed wonder over the deep concern of his fellow liberals for Sacco and Vanzetti. "I cannot but ask myself why there is so much greater interest in Red than Black. A thousandfold worse cases of Negroes come up from time to time, but the world does not worry over them."

Sacco and Vanzetti were scheduled to die in the electric chair on Monday, August 22, 1927. Europe erupted. In Paris, 15,000 rioted and a small army of 5,000 Communists stormed the American embassy while another mob attacked nightclubs in Montmartre. Twelve thousand demonstrated in Hyde Park in London. In Geneva, crowds attacked the League of Nations Palace and the American consulate. There was mob violence in Copenhagen, in Leipzig, in Buenos Aires, in Lyons, in Johannesburg, in Sidney. Ironically only Italy, in the iron grip of Mussolini, was quiet.

The first man to be strapped into the chair was neither Sacco nor Vanzetti, but Celestino Medeiros. Groggy from overeating at his "last meal," Medeiros died in silence. At eleven minutes after midnight, Nicola Sacco entered the chamber. The Associated Press reporter present described his manner as "defiant." Taking note of the witnesses, Sacco nodded. "Good evening, gentlemen," he said. His last words were "Viva l'anarchia!" Long live anarchy! He was pronounced dead at 12:19.

If Sacco had been calm, Vanzetti was almost casual. He shook the warden's hand and then addressed the witnesses. "I am," he said, "an innocent man." The fish peddler, who had often in his letters compared his fate with Christ's, selected his last words carefully. "I wish to forgive some people for what they are doing to me." Some people, but not all. For Bartolomeo Vanzetti, Christian charity had its limits. At 12:26 he was dead.

In the Boston headquarters of the Sacco-Vanzetti Defense Committee, Mary Donovan turned to the secretary-treasurer, Joseph More. "Lock the doors, Joe," she said. "The work is over."

On August 28, Mary Donovan delivered the eulogy. "You, Sacco and Vanzetti, are the victims of the crassest plutocracy the world has known. . . . In your martyrdom we will fight on and conquer!"

In 1932 a bomb destroyed the home of Judge Webster Thayer and seriously injured his wife.

On the twentieth anniversary of the executions, Albert Einstein issued a statement from his home in Princeton which read in part: "At that time [during the Sacco-Vanzetti case] the desire for justice was as yet more powerful than it is today, although it did not triumph. Too many horrors have since dulled the human conscience. Therefore, the fight for the dignity of man is particularly urgent today. May Sacco and Vanzetti continue to live as symbols in all those who strive for a better morality in public affairs."

Shortly after Sacco and Vanzetti were electrocuted, the *Boston Transcript* said: "Massachusetts has narrowly escaped a lynching. . . . That it was the community and not the individual that was to be lynched in no wise affects the principle of this case."

> The deaths of Sacco and Vanzetti were front-page news, but not for long. The press turned its attention to the heroics of Charles Lindbergh and a disastrous flood of the Mississippi River. In Chicago, Jack Dempsey was preparing to fight Gene Tunney for the heavyweight title. The Mah-Jongg fad had been replaced by a craze for contract bridge, and all America was singing the latest song hit, "Barney Google With the Goo-Goo-Googly Eyes."

Bibliographical entry

Winston, Mark. "The Sacco—Vanzetti Case," <u>Famous American Trials</u>, George Hodnovich and Wendell Banks, eds. Boston: Small, Brown & Company, 1959, pp. 201—212.

Note: At times one or more persons will collaborate on the editing of a work. Above we have two editors, George Hodnovich and Wendell Banks, who have taken the works of several authors on the subject of famous trials. Mark Winston's work is just one, and is the one particular work cited in the bibliographical entry above. If you were to refer to the book *Famous American Trials* as a source, but not to any particular work within it, you would then list the entry in the bibliography in this manner:

Hodnovich, George, and Wendell Banks, eds. <u>Famous</u>
 <u>American Trials</u>. Boston: Small, Brown & Company,
 1959.

Initial footnote entry
 ¹Mark Winston, "The Sacco—Vanzetti Case," <u>Famous</u>
<u>American Trials</u>, p. 210.

Excerpt from *What Happened at South Braintree?*
by Robert Carr

New Brunswick, N.J.: Queens University Press, 1963. Pp. 213–219.

The confession of Celestino Medeiros to the South Braintree holdup-murder was, of course, an acute embarrassment to the Commonwealth of Massachusetts in 1925, as it is for detractors of Sacco and Vanzetti today, for the simple reason that Medeiros' account of the crime was infinitely more logical than the theory argued by the prosecution at the Dedham trial. Yet, before contrasting the young Portuguese's story with the absurd idiocies put forth by the authorities, it would be wise to inquire into the circumstances under which Medeiros' statement was made.

When he volunteered the confession, Medeiros had already been convicted of first-degree murder in the slaying of a Wrentham cashier during a crime completely similar to the South Braintree robbery. In fact, his partner in that holdup, James Weeks, later said that Medeiros had made use of his experience at South Braintree in planning the Wrentham job. The young gangster's first written confession was a brief note smuggled into Sacco's cell in a magazine on November 18, 1925. Prior to this he had made several attempts to communicate with Sacco, all rebuffed because Sacco feared Medeiros was a police spy. The timing of Medeiros' actions is important because they came after his first conviction but while his attorney's motion for a new trial was pending.

It has been suggested that Medeiros confessed to the South Braintree crime only to delay his execution on the Wrentham murder, but the facts clearly disprove this. At the time he made his original confession, Medeiros stood an excellent chance of winning a new trial on the Wrentham charge and going scot-free. Nothing could prejudice his motion for a new trial more than a new confession to yet another murder. That this was understood by both sides is obvious from the fact that, by special agreement with the authorities, the Medeiros confession was kept secret until his new trial was granted and completed.

But if the desire to prolong his life did not motivate Medeiros, perhaps he confessed in the hope of financial reward from the Sacco-Vanzetti Defense Committee. This accusation, too, is merely foolish. Medeiros, in fact, never received a dollar of defense fund money, and even the Commonwealth acknowledged there was no proof that "aid of any description had been promised to Medeiros."

Having now disposed of all possible motives Medeiros might have had for lying, we are led to the conclusion that his confession was the truth. But before we accept this explanation, let us take a hard look at his story. Medeiros claimed that in 1920, when at the tender age of eighteen he was already a hardened criminal, he had fallen in with a gang of Italians from Providence whose felonious specialty was robbing freight cars. He refused to identify the gang, but admitted one of the companies they victimized regularly was the Slater & Morrill Shoe Company of South Braintree. It is logical to assume, therefore, that the gang had a contact inside Slater & Morrill to tip them off when large consignments of shoes were to be shipped to Providence. The same confederate could easily have set up the April 15 payroll robbery.

In a Providence speakeasy, a few days before April 15, the gang invited Medeiros to join in the South Braintree job. His role was a simple one: to remain in the back seat of the getaway car and fire at the crowd if they attempted to rush the vehicle. To discourage pursuit, the gang used two cars. Medeiros and four others drove from Providence to a patch of woods near Randolph, Massachusetts, in a stolen Hudson automobile. At Randolph they took the Buick to South Braintree, arrived about noon and took up their positions, Medeiros remaining in the car.

Medeiros described his confederates as four Italians and "a slim fellow with light hair" who did the driving. Of the four Italians, "two were young men from 20 to 25 years old, one was about 40, the other about 35. All wore . . . caps. Two of them did the shooting—the oldest one and another." After the crime they abandoned the Buick at Randolph and returned to Providence in the Hudson. Despite persistent questioning, Medeiros steadfastly refused to name the members of the gang, but on one point he was insistent. "Sacco and Vanzetti had nothing to do with this job."

If Medeiros was reluctant to "rat" on his pals, his Wrentham partner, James Weeks, did not share his sense of underworld ethics. Serving a life sentence in the state prison at Charlestown, Weeks talked freely with defense investigators. "Medeiros often told me about the South Braintree job," Weeks deposed. It had been pulled by the Joe Morelli gang, a notorious Providence mob. According to Weeks' memory of Medeiros' story, the men actually involved in the holdup were Joe Morelli, the gang leader, his brothers Mike and Butsy, and a man named Bill. Weeks did not mention two other hoodlums who were later tied closely to the crime. One, Antonio Mancini, owned a Star 765mm. pistol, the exact make and calibre as the gun which had fired five of the six bullets found in the bodies of the slain paymaster and guard. The other, known as Steve the Pole, fit the description of the Buick's driver given by Medeiros and by numerous witnesses for both the defense and the prosecution at the Sacco-Vanzetti trial.

Once on the trail of the Morelli gang, the investigators began building an impressive case against them. Medeiros had said that one of the men who did the shooting was the oldest Italian, aged "about 40." Joe Morelli had been 39 in 1920. He bore a remarkable similarity in appearance to Sacco. Two eyewitnesses identified him as the gunman who shot the fatal bullet into the guard. That bullet came from a Colt .32 pistol. In 1920 Joe Morelli had owned a Colt .32. Imprisoned at Leavenworth, Joe whined that he was being framed, but the facts were unanswerable.

There was never any doubt that the car used at South Braintree was a Buick. Mike Morelli had been seen driving a Buick by the New Bedford police in 1920, and the car had strangely vanished immediately after the Slater & Morrill holdup. An eyewitness came forward who confirmed that the blond man hovering near the Buick before the murders was Steve the Pole. Medeiros had noted that the gang wore caps, and a cap was lost by one of the gunmen during the shooting. Medeiros himself suddenly possessed a $2,800 bank account after the holdup, and $2,800 would have been approximately his share of the Slater & Morrill loot.

Obviously there was more than enough evidence, both circumstantial and direct, to insure a swift indictment of the Morelli gang for the South Braintree crime under ordinary circumstances. But these were not ordinary circumstances. Sacco and Vanzetti already stood convicted of these murders. If the Medeiros-Morelli theory was true, then Sacco and Vanzetti were innocent. Clearly these men, who had been rotting for six years in prison, were victims of a blatant and out-rageous injustice. Clearly these two little anarchists were being rail-roaded to their deaths out of prejudice and fear by the very men and institutions which were sworn to protect their rights, in the nation which prided itself above all things on doling out "liberty and justice for all." The world, already seething with anger at the plight of Sacco and Vanzetti, could have put no other interpretation on the case.

It is particularly revealing to place side by side the evidence gath-ered against the Morelli gang and that used to convict Sacco and Van-zetti. This is precisely what defense counsel William Thompson did in his brief to the Supreme Judicial Court appealing Judge Webster Thayer's denial of the Medeiros motion for a new trial.

Everything about the South Braintree holdup, the use of two cars to cover the trail, the employment of additional thugs to prevent inter-ference from the crowd, the fact that the job was "cased" in advance, probably by a confederate working inside Slater & Morrill, every detail indicates that the crime was the work of a gang of professional thieves. The Morellis, quite obviously, were a gang of professional thieves, and their history of hijacking Slater & Morrill shipments makes it highly probable they had a contact in the factory. By contrast, Sacco and Vanzetti at the time of their arrests were men without criminal records or underworld connections. Vanzetti, the sometime fish peddler, was a wanderer, a dreamer and would-be political agitator. Sacco, a solid family man with a good job and a savings account, is an even less likely candidate for gangsterism.

The only motive the state could concoct for Sacco and Vanzetti was robbery for personal gain, yet none of the stolen money was ever traced to them, nor was there ever any evidence of a display of sudden wealth by them after the crime. The Morellis, on the other hand, faced trial in Federal court soon after April, 1920, and were desperate for funds to finance their bail and defense. And Medeiros, who later not only confessed but cleared Sacco and Vanzetti, banked $2,800 im-mediately after the holdup. Moreover, as Thompson pointed out, the alibis presented by the Morellis were "full of contradictions," while those of the two anarchists had been "testified to by many reputable witnesses." .

The case against Sacco and Vanzetti thus boils down to three major issues: eyewitness identifications, ballistics evidence, and the question of "consciousness of guilt." On the first, the following facts should be noted: (1) The prosecution's witnesses did not identify Sacco and Vanzetti from lineups. Rather, each defendant was forced to stand alone in the center of a room and to assume certain postures which the real killers had taken. (2) Several of the government witnesses had made "positive identifications" of known criminals from mug shots prior to the arrests of Sacco and Vanzetti, and afterwards changed their testimony. Others who had been uncertain of their identifications during the grand jury hearing became strangely "positive" at the trial. (3) Some witnesses had viewed the crime under almost impossible circumstances. For instance, Mary Splaine, a Slater & Morrill book-keeper, identified Sacco as the man she had seen in a moving car for a few seconds through a second-floor window from a distance of eighty feet! And Louis Pelser, a worker in the nearby Rice & Hutchins factory, claimed he had seen Sacco shoot the guard at the same moment that, two of his co-workers swore, he was cowering under a bench. (4) In addition to all this, the defense was able to produce more witnesses who swore Sacco and Vanzetti were *not* among the robbers than the prosecution could produce to identify them.

Against this, simply contrast the uncontradicted testimony of five eyewitnesses. Two identified Joe Morelli, two more fingered "Steve the Pole" Benkosky, the fifth placed Antonio Mancini at the scene. You should observe that the Medeiros-Morelli theory accounts for every member of the murder party, while the prosecution's thesis could account for only two, Sacco and Vanzetti.

The ballistics evidence demonstrated that two guns had been used in the killings. Of the six bullets found in the victims' bodies, five had been fired from a Star 765mm. and one from a Colt .32. As we have seen, Mancini owned a Star and Joe Morelli a Colt at the time of the holdup. It is true that Sacco also owned a Colt, and that the Commonwealth offered the testimony of two experts to the effect that the slug that had killed the guard had come from Sacco's gun. But the two expert defense witnesses disagreed, and one of the prosecution's experts, a respected state police captain, clarified his evidence after the trial, explaining that he believed only that the bullet had been fired from a Colt .32. He had not meant to imply that there was any proof the murder weapon was, specifically, Sacco's Colt. In his opinion there was no such proof.

Certain facts are clear. Had the police captain's testimony been understood during the trial, he would have been a witness *for* Sacco and Vanzetti, not against them. No sound evidence was produced at the trial to prove the fatal bullet was fired from Sacco's gun. And the prosecution's theory of the crime, in any event, accounts for only *one* of the six murder bullets, while the Medeiros-Morelli theory explains *all six*.

As for the question of "consciousness of guilt," it should be explained at once that, if Sacco and Vanzetti lied to the police at the time of their arrests, so did the members of the Morelli gang when confronted with the evidence against them in the Slater & Morrill robbery. But there are important differences. Consciousness of guilt, to be used as proof in a criminal case, must be consciousness of guilt *of the crime of which the defendants are accused.* Otherwise it is not admissible evidence. What this means, very simply, is that the lies of Sacco and Vanzetti to the police are in no way proof of their guilt in the South Braintree murders *unless* it can be demonstrated that they knew at the time they lied that they were under suspicion of those murders. And the undisputed fact is that, during the hours immediately following their arrests, when Sacco and Vanzetti were lying to the police, they were never once accused of the homicides or questioned directly about them. They were, however, questioned repeatedly about their radical activities and beliefs, and they lied simply because they *were* guilty of radical activity and they were conscious of that guilt.

Here lies the real tragedy of Sacco and Vanzetti. Their defenders at the time, and for decades since, have maintained that they were convicted of murder not because they were guilty but because they were radicals, and in a very real sense this is true. But it is not true in the sense that the liberals and intellectuals think it is true. They maintain that, caught up in the poisonous anti-radical atmosphere of the early 1920's, inflamed by "highly prejudicial cross-examination as to draft evasion and anarchistic opinions and associations" by the prosecution, brainwashed by the "patriotic speeches and charge" of the judge, the Sacco-Vanzetti jury brought in a verdict of guilty based on their own bigotry and against the evidence.

The jurors, of course, denied this. The liberals, of course, disbelieve them, but that disbelief is rooted in their own liberal prejudices. Juries, like defendants, have the right to be presumed innocent until proven otherwise. Nor was the verdict of guilty clearly against the evidence. The testimony of the eyewitnesses was contradictory and confused. The testimony of the alibi witnesses and the ballistics experts was contradictory and confused. Only in the matter of "consciousness of guilt" could the evidence have seemed clear to the jury (and it was the opinion of Judge Thayer that this was the evidence which cinched the verdict). Sacco and Vanzetti had lied to the authorities. They admitted those lies on the witness stand. Those lies had a fatal effect on the jury.

In fairness to the much maligned Thayer, he seems to have made an attempt to explain the fine, legal points appropriate to the issue of consciousness of guilt. But fine, legal points are often lost on a jury. What the verdict might have been had the jury been aware of the Medeiros confession and the Morelli theory can only be guessed. But Medeiros did not confess, and the Morellis were not accused, until more than four years after the Sacco-Vanzetti trial. And when the Morelli gang was confronted with the Medeiros confession they lied. Using the same principle of consciousness of guilt, the Morellis must be considered guilty. For the Morellis lied while fully aware that they were under suspicion of the South Braintree murders.

It remains only to inquire what attitude the authorities took toward the Medeiros confession. That attitude is summed up succinctly by Thompson's brief: "Seriously offered statements and affidavits of Morellis denying participation in crime. Declined request of defendants' counsel to interview *all witnesses* jointly to avoid vulgar contest of affidavits. Declined to investigate."

"Declined to investigate." The attitude of the government was summed up in that simple, three-word phrase. On the 23rd of August, 1927, Sacco and Vanzetti were executed. Ironically, the third man killed with them was Celestino Medeiros.

Bibliographical entry

Carr, Robert. <u>What</u> <u>Happened</u> <u>at</u> <u>South</u> <u>Braintree?</u>, New Brunswick, New Jersey: Queens University Press, 1963. Pp. 213–219.

Initial footnote entry

[1]Robert Carr, <u>What</u> <u>Happened</u> <u>at</u> <u>South</u> <u>Braintree?</u>, p. 215.

Sacco-Vanzetti Reconsidered

by Lon Quinncannon

Trial Magazine, vol. 12, September, 1970, pages 219–228.

The only question I intend to address myself to in this article is: were Nicola Sacco and Bartolomeo Vanzetti innocent or guilty of the holdup-murders of Frederick Parmenter and Alessandro Berardelli

The Sacco-Vanzetti Case

on April 15, 1920, in South Braintree, Massachusetts? It is important to make this clear at the outset, because every other writer who has ever dealt with this controversial, emotion-charged case has allowed this question of guilt or innocence to become hopelessly entangled with and confused by other issues which are at once inflammable, irrelevant and misleading. I am not concerned with the American public's state of mind during the trial, nor with world opinion following it. I am not concerned with any alleged prejudice on the part of the jury or misconduct by the trial judge. These issues must be entirely separated from that of innocence/guilt, as must the issue of the accused men's anarchist activities except as it relates to the question of "consciousness of guilt." Unless we agree, you and I, to concentrate exclusively on the evidence directly related to the crime and its commission, a dispassionate and objective investigation of the murders will be no more possible for us today than it was fifty years ago.

Sacco and Vanzetti were convicted of first-degree murder by a jury in Dedham in July of 1921. Since then new facts have been discovered and new evidence has been offered. Some trial testimony has seemingly been confirmed; some has been called into serious question. The passage of time now allows us to reexamine the evidence and, forming a jury of two, reach a final verdict. If we are to act as a jury, however, we must remember the two conditions imposed on any jury under the law. We must assume the innocence of the defendants unless and until they are proved guilty, and their guilt must be proved beyond any reasonable doubt. It is not enough to say they are possibly guilty, or even probably so. If there is any reasonable doubt of guilt, we must find for acquittal.

The difference between circumstantial and direct evidence should also be explained. The former refers to the presence of a circumstance or set of circumstances from which a jury might reasonably infer the fact of guilt or innocence. For example, a murder might be committed without any eyewitnesses to it, but if a man were found standing over the victim with a knife in his hand and covered with blood, a jury might infer from these circumstances that the man so found was the murderer. Direct evidence, on the other hand, is the direct testimony of witnesses as to what they saw and heard. In the Sacco-Vanzetti trial, the major pieces of circumstantial evidence were three: the Harrington & Richardson .38 revolver found on Vanzetti, which the prosecution attempted to trace to Berardelli; the cap found beside Berardelli's body, which the prosecution tried to prove belonged to Sacco; and

Sacco's .32 Colt, which the prosecution sought to connect with one of the murder bullets. All the testimony of alibi witnesses and eyewitnesses to the crime falls into the category of direct evidence.

In detective fiction, circumstantial evidence is always misleading. As any avid reader of whodunits knows, when a character in a novel is discovered kneeling beside a corpse with his fingerprints all over the murder weapon, you may be absolutely certain he is completely innocent. It would be a serious mistake, however, to judge life by what we read in fiction. In actual criminal cases, it often occurs that circumstantial evidence is more trustworthy than direct testimony. True, circumstances can be misinterpreted, but witnesses can be confused, or frightened, or bullied, or bribed. Since there is reason to believe that all four may have been tried on the witnesses in the Sacco-Vanzetti case, it would be sensible to look first at the circumstantial evidence offered.

Against Vanzetti there was very little. When arrested, he had been carrying a loaded revolver and four shotgun shells. The revolver corresponded in make and caliber to a gun owned by the dead payroll guard, Berardelli, which was not found on his body. The prosecution theorized that Vanzetti's weapon was taken from the guard during the crime. If this could be proved, it would tie the fish peddler to the Slater & Morrill holdup. But the prosecution had hard going. They proved Berardelli had possessed a .38 Harrington & Richardson and that on March 20, 1920, twenty-six days before his death, the guard had brought the gun to the Iver Johnson Company to have a new hammer put in. But had Berardelli ever reclaimed the revolver? His widow didn't know. Her husband had "returned the [claim] ticket to Mr. Parmenter," she said, "and I don't know if Mr. Parmenter got it for him, but I know Mr. Parmenter let him take another one." Under cross-examination she acknowledged that this substitute gun had a "black handle" and "looked like" the one he had taken for repairs. The revolver found on Vanzetti had a silver handle.

George Fitzemeyer, an Iver Johnson gunsmith, testified he had replaced the hammer in Berardelli's gun and that the hammer in the gun carried by Vanzetti was new. Two defense experts denied this last statement, one of them, James E. Burns, showing the jury that the face of the hammer had been worn smooth and shiny by long use. James Jones, the Iver Johnson manager, admitted he had no record that Berardelli had picked up the gun, but also no record that it had been sold. In short, though the revolver was gone, Jones had no idea where.

SECTION IV: PROJECTS IN INVESTIGATION

The Sacco-Vanzetti Case

The defense, in its effort to prove Vanzetti had purchased the weapon legitimately, had trouble with contradictory testimony, but the burden of proof did not lie with the defense, and the prosecution failed to show a connection between Vanzetti's revolver and Berardelli. As for the four shotgun shells, their only importance lay in the fact that witnesses had seen a long gun at the South Braintree holdup. But they were unsure whether this was a shotgun or a rifle, and in any event all the bullets found in the victims' bodies had been fired from sidearms.

All attempts to connect Sacco with the cap dropped by the killer proved equally futile. The only witness who could have identified the cap as Sacco's was his boss, George Kelley, who stubbornly refused to do so. But the ballistics evidence against Sacco was an entirely different matter. At the trial, the prosecution introduced two expert witnesses to testify that the bullet which killed Berardelli had been fired from the pistol found on Sacco. One of them, Captain William Proctor of the Massachusetts State Police, later in effect switched sides, but Proctor's status as a gun expert was questionable anyway since he was unable to dismantle and reassemble a pistol while on the stand. The other, Charles Van Amburgh, a former policeman employed by the Remington Arms Company, was of far greater importance to the jury.

The science of ballistics is based on the individuality of the markings to be found on all firearms, on the breech-block and firing pin, and within the barrel. Markings on the first two leave distinctive scars on the shell, while markings inside the barrel cause unique grooves on any bullet fired from the gun. Thus, shells and bullets fired from the same weapon will show identical scratches. These scratches are as individual and unique as fingerprints.

The methods of obtaining ballistic identification were fairly primitive in 1921, chiefly because the comparison microscope had not yet been invented and the experts were forced to rely on the compound microscope. Under the latter, the fatal bullet (marked III by the police and spoken of throughout the trial as "bullet number three) could be compared with test bullets fired from Sacco's pistol only by placing each under separate microscope viewers. One could make a comparison of bullets (or shells) only by alternately opening and closing first the right and then the left eye. It was impossible to see both bullets simultaneously. The invention of the comparison microscope made it possible to fuse the right half of one bullet with the left half of another into a single image. If the two bullets thus observed had been fired from the same gun, the composite image produced in the microscope would appear as a single bullet. The marks and grooves from the murder bullet would blend completely with those of the test bullet in such a way that no observer could tell where one left off and the other began. The identification would be as certain as matching two halves of the same fingerprint.

The comparison microscope was not used in ballistics until 1925 and not introduced into the Sacco-Vanzetti case until 1927, but it confirmed the findings of Van Amburgh. In tests conducted by Colonel Calvin Goddard in 1927, and repeated in 1961 by Colonel Frank Jury, former head of the New Jersey State Police Firearms Laboratory, and Jac Weller, honorary curator of the West Point Museum, it was proved conclusively that a shell found near Berardelli's body and the bullet which killed the guard had both come from the Colt .32 found by the police in the possession of Nicola Sacco at the time of his arrest.

It has been claimed by defenders of Sacco and Vanzetti that the ballistics evidence produced subsequent to their trial was invalid because the bullet exhibits could have been switched after the trial by the police. The argument against this charge makes two points, one of which is valid. The first is that the police would not stoop so low as to falsify evidence in a capital trial. To those whom a study of capital trials has taught better, this position is ridiculous. But the second argument is far sounder. It is simply that a switch in exhibits would have been impossible because the bullets and shells in question were scraped with identifying marks immediately after the South Braintree crime, and these marks are evident in all photographs of the important bullets and shells made subsequent to the murders. There can be no question that the bullet which killed Berardelli, and the shell from which it was fired, came from the .32 Colt pistol found in the pocket of Nicola Sacco.

The direct testimony was even more muddled than the circumstantial evidence. It dealt primarily with the question of whether or not Sacco and Vanzetti could be identified by eyewitnesses and with defense efforts to prove alibis for the day of the crime. Nothing could be so withering to a belief in the value of eyewitness testimony as a study of the direct evidence given in this case.

Seven people swore they saw Sacco at South Braintree on April 15. Seven others swore that he was in Boston on that day. Four people insisted that Vanzetti had ridden in the getaway car. But five others said they had been buying fish from him in Plymouth while the holdup was taking place. Against the eleven witnesses who put either Sacco or Vanzetti in South Braintree, the defense produced over a dozen who swore that neither man was in the gang. Unfortunately not one of this mob of witnesses stands out as unimpeachable. In all cases the testimony is either confused, contradictory or suspect.

On behalf of the prosecution, it can be stated that Vanzetti's alibi witnesses were all personal friends, and that the defense relied chiefly on a thirteen-year old boy who looked up to the fish peddler as a father figure and who admitted rehearsing his testimony until he had memorized it "like a piece at school." Yet the defense might argue it was natural for a man to spend a day among his friends, and the fact that testimony is memorized does not prove it is false. As for Sacco's alibi, it was almost entirely provided by prominent radicals active on the Sacco-Vanzetti Defense Committee. Two of these, Felice Guadenagi and Antonio Dentamore, claimed to recall meeting Sacco in Boston on April 15 because that was the date of a banquet to which they had both been invited. But Guadenagi said they had met Sacco at 11:30 in Boni's restaurant and that the banquet was held in the evening. Dentamore testified he had gone to the banquet at noon and later been introduced to Sacco by Guadenagi at 2:45 in Ciordani's coffee house.

Sacco, who had claimed to be at work on the murder day until this was disproved, then told the story of going to Boston to obtain a passport. He had no passport to corroborate this tale, but explained he was refused one because he had brought the wrong size photograph. A clerk at the Italian consulate, Guiseppe Andrower, said he remembered Sacco, but he acknowledged that he dealt with 150 to 200 people on an average day, and there was no written record to substantiate Sacco's story. Having returned to Italy, Andrower could not be present in court, but his deposition was read into the record by the defense.

Though Vanzetti's witnesses were friends who might have been willing to lie for him, their stories had the advantage of simplicity and the appearance of sincerity, as did the fish peddler's own testimony. At one point in his cross-examination, when the District Attorney expressed doubt about his alibi, Vanzetti shouted, "Yes, yes, yes, sure, and you can be sure that I can remember that I never kill a man on the 15th, because I never kill a man in my life."

In contrast, Sacco's alibi was complicated and his witnesses contradictory. The passport story was not advanced until months after his arrest, when he had already been caught in one lie. Still, in fairness to both defendants, it should be stressed that the prosecution's eyewitnesses were a sorry lot. Some were shady characters. Some told different stories at different times under oath. Some had had no real opportunity to view the crime or the criminals. Some had given descriptions which did not fit the defendants. Some, it was claimed, had privately admitted they could not really identify any of the gang. Of the four who fingered Vanzetti, one said he was driving the murder car though Vanzetti could not drive, and another said he had spoken without an accent, a feat which was clearly impossible for the Italian-born immigrant.

There is one witness whose identification is, perhaps, more trustworthy. Louis Pelser had watched the murder of the guard, Berardelli, from a first-floor window in the nearby Rice & Hutchins factory, a distance of only seven feet. In court he named Sacco as the killer. He admitted telling a defense investigator that he had waited out the shooting crouched under a bench and therefore could not make an identification, but on the stand he said this was a lie told to avoid being called as a witness. Pelser was a sufficiently accurate observer to provide the police with the exact license number of the getaway car. Was his identification of Sacco equally accurate? You, who are now the jury, must decide.

The issue of "consciousness of guilt," about which much has been said at the trial and since, is really not worth all the attention that has been wasted on it. When they were taken into custody, Sacco and Vanzetti lied to the police. The prosecution argued this fact as proof of their guilty knowledge of the South Braintree murders. The defense contended the lies were motivated by their fear of arrest for radicalism. The key point, of course, is when precisely the two men were first made aware they were under suspicion of the Slater & Morrill holdup. Under questioning by his attorney, Vanzetti insisted he had no idea he was suspected of murder at the time he lied to the police.

Q. Did either Chief Stewart at the Brockton police station or Mr. Katzmann tell you that you were suspected of robberies and murder? A. No.

Q. Was there any question asked of you or any statement made to you to indicate to you that you were charged with that crime on April 15? A. No.

Q. What did you understand, in view of the questions asked of you, what did you understand you were being detained for at the Brockton police station? A. I understand they arrested me for a political matter.

SECTION IV: PROJECTS IN INVESTIGATION

The Sacco-Vanzetti Case

Q. You mean by reason of the questions asked of you? A. Because I was asked if I am a socialist, if I am I.W.W., if I am a Communist, if I am a radical, if I am black-hander.

Vanzetti had been asked by the police for his whereabouts on "the Thursday before that Monday (April 19)"; that is, the murder day. He had answered that he could not remember, but apparently there was no direct reference to South Braintree during his interrogation. Sacco, on the other hand, was specifically questioned about the factory holdup on the day following his arrest. He admitted knowing about the crime, claiming to have read about it in the newspaper, and immediately afterwards he lied about being at work on April 15. All this Sacco acknowledged on the stand during his trial. In other words, while it is not at all clear when Vanzetti was told he would be charged with murder, it is evident that Sacco understood that his arrest was connected with the South Braintree robbery, and that he then gave a false alibi to the authorities. This is the only conclusion that can be drawn about "consciousness of guilt" from a close reading of the trial record.

Before considering a verdict, we must look at additional evidence which was unknown to the original jury. Five years after the trial, the defense offered a new theory of the crime. Celestino Medeiros, a convicted murderer awaiting retrial, sent a one-sentence confession to Sacco's jail cell just thirty minutes after being shown a financial report of the Sacco-Vanzetti Defense Committee. He put nothing more into writing, however, until after his second trial also ended in conviction. Then, in the shadow of the electric chair, Medeiros sought to hold off his execution by signing a detailed confession. So long as the possibility existed that Medeiros might be an important witness in the Sacco-Vanzetti case, his life would be spared by the state.

It is indicative of the desperate plight of the defense that the Medeiros confession was ever taken seriously. He was wrong about the date of the crime and the caliber of the guns used in the holdup. He said the gang did not arrive in South Braintree until noon when they had been seen in town as early as 9:18, and several more times during the morning. He claimed the stolen cash was in a black satchel when it was in fact in two metal boxes. He was unable to give any description of the holdup scene, and his account of the escape route was at odds with the independent testimony of several witnesses who saw the car after the robbery. The list of discrepancies between Medeiros' statement and the known facts is endless.

Medeiros refused to name the other gang members, but another convict told defense investigators that the crime had been engineered by the Joe Morelli gang of Providence. Morelli, imprisoned in Leavenworth, denied the charge, as well he might out of professional pride if nothing else. For the Morellis were professional hoodlums, and the Slater & Morrill holdup was as sloppy and amateurish a crime as ever disgraced the underworld. The criminals had blown the chance to grab the entire $30,000 payroll from a lone Railway Express agent when the money first arrived on the 9:18 train. Instead they had meekly watched the agent carry the cash from the railroad station to his office and then hung around South Braintree, making themselves conspicuous, for almost six hours, waiting for a chance to steal half the original loot.

The execution of the holdup was slovenly. Although at least three of the thugs were armed and as many as twenty shots may have been fired at the victims, only six bullets hit anything, five of them from the same pistol. Witnesses saw Berardelli's killer stand over his fallen body and fire four shots at point-blank range, yet only one slug found its mark. If the robbers were not sharpshooters, neither were they mechanics. Although one of them worked on the engine of the getaway car for hours, two of its cylinders were missing and it chugged and lurched away from the bloody scene with no more speed than a kiddie-car.

The rest of the "evidence" supporting the Medeiros-Morelli theory is slender. An attempt was made to connect a hood named Antonio Mancini with the killings because he had committed murder in New York in February, 1921, with a gun of the same caliber as that which had fired the five unexplained shots in South Braintree. But thousands of similar weapons were in existence, and there was no evidence to link Mancini to the Morelli mob. It was argued that the holdup men must have had a confederate inside Slater & Morrill to plan the crime, yet no employee of the factory was ever connected to the Morellis, whereas Ferruccio Coacci, a known associate of Sacco and Vanzetti, had worked at the plant until three days before the robbery. The point was made that none of the stolen money was ever traced to Sacco and Vanzetti, but that loot would have been earmarked for the treasury of the radical cause, not the pockets of the defendants. Any way you look at the facts, the Medeiros-Morelli theory falls apart.

We are ready to sum up the evidence and reach a verdict. Against Vanzetti, no solid circumstantial evidence exists. The pistol found in his possession was never proved to be Berardelli's gun. Only the contradictory testimony of four dubious witnesses exists to place him at the crime scene. His alibi is provided by friends, but there is no valid reason to disbelieve them. Consciousness of guilt is not a factor since it is unproved that he knew he was suspected of murder at the time he lied to police. It is, of course, possible that he was guilty, but there is more than a little cause for a reasonable doubt, and innocence must be assumed until guilt is proved.

Sacco presents a different case altogether. Solid ballistics evidence proves conclusively that his Colt pistol was the murder weapon in the death of the guard, Berardelli. By his own admission, he lied to the authorities after being questioned about the Slater & Morrill holdup, thus we have proof of consciousness of guilt. His Boston alibi is advanced only after his first story has been disproved, and it is unsupported except by the doubtful testimony of interested witnesses who contradict each other on significant points. He is identified as Berardelli's killer by the most trustworthy of the prosecution's eyewitnesses.

The final verdict: Nicola Sacco is guilty beyond a reasonable doubt of murder in the first degree. Bartolomeo Vanzetti is not guilty. If you do not agree, then our jury is hung. If you agree, then perhaps the truth has at last been found.

Bibliographical entry

Quinncannon, Lon. "Sacco–Vanzetti Reconsidered," Trial
    Magazine, 12:219–228, September, 1970.

Initial footnote entry

[1]Lon Quinncannon, "Sacco–Vanzetti Reconsidered,"
Trial Magazine, September, 1970, p. 222.

Did Sacco and Vanzetti Receive A Fair Trial?
by Clayton Morris

New York Evening Herald, November 15, 1971, pages 28–35.*

In any debate over the Sacco-Vanzetti case the dispute invariably boils down to two basic questions: First, did Sacco and Vanzetti receive a fair trial or were the judge and jury prejudiced against them

*Omit the first "2" (200) from the text page number when cross-referencing this article, since it appears in a newspaper.

because they were anarchists and draft dodgers? Second, were Sacco and Vanzetti guilty or innocent of the murders at South Braintree? If you know a man's opinion on one of these questions, you can infallibly predict his opinion on the other. If he believes that the court was bigoted and the trial unfair, he is certain also to insist on the innocence of the defendants. If he maintains that the trial was evenhanded and the court objective, then he is sure to argue that Sacco and Vanzetti were guilty.

I have always found this circumstance fascinating for what it reveals about the mental and emotional state of those who take sides on this controversial case. For it should be clear at once to any rational observer that there is *absolutely no logical connection* between these two issues.

It is not necessary to believe that Sacco and Vanzetti were innocent in order to contend that their trial was tainted with prejudice. Obviously it is just as possible for a guilty man to receive an unfair trial as for an innocent man. An excellent example is Celestino Medeiros, the young thug whose "confession" to the Slater and Morrill holdup embroiled him in the Sacco-Vanzetti uproar. Medeiros was unquestionably guilty of killing an aged cashier during a bank stickup in Wrentham, and the jury at his first trial convicted him. But the judge had failed to remind the jury of one of the most basic principles of law, that a man is presumed innocent until proven guilty. Thus, though the accused was guilty, the trial was unjust, and it was the ruling of the Supreme Court that Medeiros be awarded a new trial.

That the judge, Webster B. Thayer, was personally against the defendants seems unfortunately evident. Investigators for the defense were able to obtain numerous affidavits from friends and acquaintances of the judge indicating that, outside of his court, Thayer recklessly referred to Sacco and Vanzetti as "anarchistic bastards" and "dago sons of bitches" among other charming terms. The question is, did Thayer permit his personal bigotry to influence his conduct at the trial? I am sorry to say that, based on my own, hopefully impartial, reading of the transcript, I am forced to believe he did.

The Sacco and Vanzetti case was tried against a background of national tension resulting from a succession of radical bombings and government retaliation through massive arrests and deportation of aliens. The radical movement was not unified. There were ideological differences between the Communists and the anarchists, between the anarchists and the Bolsheviks. Vanzetti, for example, strongly disapproved of the Russian revolution. But these philosophical distinctions were too fine to be understood by the general public, which lumped all leftists together as "radicals."

Sacco and Vanzetti were anarchists. As such, they were also, or at least they claimed to be, pacifists. Thus they had been "slackers," 1920's slang for draft dodgers, and had fled to Mexico during World War I to avoid serving in the military. In view of this, Judge Thayer's repeated references to patriotism during the trial, and especially his comparisons of a juror's patriotic duty with that of a soldier, must be considered deliberately prejudicial. Thayer sounded this theme as early as his address to the first panel of prospective jurymen:

> It is not a sufficient excuse that the [juror's] service is painful, confining and distressing. It is not a sufficient excuse that a juror has business engagements and other duties more profitable and pleasant than he would rather perform, for you must remember the American soldier had other duties he would rather have performed than those that resulted in his giving up his life upon the battle-fields of France, but he, with undaunted courage and patriotic devotion that brought honor and glory to humanity and the world, rendered the service and made the supreme sacrifice. He answered the call of the Commonwealth.

> So, gentlemen, I call upon you to render this service here that you have been summoned to perform with the same spirit of patriotism, courage and devotion to duty as was exhibited by our soldier boys across the seas.

During the cross-examination of both defendants, Thayer allowed the district attorney, Frederick G. Katzmann, to hammer home to the jury that Sacco and Vanzetti had been slackers. This was especially true of Sacco, who got a rough going over despite the constant objections of his attorney, Jeremiah McAnarney. Sacco had said he originally came to America because he loved a free country. Katzmann demanded to know if he still loved America when he went to Mexico to beat the draft.

> Question (by Mr. Katzmann). Did you love this country in the last week of May, 1917? Answer (by Sacco). That is pretty hard for me to say in one word, Mr. Katzmann.

> Q. There are two words you can use, Mr. Sacco, yes or no. Which one is it? A. Yes.

> Q. And in order to show your love for this United States of America when she was about to call upon you to become a soldier you ran away to Mexico?

> Mr. McAnarney. Wait.

The Court. Did you?

Q. Did you run away to Mexico?

The Court. He has not said he ran away to Mexico. Did you go?

Q. Did you go to Mexico to avoid being a soldier for this country that you loved? A. Yes.

It was possible, of course, that the jury's knowledge of the defendants' anarchism might create a bias, but the issue had necessarily to be introduced into the trial to explain why Sacco and Vanzetti showed "consciousness of guilt" after being arrested. But the issue of draft dodging had absolutely no relevance to the charge of murder. In my own view, the defense blundered in introducing it during direct examination, thus giving Katzmann the opportunity to place such stress on it in cross-examination. For Thayer to have permitted the prosecutor to go so far in a line of questioning which was at once both immaterial and prejudicial is inexcusable. Worse yet, the judge made patriotism the keynote of his final charge to the jury.

> Mr. Foreman and gentlemen of the jury—you may remain seated—the Commonwealth of Massachusetts called upon you to render a most important service. Although you knew that such service would be arduous, painful and tiresome, yet you, like the true soldier, responded to that call in the true spirit of supreme American loyalty. There is no better word in the English language than "loyalty." For he who is loyal to God, to country, to his state and to his fellow men, represents the highest and noblest type of true American citizenship, than which there is none grander in the entire world. . . . For this loyalty, gentlemen, and for this magnificent service that you have rendered to your state and to your fellow men, I desire, however, in behalf of both to extend to each of you their profoundest thanks, gratitude, and appreciation.

Through all his pompous rhetoric, the judge's meaning rang loud and clear. The jurors were loyal Americans who had done their duty to their country as nobly as the soldiers who died on the fields of France. Sacco and Vanzetti, by implicit contrast, were shirkers who had enjoyed their adopted country's freedoms and deserted her in her hour of need. Faced with the prospect of dodging bullets in France, they had chosen instead to dodge the draft in Mexico.

Nor is this all the evidence of Thayer's prejudicial conduct of the trial. Although both defendants repeatedly petitioned him for separate trials, the judge, refusing to explain his reasons, denied all such motions. Separation of the cases would surely have benefited Vanzetti, against whom the prosecution had far shakier evidence. In addition,

The Sacco-Vanzetti Case

Thayer threatened to allow testimony showing Vanzetti had had to produce an alibi in another criminal case if the defense tried to introduce any evidence of "good character" of either defendant. The exclusion of "good character" witnesses by a judge who permitted so much immaterial testimony tending to show "bad character" is outrageous.

On at least two occasions, Thayer indulged himself in prejudicial cross-examination of witnesses. One, Harry Kurlansky, had been called to discredit Mrs. Lola Andrews, who had made a positive identification of Sacco. Kurlansky testified he had spoken to Mrs. Andrews as she was returning from the jail. "The government took me down and want me to recognize those men," he quoted her as saying, "and I don't know a thing about them. I have never seen them and I can't recognize them." At about this point the judge interrupted.

> The Court. Mr. Witness, I would like to ask one question. Did you attempt to find out who this person was who represented the Government who was trying to get her to take and state that which was false?
>
> The witness. Did I what?
>
> Mr. McAnarney. What is that question?
>
> The Court. Did you try to find out who it was who represented the Government?
>
> The witness. No.
>
> The Court. Why not?
>
> The witness. Well, it didn't come into my mind. I wasn't sure, you know. It didn't . . .
>
> The Court. Did you think the public interest was served by anybody representing the Government to try to get a woman . . .
>
> The witness. I don't think of anything . . .
>
> The Court. . . . to identify somebody?
>
> The witness. I don't think of anything at all.

The effect of Thayer's interference was to turn the jury's attention from the relevant question of whether Lola Andrews had falsely identified Sacco to the irrelevant question of why Kurlansky had not found out the name of a policeman. Kurlansky's complete confusion must have had an impact on the jury.

One of the South Braintree gunmen had lost a cap at the scene. The prosecution maintained that the cap belonged to Sacco, but they had only one witness to prove a connection between Sacco and the cap, and he was a very reluctant witness. George T. Kelley, Sacco's boss, would swear to nothing except that Sacco sometimes wore a cap to work, that he had seen it "hanging up on a nail in the distance," and that "it was similar in color" to the cap lost by the killer. This was hardly a positive identification, but the assistant district attorney, Harold P. Williams, attempted to introduce the cap into evidence anyway. The defense, naturally, objected. Instead of ruling on the objection immediately, Judge Thayer again intruded.

> The Court. I would like to ask the witness one question: whether—I wish you would ask him, rather—according to your best judgment, is it your opinion that the cap which Mr. Williams now holds in his hand is like the one that was worn by the defendant Sacco?
>
> Mr. Moore. I object to that question, your Honor.
>
> The Court (to Mr. Williams). Did you put it? I would rather it come from Mr. Williams. Will you put that question?

Thayer seems to have been determined to admit the cap in evidence, but Kelley's refusal to connect the cap with Sacco created a problem. On the basis of the witness's testimony thus far, the judge had no choice but to sustain the defense objection. This meant that the cap could not be used in evidence. Rather than make such a ruling, Thayer suggested a question to the prosecution which, if answered in the affirmative, would enable him to admit the cap. Williams, taking the hint, repeated the question in almost the same words: "Mr. Kelley, according to your best judgment, is the cap I show you alike in appearance to the cap owned by Sacco?" But the witness was stubborn. "In color only," he answered. But the judge was stubborn too.

> The Court. That is not responsive to the question. I wish you would answer it, if you can.
>
> The witness. I can't answer it when I don't know right down in my heart that that is the cap.
>
> The Court. I don't want you to. I want that you should answer according to what is in your heart.
>
> The witness. General appearance, that is all I can say. I never saw that cap so close in my life as I do now.
>
> The Court. In its general appearance, is it the same?

Kelley surrendered. "Yes, sir," he said. Thayer was anxious that the record show the question had been asked by Williams, not by himself. Williams obediently repeated the question and Kelley his answer. Then Williams again offered the cap in evidence. The judge sat back. "Admitted," he said.

The Sacco-Vanzetti Case

The result of this incredible manipulation of testimony by the bench was that, in spite of the prosecution's failure to prove any connection between the cap and the defendant, the cap was made to appear to the jury an important piece of evidence against Sacco. Thayer had violated his impartiality. He had not only allowed the prosecutor to cross-examine his own witness, he had insisted upon it, and had, in fact, conducted the questioning himself. He had transformed a meaningless cap into a damaging prosecution exhibit. Finally, as proof that he knew perfectly well what he was doing, he had tried to juggle the trial transcript to conceal his own part in Kelley's examination.

From beginning to end, Sacco and Vanzetti suffered from the incompetence of their attorneys. Their first chief counsel, Fred Moore, was a bungler and a bully who thought nothing of framing evidence and employed a crew of hoodlums as "investigators" to terrify or blackmail those witnesses who could not be bribed. After their convictions, Sacco's and Vanzetti's best hope for a new trial lay always in a charge of prejudice against Webster Thayer, but their lawyers never saw that hope or made that charge until it was too late. Instead, Moore wasted over three years in appeals based on the phony testimony of witnesses who had been either browbeaten or bought.

Typical of Moore's methods was his attempt to destroy ballistics evidence important to the Commonwealth's case against Sacco. In 1923 Moore hired a charlatan named Albert H. Hamilton as his new ballistics "expert." Shortly thereafter Hamilton appeared in Thayer's office with two Colt pistols which he said he wanted to compare with the gun found on Sacco. Under the judge's watchful but undiscerning eye, Hamilton treated Thayer to a sophisticated version of the old shell game, dismantling and reassembling the three pistols to demonstrate how the parts of a gun could be interchanged. In the confusion, Hamilton palmed the barrel of Sacco's pistol and attached it to one of his own guns. Moore's "expert" was almost out the door with the incriminating barrel when the suspicious judge demanded that all three weapons be left in his custody. It was not, however, until weeks later that Thayer realized Moore's man had come within an ace of absconding with the only important circumstantial evidence connecting Sacco with the crime. Small wonder, then, that all Moore's tricks accomplished was to reinforce Thayer's certainty that his actions from the beginning had been justified.

Fred Moore's successor, William G. Thompson, was a skillful and ethical attorney who might have seen the importance of an appeal on the ground of Thayer's prejudice had he not been sidetracked by the "confession" of Celestino Medeiros. Though the Medeiros confession was hopelessly contradictory and inaccurate, Thompson, acting more in despair than in wisdom, consumed almost a year of precious time trying to obtain a new trial on its strength. When the attempt failed Thompson resigned, and Thayer took the opportunity, on April 9, 1927, nearly six years after their convictions, to sentence Sacco and Vanzetti to the electric chair. Not until four months later did the defense finally base an appeal on the judge's prejudice. The motion was doomed automatically by a technicality in Massachusetts law which forbade any motion for a new trial once sentence had been imposed. For Sacco and Vanzetti it was too late.

The execution of Sacco and Vanzetti was a travesty of justice and a tragic blot on this nation's history. I do not say this because I believe Sacco and Vanzetti were innocent. On the contrary, I find the recent scholarship of such men as Francis Russell, David Felix and Lon Quinncannon more than convincing when it suggests that Sacco was certainly guilty and Vanzetti possibly, if not probably so. I indicated earlier that I do not consider a belief in the innocence of the defendants necessary to a conclusion that these men did not receive a fair trial. I would go further. Even if Sacco and Vanzetti were clearly and unquestionably guilty of murder in the first degree, they deserved a new trial, for they did not receive justice.

The importance of the Sacco-Vanzetti case, the factor which has kept it a lively issue for more than half a century, is that it was a political trial on a nonpolitical charge. The danger of a miscarriage of justice is always present under such circumstances; the cry of injustice is always imminent, whether the defendants be 1920 "radicals" and "anarchists," or 1970 "Communists," "Weathermen," or "Black Panthers." If there are Webster Thayers among us, they must be rooted out, not nurtured and protected. This country cannot afford another Sacco-Vanzetti case.

Bibliographical entry

Morris, Clayton. "Did Sacco and Vanzetti Receive a Fair Trial?" New York Evening Herald, November 15, 1971, pp. 28–35.

Initial footnote entry

[1]Clayton Morris, "Did Sacco and Vanzetti Receive a Fair Trial?" New York Evening Herald, November 15, 1971, p. 30.

SELECTED BIBLIOGRAPHY FOR SECTION IV

All the articles and reviews in Section IV have been created by the text authors to fulfill the purposes of the exercises. But the student should be aware that numerous periodical and newspaper sources are available for further research. The following entries are the principal *secondary* sources the authors consulted in creating the text articles. The authors also consulted numerous *primary* documents associated with each case.

The Lindbergh Kidnapping

Waller, George. *Kidnap*. New York: The Dial Press, 1961. Principal secondary source. Extremely useful, but slanted toward prosecution.

Whipple, Sidney B. *The Trial of Bruno Richard Hauptmann.* New York: Doubleday & Co. Inc., 1937. Good contemporary account.

The Salem Witch Trials

Burr, George L., ed. *Narratives of the Witchcraft Cases.* New York: Barnes and Noble Books, 1972. Finest collection of primary sources, including writings of the Mathers and Robert Calef.

Hansen, Chadwick. *Witchcraft at Salem.* New York: George Braziller, Inc., 1962. Most recent study, but conclusions based on questionable evidence.

Starkey, Marion L. *The Devil in Massachusetts.* New York: Alfred A. Knopf, Inc., 1949. Breezy narration of trials, with emphasis on psychological aspects.

Upham, Charles N. *Salem Witchcraft.* New York: Frederick Ungar Publishing Co., Inc., 1969. The classic nineteenth-century account.

The Lizzie Borden Case

Lincoln, Victoria. *A Private Disgrace: Lizzie Borden by Daylight.* New York: G. P. Putnam's Sons, 1967. See simulated review on text pages 192–194.

Pearson, Edmund. *Studies in Murder.* New York, The Macmillan Company, 1924. Very readable general study of case.

Porter, Edwin H. *The Fall River Tragedy.* Fall River, Mass.: George R. H. Buffinton, 1893. Though out of print, the principal secondary source for all subsequent studies of the case.

The Sacco-Vanzetti Case

Ehrmann, Herbert B. *The Untried Case: The Sacco-Vanzetti Case and the Morelli Gang.* New York: Vanguard Press, Inc., 1933. The defense argues for the Morellis' guilt.

Felix, David. *Protest: Sacco-Vanzetti and the Intellectuals.* Bloomington: Indiana University Press, 1965. Excellent study of the social and political aspects of case.

Frankfurter, Felix. *The Case of Sacco and Vanzetti: A Critical Analysis for Lawyers and Laymen.* Boston: Little, Brown and Company, 1927. The most famous contemporary statement of the liberal position.

Russell, Francis. *Tragedy in Dedham: The Story of the Sacco-Vanzetti Case.* New York: McGraw-Hill, Inc., 1971. Superb study in which recent ballistics evidence casts new light on the crime.

Weeks, Robert P. *Commonwealth vs. Sacco and Vanzetti.* Englewood Cliffs, N.J.: Prentice-Hall, Inc., 1958. Contains lengthy excerpts from original documents, including indictment, trial, appeals transcripts.

Appendices

Punctuation and Grammar

Introduction

Punctuation, we have said, is the referee of written language. It maintains order. Like the referee, you may sometimes hate it but without it you have chaos. We have placed our emphasis on the functions performed by punctuation in the belief that when function is understood the rules are easier to remember and apply.

The most persistent problems of punctuation and grammar are dealt with here: comma usage, run-on sentences, subject-verb agreement and pronoun-referent agreement. Included also are checklists for such things as capitalization, common typing constructions, term-paper abbreviations and correction symbols. You may use this Appendix as a systematic review of writing mechanics or as a reference handbook when you need quick answers.

The Comma

Before considering the rules for using commas, do the following exercises. Each passage is completely punctuated except for its commas. Read each passage through silently once or twice until you are thoroughly familiar with its content. Then read it aloud as often as necessary. Insert a comma where an oral pause seems natural.

1. On Sunday November 20 1817 the nightmare began. The look-out at the masthead was scanning the horizon when at about 8 o'clock he discovered a shoal of whales off the lee bow. The usual cry "There

she blows'' echoed through the morning air. When our ship had reached within half a mile of the place where the whales were sighted all our boats were lowered in pursuit. The ship in the meantime was brought to the wind to wait for us.

2. I had the harpoon in the first boat. When we reached the spot where we thought they were nothing could be seen. We lay on our oars in anxious anticipation and soon a whale rose and spouted a short distance away. I made for the beast came up beside him and hurled the harpoon. Feeling the spear in him he threw himself in an agony toward the boat. A severe blow from his tail struck the boat and stove a hole in her. I seized the hatchet and cut the line. The whale which was thrashing violently was thus separated from the boat. Finding the sea pouring in I ordered Johnson the bowman to bail and the rest to pull immediately for the ship.

3. We were troubled by high winds rough seas and the danger of capsizing but we managed to reach the ship. As I scrambled aboard I saw a huge sperm whale of a length so it seemed to me of about eighty-five feet. He broke water about twenty rods off our weather bow and was lying quietly with his head in the direction of the ship. He spouted two or three times and then suddenly charged at us. I shouted an order to young Tom the boy at the helm hoping to turn the ship in time. The words were scarcely out of my mouth when the whale came down upon us with full speed and struck the ship with his head just aft of the fore-chains with an appalling and tremendous crash. The ship brought up as suddenly and violently as if she had struck a rock and trembled for a few seconds like a leaf.

4. Longstreet the third mate shouted ''Mr. Chase we are lost!'' I ordered the pumps to be rigged at once although I could already see the head of the ship gradually settling down in the water. Again the monster broke water apparently in convulsions about one hundred rods to leeward. He was enveloped in sea-foam which his continual and violent thrashing had created around him and I could see him smite his jaws together as if insane with rage and fury. The ship had settled down a considerable distance in the water and I gave her up as lost. I had just ordered the longboats lowered when I heard a man at the hatchway cry ''Here he is Mr. Chase! He is attacking us again!'' I turned and saw him coming with twice his ordinary speed and it seemed to me at that moment with mad vengeance in his appearance. The surf flew in all directions and his path toward us was marked by a white foam

whipped by the violent thrashing of his tail. Then the ship took her second shuddering shock. We shoved our boats as quickly as possible into the water and launched off clear of the ship. We were scarcely away before the ship fell over to windward and sank below the surface of the sea.*

Certain generalizations about the comma can be stated with a fair degree of certainty. Before reviewing the exercises you have just completed, study these statements:

1. The comma is the most common, complex and troublesome of all marks of punctuation. The comma performs more functions and is governed by more rules than any other mark.

2. The comma occurs only in the interior of a sentence, never at its conclusion. Its many different uses can, therefore, be effectively reduced to one: *the comma is used to separate units of words from one another within a sentence.* Another way to say this is that a comma is used to separate *thoughts* from one another within a sentence.

3. There are three principal reasons for using commas to separate units of words:
   a. to show the reader the relationship between separate thoughts within a sentence.
   b. to avoid confusing the reader as to the meaning of the sentence.
   c. to indicate to the reader the proper places within a sentence to pause, or, if reading aloud, to draw a breath.

All three of these will be explained further and demonstrated; however, something should be said here about the importance of (c). It may seem to you that the first two reasons are much more important than the last, but keep in mind that it is only in the last fifty years or so that reading aloud has gone out of style. Before the advent of radio, and later of television, it was common for families to be entertained in the evening by one member reading

---

*The tragedy described here actually occurred. The passages have been freely adapted from the first-hand account of the shipwreck of the whaler *Essex* by her first mate, Owen Chase. The crew escaped in three boats under the command of Chase, Captain Pollard, and the second mate. Chase's boat was picked up at sea, as was that of Pollard, but not before two of its men died insane and were devoured by the survivors. Of the third boat nothing was ever heard.

a book aloud to the others. If today almost all our reading is done silently, we still pause mentally when a comma appears, just as we would pause orally if reading to an audience.

Furthermore, it is vital to remember that there is a close connection between oral pauses and punctuation. The latter is the written substitute for the former. When speaking or reading aloud, we have two principal reasons for pauses (aside from the occasional need to breathe). The first is to show the listener the relationship between separate thoughts. The second is to avoid confusing the listener as to the meaning of what we are saying or reading. Thus the relationships among these three reasons for comma usage are extremely close.

4. Unlike almost every other punctuation mark, the comma is often optional rather than required. While some comma rules demand that the mark be used, others are flexible, with the choice of whether to use the comma or not left up to the writer. More and more the modern trend is to use the comma less and less.

5. Many errors involving the comma arise from the failure to use it rather than the improper insertion of the mark.

6. Keeping all these points in mind, as we review the exercises concentrate less on the "rules" of comma usage than on the *actual function* of each comma in the narrative.

Uses of the comma illustrated

Here are the solutions to the exercises you completed earlier. Each portion of the text is reprinted with the commas inserted and numbered for identification. After each extract, there is an explanation of the reasons for the commas and some rules.

On Sunday,[1] November 20,[1] 1817,[1] the nightmare began.

1. These three commas separate all parts of a date from the rest of the sentence. Few students have difficulty placing the first two, but the third comma is often omitted. Remember:

☐ *A comma should be placed after each part of a date.*

Commas would also be used if the sentence read, "In November, 1817, the nightmare began."

A closely related rule is:

☐ *A comma should be placed after each part of an address.*

For example: The house at 32 Maple Street, Springfield, Illinois, was sold yesterday.

These rules are conventions and are therefore required.

The lookout at the masthead was scanning the horizon when,[2] at about 8 o'clock,[2] he discovered a shoal of whales off the lee bow.

2. The phrase "at about 8 o'clock" is set off by commas. To understand why, look at what the writer is doing in this sentence. His main purpose is to communicate to you that the lookout discovered a shoal of whales. He has decided (a) to give you an additional piece of information about this discovery, the time when it happened, and (b) to place that information in the middle of his sentence. Note two things about this phrase. First, it *interrupts* the communication of the main thought in the sentence. Second, it gives you information about that main thought.

Recall our discussion of modifying words in the segment on Context in Section II. We noted that a modifier is a word which *limits the meaning* of another word, making the meaning of the other word more precise. "Run swiftly" communicates a more precise meaning than the verb "run" alone. A "sloppy eater" tells more than the noun "eater" by itself.

Notice that, just as single words can be used to limit the meanings of other single words, *units of words can be used to limit the meanings of other units of words.* In this sentence, the phrase "at about 8 o'clock" limits the meaning of the main thought by telling *when* the action of the sentence occurred. The phrase tells when the whales were discovered.

If we seem to be spending too much time on these two little commas, bear with us; we are trying to explain the most complicated of all rules of comma placement.

We have established two facts about this phrase: it *modifies* the main thought or action of the sentence; and, because it is placed in the middle of the sentence, it *interrupts* the communication of the main thought or action. One more fact must be made clear. Although the phrase gives the reader additional information about the main action of the sentence, and although that information may be interesting, it is not crucial to a clear understanding of the main action. In other words, it is not necessary to know the time at which the whales were sighted in order to understand that they *were* sighted. To demonstrate this, simply read the sentence without the modifying phrase. "The lookout at the masthead was scanning the horizon when he discovered a shoal of whales off the lee bow." Even with the phrase omitted, the sentence makes perfectly good sense.

Because the phrase does not give information essential to understanding the main thought or action, the grammarian calls it a *nonessential modifying phrase*. Because it is placed in the middle of the sentence and interrupts the communication of the main thought or action, the grammarian calls it an *interrupting unit* or a *parenthetical expression*. In the exercise, the phrase must be set off by commas for both reasons, although either one would be reason enough. Remember:

☐ *All nonessential modifying word-units should be separated from the rest of the sentence by commas.*

☐ *All interrupting units (or single words used to interrupt a sentence) should be set off by commas.*

Study the samples below. The modifying word-units are in italics; if nonessential, they are set off by commas.

It is beginning to look as if the Green Bay Packers, *who dominated professional football in the 1960's,* are going to stage a comeback this season.

John Adams, *who was the first tenant of the White House,* is the elder half of America's only father-and-son team of Presidents.

People *who are fair skinned* are more likely to get sunburned.

Obviously, proper nouns usually do not require modification; general nouns often do. The proper names of the Green Bay Packers and John Adams serve to identify them fully, so the modifiers are nonessential. In these two samples, the sentences do not change meaning if the modifiers are omitted. In the third sample, the writer does not mean *all* people, but only those with fair skin. The modifier is essential; the meaning would be lost by omitting it. Use no commas.

Note that the first sample is a better sentence than the second because the information given in the modifying word-unit is *relevant* to the meaning of the entire sentence. To understand what the writer means by the word "comeback," it is helpful to know that the Packers once ruled the league. By contrast, the fact that John Adams was the first man to occupy the White House, while interesting, adds nothing to clarify the rest of the sentence. Modifying word-units are often nonessential, but they should never be irrelevant.

The usual cry,[3] "There she blows,"[3] echoed through the morning air.

3. As with dates and addresses, most students know that:

☐ *All direct quotations should be set off from the rest of the sentence by commas.*

The function of these commas is to separate the direct quotation clearly from the rest of the sentence for the reader's eye. Notice that the commas both immediately precede and immediately follow the direct quotation. The most common error is to place the following comma outside the quotation marks. Remember this simple rule: *all commas are always placed* inside *the quotation marks.*

When our ship had reached within half a mile of the place where the whales were sighted,[4] all our boats were lowered in pursuit.

4. The main purpose of this sentence is to tell you that "all our boats were lowered." Before the writer communicates this fact, however, he chooses to give you additional information in a long word-unit placed at the beginning of the sentence. This additional information modifies the main action of the sentence by telling you when the boats were lowered. They were lowered "when our ship had reached within half a mile of the place where the whales were sighted." (See also the rule under 16.)

The situation is very similar to that discussed above under number 2. The main difference is the placement of the modifying word-unit at the beginning of the sentence instead of in the middle. It is an *introductory* word-unit rather than an interrupting word-unit, but the modifier is again nonessential; that is, the additional information in the introductory unit is not needed to make the meaning of the main part of the sentence clear. This is the rule:

☐ *Introductory word-units should be separated from the main part of the sentence by a comma.*

The ship,[5] in the meantime,[5] was brought to the wind to wait for us.

5. The phrase "in the meantime" is both *interrupting* and *non-essential.* (See the rules under 2.)

I had the harpoon in the first boat. When we reached the spot where we thought they were,[6] nothing could be seen.

6. The clause "When we reached the spot where we thought they were" is *introductory* to the main part of the sentence. (See the rule under 4.)

We lay on our oars in anxious anticipation,[7] and soon a whale rose and spouted a short distance away.

7. This sentence is made by putting two main actions together and joining them with the word "and." The two main actions are "we lay on our oars" and "a whale rose and spouted." This is a common sentence construction. In addition to "and," words used to join two main actions into one sentence are "but," "for," "or," "nor," "so," "yet." The comma functions to emphasize the distinction between the two main actions for the reader's eye, and thus for his mind.

☐ *Use a comma to separate main actions joined together in the same sentence by* and, but, for, or, nor, so, yet.

This rule is often optional. The comma need not be used if the sentence is short enough to read comfortably and naturally in one breath.

I made for the beast,[8] came up beside him,[8] and hurled the harpoon.

8. The rule for these commas is:

☐ *Use commas to separate words or units of words in a series.*

The sentence communicates three actions in a series. A comma is needed to separate the first two actions. The comma before the final item in a series is optional and can be omitted unless some confusion in meaning would result. Similarly, commas separate words in a series: *men, women, boys, and girls; the red, white, and blue flag; one, two, or three units.* (The last comma in each series is optional.)

Feeling the spear in him,[9] he threw himself in an agony toward the boat.

9. The rule applied here is the one governing introductory word-units. (See under 4.)

A severe blow from his tail struck the boat[10] and stove a hole in her.

10. No comma should be used in the space marked 10. At first glance, it may seem to you that the rule governing the separation of main actions (discussed under 7) requires a comma here. The rule does not apply to this sentence because here both actions are performed by the same subject (the "blow").

There is a simple way to test for whether or not to use a comma in cases like this. Remove the connecting word (in this case "and") from the sentence. Then write the two remaining parts of the sentence as if they were separate sentences. If they make sense as separate sentences, the rule applies and the comma should be used. If one of them does not make sense as a separate sentence, do not insert the comma.

Look at these two examples. "We lay on our oars in anxious anticipation." (Makes sense.) "Soon a whale rose and spouted a short distance away." (Makes sense.) *Conclusion:* Comma should be used. "A severe blow from his tail struck the boat." (Makes sense.) "Stove a hole in her." (Does not make sense.) *Conclusion:* Do not use a comma.

The difference between the two sample sentences, as you may have observed, is that although each tells you of two separate actions, the actions of the first sentence are performed by separate subjects, "we" and "a whale." In the second sentence, the two actions are performed by the same subject, the "severe blow."

I seized the hatchet and cut the line. The whale,[11] which was thrashing violently,[11] was thus separated from the boat.

11. The rule applied here is the one governing interrupting word-units. (See under 2.)

Finding the sea pouring in,[12] I ordered Johnson,[13] the bowman,[13] to bail and the rest to pull immediately for the ship.

12. The rule applied here is the one governing introductory word-units. (See under 4.)

13. To understand what these commas are doing here, you must first understand what an appositive is. An *appositive* is a noun or pronoun which has the same meaning as another noun or pronoun and is placed immediately after it in a sentence. In the sentence from the exercise, Johnson *is* the bowman. The words "Johnson" and "bowman" refer to the same man and, therefore, convey the same meaning. Since "the bowman" is placed immediately after "Johnson" in the sentence, it is an appositive. This is the rule:

☐ *Use commas to set off an appositive from the rest of the sentence.*

The function of the commas is to avoid confusion. If they were omitted, the reader might assume that Johnson and the bowman were two different people. The commas make clear that both words refer to the same man. Study the following samples. The appositives are in italics.

I have no intention of paying my mechanic, *"Honest John" Grogan,* the ransom he is demanding for the safe return of my car.

Al Freeman, *the sales manager at Merrimac Inc.,* just became a grandfather.

Let's be grateful that the ecologists, *those people we all ignored for years,* have finally begun to be heard.

George Washington, *our first President,* had wooden teeth.

We were troubled by high winds,[14] rough seas,[14] and the danger of capsizing,[15] but we managed to reach the ship.

14. The rule applied here is the one governing items in a series. (See under 8.)

15. The rule applied here is the one governing the separation of main actions. (See under 7.)

As I scrambled aboard,[16] I saw a huge sperm whale of a length,[17] so it seemed to me,[17] of about eighty-five feet.

16. The rule applied here governs introductory word-units (discussed under 4); however, this comma is strictly optional. When an introductory unit is short, less than six words, it is normally possible to omit the comma unless that would confuse the meaning of the sentence. Since the recent trend is to use fewer commas, this comma would normally not be used. It is not, however, wrong to place a comma here.

17. The rule applied here is the one governing interrupting word-units. (See under 2.)

He broke water about twenty rods off our weather bow[18] and was lying quietly with his head in the direction of the ship.

18. No comma should be used here. See the discussion under 10.

He spouted two or three times and then suddenly charged at us. I shouted an order to young Tom,[19] the boy at the helm,[19] hoping to turn the ship in time.

19. The rule applied here is the one governing appositives. (See under 13.)

The words were scarcely out of my mouth when the whale came down upon us with full speed and struck the ship with his head just aft of the fore-chains with an appalling and tremendous crash.[20]

20. Although this sentence is quite long, it is not interrupted by commas. This is an example of the writer using punctuation as a tool to increase the effectiveness of his communication of ideas. The sentence describes a swift and violent action, the ramming of the ship by the whale. To increase the reader's sense of the sudden speed of this action, the writer does not allow any pauses in the sentence. Read the sentence aloud. Since it contains

no commas, it does not permit you to pause for breath. This forces you to increase the speed at which you are reading (so as to reach the period and take a breath) and thus increases your sense of the speed of the action described. The same effect is obtained even if you read the sentence silently.

> The ship brought up as suddenly and violently as if she had struck a rock[21] and trembled for a few seconds like a leaf.

21. No comma is needed here. See the discussion under 10.

> Longstreet,[22] the third mate,[22] shouted,[23] "Mr. Chase,[24] we are lost!"

22. The rule applied here is the one governing appositives. (See under 13.)

23. The rule applied here is the one governing the use of commas to introduce direct quotations. (See under 3.)

24. This serves to introduce another rule:

☐ *Expressions of direct address are set off by commas.*

Since the third mate addresses the writer as "Mr. Chase," the expression of direct address must be separated from the rest of the sentence by commas. The function of the comma is to avoid confusion. By showing that Mr. Chase's name is used in direct address, the comma tells the reader that the speaker is talking *to* Chase, not *about* him.

> I ordered the pumps to be rigged at once although I could already see the head of the ship gradually settling down in the water.[25]

25. Compare the following sentence with the one from the exercise. "Although I could already see the head of the ship gradually settling down in the water, I ordered the pumps to be rigged at once." As you can see, it merely reverses the order of the word-units so that the main action of the sentence occurs after an introductory word-unit. Had the sentence in the exercise been written this way, the comma after "water" would be required by the rule governing introductory word-units. However, because the main action of the sentence is placed first, the comma is only optional, and it is preferable to omit it.

Again the monster broke water,[26] apparently in convulsions,[26] about one hundred rods to leeward.

26. The rule applied here is the one governing interrupting word-units. (See under 2.)

He was enveloped in sea-foam which his continual and violent thrashing had created around him,[27] and I could see him smite his jaws together as if insane with rage and fury. The ship had settled down a considerable distance in the water,[27] and I gave her up as lost.

27. The rule applied here is the one governing the separation of main actions discussed under 7. Because the second part of the second sentence is short, the comma there is optional.

I had just ordered the long-boats lowered when I heard a man at the hatchway cry,[28] "Here he is,[29] Mr. Chase! He is attacking us again!"

28. The rule applied here is the one governing direct quotation. (See under 3.)

29. The rule applied here is the one governing direct address. (See under 24.)

I turned and saw him coming with twice his ordinary speed and,[30] it seemed to me at that moment,[30] with mad vengeance in his appearance.

30. The rule applied here is the one governing interrupting word-units. (See under 2.)

The surf flew in all directions,[31] and his path toward us was marked by a white foam whipped by the violent thrashing of his tail.

31. The rule applied here is the one governing separation of main actions. (See under 7.)

Then the ship took her second,[32] shuddering shock.

32. Here the comma gives extra weight to the second modifier, *shuddering*. As a similar example, compare *the big red house* and *the big, red house*.

We shoved our boats as quickly as possible into the water[33] and launched off clear of the ship. We were scarcely away before the ship fell over to windward[33] and sank below the surface of the sea.

33. No commas are needed here. (See under 10.)

RECAPITULATION OF COMMA RULES

1. A comma should be placed after each part of a date and after each part of an address.
2. All nonessential modifying word-units should be separated from the rest of the sentence by commas.
3. All interrupting units (or single words used to interrupt a sentence) should be set off by commas.
4. All direct quotations should be set off from the rest of the sentence by commas.
5. Introductory word-units should be separated from the main part of the sentence by a comma.
6. Use a comma to separate main actions joined together in the same sentence by *and, but, for, or, nor, so, yet.*
7. Use commas to separate words or units of words in a series.
8. Use commas to set off an appositive from the rest of the sentence.
9. Expressions of direct address are set off by commas.

FOLLOW-UP

1. *In the following paragraphs all the commas are placed correctly and identified by letters of the alphabet. On a separate sheet of paper, match the commas with the number of the rule being applied. Then check the answers at the bottom of page 254.*

a. I hate mowing the lawn,[A] washing the car,[B] and walking the dog,[C] but the worst job of all is taking out the garbage. My mother never says,[D] "Harry,[E] take out the garbage,"[F] when she wants it done. My mother,[G] who isn't very subtle,[H] drops hints like,[I] "Harry,[J] the garbage bag is full." Whenever I get comfortably settled in front of the television or finally work up the will power to do some homework,[K] dear old Mom,[L] with her great sense of timing,[M] discovers that the garbage bag is full. I complain as loudly as possible,[N] but I get up and go out to struggle with melon rinds,[O] chicken bones,[P] milk cartons and lemon peels.

b. Dear old Mom,[A] who has had years of experience with trash,[B] has developed her own technique for filling garbage bags. First she puts something wet in the bottom of the bag,[C] and the result,[D] as my bitter experience has proved,[E] is that the bottom soaks through and drops out before I reach the trash can. When the bag is completely sopping,[F] my mother puts in the messiest stuff imaginable,[G] usually coffee grounds or left-over oatmeal,[H] something that's impossible to pick up after the bag breaks. Finally,[I] to guarantee that the bag will break,[J] she puts the heaviest trash on top. When Abraham Lincoln was my age he would walk five miles to borrow a book and ten miles to return a nickle change,[K] and they elected him President. I guess if he'd ever had to walk ten feet with my mother's garbage they'd have made him king.

2. *Working with another student as your partner, select some unedited first drafts from your folder. The instructor will have copies made for your partner. Read your papers aloud while your partner listens for your natural pauses and inserts (or removes) commas in his copy. Go over the papers together and try to determine which comma rules you are applying. The nine rules we have listed cover most but not all uses of the comma, so do not be surprised if one or two of your commas cannot be explained by any of the rules. Repeat the editing process with your partner's paper. Then check your work with the instructor.*

The Semicolon and the Run-on Sentence

Before we consider the semicolon (;) and the problem of the run-on sentence, take the following quiz.

For each of these word-units simply note whether it is a complete sentence or not. Write your answers on a separate sheet of paper. The correct answers will be given to you later.

1. Beyond the fact that Tom Harrison is a swindler, an outrageous liar, and a nincompoop.

2. Get out of here!

3. Did you know that tomatoes are more fattening than ice cream?

4. Some days it doesn't pay to get out of bed.

5. Even though you were once in France for three whole days.

6. On top of everything else, he doesn't even have the money he owes me.

7. Six months in a rest home with plenty to eat and the birds singing.

8. Although the surf is up and the sun is shining.

9. Whether or not you complete the test successfully.

10. Keeping the house in order, trying to shop for the best values, putting three meals on the table for five hungry kids, and doing the best I can to hold this family together!

11. Are you coming to the movie or not?

12. In spite of getting a good night's sleep the night before.

13. To keep yourself in the best possible condition.

14. Don't tell me she still isn't ready to go!

15. I'd swap my whole collection of *Porky Pig* comics for a first edition of *Plastic Man Meets the Green Ghouls from Saturn*.

16. After Bill and Jeff left the house.

17. When you told me what Marge had said about Alice.

18. Perhaps doing assignments on time and studying hard for your examinations for a change.

19. Medicine or possibly law.

20. Because the train was late in arriving.

Here is a final, related question. Select the answer which best concludes this statement: A word-unit is a complete sentence if (a) it begins with a capital letter and ends with a period, question mark or exclamation point (b) it expresses a complete idea and makes sense (c) it contains a subject and a predicate verb.

Put your answers aside for the moment and reread the com-

Answers to paragraph a: A/7 B/7 C/6 D/4 E/9 F/4 G/2 H/2 I/4 J/9 K/5 L/3 M/3 N/6 O/7 P/7

Answers to paragraph b: A/2 B/2 C/6 D/3 E/3 F/5 G/8 H/8 I/3 J/3 K/5

ments on determining whether or not to use a comma in separating main actions (number 10 on page 247). We suggested that the most effective way to determine if a sentence expressed two complete main actions was to remove the connecting word and look at the two remaining word-units to see if they made sense as separate sentences. Study carefully the examples there.

Now reconsider the final question we just asked. The correct answer is (b). It is true that a complete sentence should begin with a capital letter and end with a period, a question mark or an exclamation point. But any group of words may be punctuated in this way and thus made to *look* like a complete sentence without actually being one. All twenty word-groups in the exercise are punctuated in this manner, yet only seven are actually sentences.

It is also true that a complete sentence must contain a subject and a predicate verb, but a word-group may contain a subject and a predicate verb and still not be a complete sentence. Seven word-groups in the exercise contain subjects and verbs but are not complete sentences. (The seven are numbers 1, 5, 8, 9, 16, 17 and 20.)

To be a complete sentence, a word-group must, above all, express a complete idea and *make sense*. It must, therefore, be *independent of its context*. This means that it must make sense to the reader even if he reads it without knowing what words precede or follow it. We have already seen, in Section II, how words often depend for their meaning on the context of the other words within which they are read. *Dependent* word-groups also *depend* for their meaning on the context of other word-groups within which they are read. Study these examples:

1. *Beyond the fact that Tom Harrison is a swindler, an outrageous liar, and a nincompoop,* I have nothing against him at all.

5. You don't know anything about Frenchmen, *even though you were once in France for three whole days.*

7. What I really need is *six months in a rest home with plenty to eat and the birds singing.*

8. *Although the surf is up and the sun is shining*, I'm not going to the beach today.

9. *Whether or not you complete the test successfully* will determine whether you pass this course.

10. What's driving me crazy is *keeping the house in order, trying to shop for the best values, putting three meals on the table for five hungry kids, and doing the best I can to hold this family together!*

12. *In spite of getting a good night's sleep the night before,* I did miserably in the tournament.

13. *To keep yourself in the best possible condition,* jog.

16. *After Bill and Jeff left the house,* it began to rain.

17. I was amazed *when you told me what Marge had said about Alice.*

18. *Perhaps doing assignments on time and studying hard for your examinations for a change* will finally get you a diploma.

19. I am planning on a career in *medicine or possibly law.*

20. *Because the train was late in arriving,* we sat around the station for almost three hours.

The only complete sentences in the quiz were numbers 2, 3, 4, 6, 11, 14 and 15. None of the other word-groups made sense until it was provided with a context, a second word-group. Look at the samples above. In every case the word-group in italics depends on the other word-group for its meaning. None of these word-groups by itself made clear sense. We can say that these are all *dependent* word-groups. By contrast, the complete sentences in the exercise are not dependent on a context. They communicate a clear meaning by themselves. It is simple logic to call them *independent* word-groups.

Note that sentences may contain dependent word-groups, but a complete sentence must contain at least one independent word-group, and it must *make sense* even if read without a context.

Run-on sentences

If this much is clear, we are ready to look at the run-on sentence. We have seen that a sentence should begin with a capital letter and end with a period (or question mark or exclamation point). *A run-on sentence is two complete sentences punctuated as if they were one sentence.* Another way to define a run-on is as two independent word-groups punctuated as if they were one. Study the following statements:

1. Never write run-on sentences they are serious errors.

2. Some students use a comma to separate independent word-groups, a comma alone is not enough.

3. There are three ways to separate independent word-groups. One is to put a period after the first unit and capitalize the first letter of the second unit.

4. You may use a comma to separate the two units, but you must also use a connecting word like *but.*

5. A third method is to insert a semicolon between the two units; use this only if the meanings of the two units are closely related.

You have noticed that the first two statements are examples of the two most common kinds of run-ons: the run-on without any punctuation and the run-on using only a comma. The last three are examples of the three methods of correcting a run-on. If the two word-groups are particularly long, it is usually best to write them as separate sentences. It is also acceptable to separate them with a comma and a connecting word (grammarians call connecting words *conjunctions*). These conjunctions include *and, but, for, or, nor, so, yet.* (See number 7, page 246, for a discussion of this use of the comma.)

Use of the semicolon is by far the least common of the three methods. The easiest way to correct the run-on is to put a dot above the misused comma and convert it into a semicolon, but the semicolon should be used only when the word-units are not especially long and only when the meanings of the two units are closely related. There are no hard and fast rules about this; it is chiefly a matter of using common sense.

It is important to understand the run-on because many instructors consider it the single most serious punctuation error. There is good reason for this. The more a mechanical error confuses the meaning you are trying to communicate, the more serious the error is. A run-on, by jamming two independent thoughts together into what looks *to the reader's eye* like a single unit, makes it difficult for the reader's mind to distinguish between the two thoughts. The effect is similar to a double-exposure photograph. When you look at a double exposure your eye has trouble distinguishing between the two images in the picture. Neither image is seen clearly. As a result, your mind cannot understand either image clearly. A run-on has the same effect of blurring two ideas in the reader's eye, and thus also in his mind. (For additional discussion of the correlation between the eye's perceptions and those of the mind, see pages 36–37.)

Other uses of the semicolon

We have mentioned one use of the semicolon, to separate independent word-units. There are two others, closely related, which should be discussed.

Normally, when two independent word-units are joined by a connecting word or conjunction they should be separated by a comma. (See the discussion of this rule on page 246, number 7.) However, *when the independent word-units themselves contain commas, they should be separated by a connecting word and a semicolon.* If you think about this rule, you will see that it is common sense to avoid confusion. Study this example:

> The champion,[A] who had trained harder for this bout than ever before in his career,[B] fought brilliantly; but McGuire,[C] with an advantage of height and weight,[D] was not to be denied the title.

By now, of course, you have mastered the comma and you knew at once that commas A and B set off a nonessential word-unit, while C and D set off an interrupting word-unit. (If this did not flash across your mind, reread number 2, pages 243–245.) The sample sentence is made up of two independent units. Each unit contains commas within itself. If the writer had used *yet another comma* to separate the two independent units of the sentence, your eye would have difficulty distinguishing between them. Therefore he used a different, stronger punctuation mark—the semicolon. Had he revised his sentence to remove the interruptive word-groups, the comma would have been used.

> The champion fought brilliantly, but McGuire was not to be denied the title.

Normally, word-units listed in a series are separated by commas. (See the rule under number 8, page 247.) However, when the word-units in a series themselves contain commas they should be separated by semicolons. Study these examples:

McGuire was driven to seek the championship by a fierce pride,[A] instilled by his manager; a simmering violence,[B] natural to him; and a constant need for money,[C] the result of his expensive habits.

Pick up Jim,[D] Larry and Bob at Bob's house; Frank,[D] Jack Adams and Jack Melton at the ball field; and Willy,[D] Les,[D] Gary and Ted at the corner of Glenwood and Oak.

Both sentences are correctly punctuated and typical of the samples used in textbooks to illustrate this rule, but please notice that they are bad sentences. Each is unnecessarily cluttered and complicated. It is fine to understand the rules of the semicolon and to use it correctly. An excessive use of the semicolon, however, often means that the writer is trying to jam too much information into his sentences. His style can become cumbersome and his meanings difficult to follow. A beginning writer is wise to use the semicolon sparingly. (Note, by the way, that commas A and B set off nonessential units, C sets off an appositive, and D separates items in a series.)

The Colon

The colon (:) has only two principal uses: it introduces formal quotations and formal promises of information. (This sentence is an example of the "formal promise of information." Information promised in the first part of the sentence is given, following the colon, in the second part.) Study these examples:

1. Study these examples: (This statement promises that examples will follow. The colon indicates to the reader that he may expect the writer to provide immediately the information he has promised.)

2. There are two things to remember when you visit New York: don't drink the water and don't breathe the air.

3. The following men have guard duty tonight: Davidson, Reynolds, Traynor and Smith.

The second use of the colon is to introduce formal quotations. A "formal quotation" is the direct quotation of written material or of a formal address or lecture (as opposed to the quotation of dialogue). (Compare this rule with the comma rule discussed in paragraph 3 on page 245.)

Study these examples:

1. In his summation before the jury, Bailey thundered: "There can be no question in the mind of any reasonable man that my client is being railroaded by the prosecution!"

2. In his latest book, Wheelwright states: "History will prove that America's greatest President was Millard Fillmore."

The Dash

The dash (—) is one of the most useful and effective marks of punctuation. It is also, unfortunately, one of the least used by student writers. Next to *clarity,* the most important effect to be aimed at by a writer is *emphasis.* Before studying the following statements, you might want to reread the discussion of punctuation as a tool to serve the writer on pages 30–35.

Interrupting word-units

Interrupting word-units are used in sentences to provide additional information about the ideas being communicated in those sentences. (Reread the discussion of interrupting word-units on pages 243–245, number 2.)

By giving the reader additional information about the main thought or action communicated by the sentence, these interrupting units modify, or limit the meaning, of the main thought or action. This is true whether the additional information is essential or nonessential. In fact the terms essential and nonessential are technical terms, useful only in determining whether or not the modifying word-unit should be set off by commas. But all interrupting modifiers, whether technically essential or nonessential, should supply the reader with additional information which it is *important* for him to know. Look at the following examples.

1. Dwight Eisenhower, who had been a five-star general in the army, warned America against the growing power of the military-industrial complex.

(We know who Eisenhower was. His name is enough to identify him. Technically, therefore, the modifying word-group is nonessential. But it is *important* to remind the reader that Eisenhower was a top-ranking military officer, whether the reader already knows it or not, because his position makes his warning against the military's power all the more significant.)

2. The United States, proud of being founded on the principal of liberty and justice for *all*, did not abolish slavery until December 18, 1865.

(Technically the modifying word-group is nonessential because we all know what the United States is without the need for modifiers. But note that if the modifying words are removed, the sentence, while it still communicates a comprehensible meaning, loses all the sarcastic sting intended by the writer. Compare the mild, merely factual tone of this sentence: The United States did not abolish slavery until December 18, 1865. It has all the irony and emotional impact of a shopping list.)

3. Congressman Logjam, who delivered an impassioned speech on behalf of law and order on Monday, was arrested on Tuesday for income tax evasion.

(Compare: Congressman Logjam was arrested on Tuesday for income tax evasion.)

4. Martin Luther King, who was a leading advocate of nonviolence, was shot to death in Memphis.

(Compare: Martin Luther King was shot to death in Memphis.)

To repeat, all interrupting modifiers, whether technically essential or nonessential, should supply the reader with information which it is *important* for him to know. This rule is followed in the four examples above. It is *not* followed in the four examples below.

1. Dwight Eisenhower, who married a girl named Mamie, warned America against the growing power of the military-industrial complex.

2. The United States, a country bounded on the north by Canada, did not abolish slavery until December 18, 1865.

3. Congressman Logjam, who roots for the Los Angeles Dodgers, was arrested on Tuesday for income tax evasion.

4. Martin Luther King, who was born in 1929, was shot to death in Memphis.

Dashes and interrupting word-units

There are three ways to set off interrupting modifying word-units within a sentence: with commas, with parentheses, and with dashes. Commas are used when the additional information is nonessential and fits easily into the structure of the sentence (see pages 244–245). Parentheses are used when the additional material is to be de-emphasized (see pages 265–266). Dashes are used in place of commas when the writer wishes to draw the reader's attention specifically to the additional information. *The dash is used to call close attention to the word-unit which it sets off.* Look at these examples:

1. Dwight Eisenhower—who had been a five-star general in the army—warned America against the growing power of the military-industrial complex.

2. The United States—proud of being founded on the principal of liberty and justice for *all*—did not abolish slavery until December 18, 1865.

3. Congressman Logjam—who delivered an impassioned speech on behalf of law and order on Monday—was arrested on Tuesday for income tax evasion.

4. Martin Luther King—who was a leading advocate of nonviolence—was shot to death in Memphis.

We can conclude that one use of the dash is *to give emphasis to interrupting modifiers which the writer considers particularly important to a communication of his meaning.*

The dash is also used to show an abrupt and premature *conclusion* or *transition* of a statement or thought:

1. "You fiend," he cried. "You filthy, horrible, loathsome—" But my fingers had closed like cords around his throat.

2. She said that the greatest curse on her family was—no, I have no right to reveal her secret.

3. "Mr. Jones, I'd like to ask for Mary's hand in—that is, your daughter and I have decided to—what I want to say, sir, is that you've raised a heck of a swell kid and—actually the point I'm trying to make is that Mary is the mother of my child—I mean, sir, the girl I want for the mother of my children—if—of course—we should have any children—sir—that is—and, so, Mr. Jones, I'd like to ask for Mary's hand in—what? No, sir, no more coffee, thank you. Mr. Jones—?"

The Ellipsis

The ellipsis (. . .), instead of the dash, should be used to indicate a *premature,* but *gradual* conclusion of a statement or thought. "I suppose you're right and yet . . . ." The speaker does not stop abruptly but trails off slowly. Notice also that you must use four dots when an ellipsis is placed at the end of the sentence. The first three dots are the ellipsis while the fourth is the period. *Ellipsis is also used to indicate omission of part of a quotation.* Often it is advisable, in quoting a source directly, to eliminate from the quotation any material which is not relevant to the topic of your paper. Too many times students quote an entire passage from a source whether the entire passage has any bearing on the subject or not. Study the following examples:

> The *original source:* "The major newspapers in New York during the mid-eighteen hundreds were the *Sun,* the *Herald,* the *Tribune* and the *Evening Tattler,* edited respectively by Moses Beach, James Gordon Bennett, Horace Greeley and Benjamin Day, each of whom had played an important role in establishing the popular press."

Suppose that the purpose of your paper is to discuss important figures in New York journalism during the nineteenth century. Your quotation might read:

> "The major newspapers in New York during the mid-eighteen hundreds were . . . edited . . . by Moses Beach, James Gordon Bennett, Horace Greeley and Benjamin Day . . . ."

Note that the ellipsis is used to replace words omitted from the *middle* of a quoted sentence. Note that when the ellipsis indicates omission of the *final* words of a sentence, the three dots of the ellipsis are joined to a fourth dot which serves as a period.

Suppose that the purpose of your paper is to discuss the important newspapers of the nineteenth century. Your quotation might read:

> "The major newspapers in New York during the mid-eighteen hundreds were the *Sun*, the *Herald*, the *Tribune* and the *Evening Tattler.* . . ."

Suppose that the purpose of your paper is to discuss one important newspaper and its editor. Your quotation might read:

> One of "the major newspapers in New York during the mid-eighteen hundreds" was "the *Evening Tattler*, edited by . . . Benjamin Day . . . ."

Quotation Marks

Quotation marks (") are used to enclose direct quotations. Most difficulties arise from not knowing whether to put other punctuation inside or outside the quotation marks. Some students try to solve the problem by putting the punctuation directly below the quotation marks. Forget it. Your instructor is on to that trick, and besides, directly below the quotation marks is just where no punctuation is ever placed. The rules are so simple anyway that you do not need any tricks.

☐ *Place all commas and periods* inside *quotation marks.*
☐ *Place all colons and semicolons* outside *quotation marks.*

Not very confusing so far, is it? The next rule is a bit more complicated but hardly complex. Study these examples:

1. Tom asked, "What time are we expected to land in San Francisco?"

2. Tom looked up at me suddenly. "What time are we expected to land in San Francisco?"

3. Was it Melville who said, "Truth, who loves to be centrally located, is found between two extremes"?

In *1* and *2* the question mark appears within the quotation marks, while in *3* it is outside. In *1* only the word-group inside the quotation marks actually forms a question. In *2* the entire sentence is a question and also a direct quotation. In sample *3*, however, the question mark is placed *outside* the quotation marks. (The question is expressed in the words "Was it Melville who said . . . .")

☐ *If the sentence that contains the quotation is a question, but the quotation itself is not a question, the question mark goes* outside *the quotation marks.*

☐ *If the quotation itself is a question, the question mark goes* inside *the quotation marks, whether or not the sentence is a question.*

The same rules hold for the exclamation point:

1. Tom cried, "We'll never reach San Francisco alive!"
2. Tom looked up at me suddenly. "We'll never reach San Francisco alive!"
3. It was *definitely* Melville who said, "Truth, who loves to be centrally located, is found between two extremes"!

When you are quoting an author who is quoting another author, enclose the internal quotation in single quotation marks:

As Professor Wright has written, "It was Dr. Hall who said that 'a single quotation mark is made on the typewriter by hitting the apostrophe key.'"

Parentheses

On page 262 we stated that there were three ways to set off interrupting word-units which contain additional information. Use commas when the interruptive unit fits easily into the structure of the sentence. Use dashes when you want to call special attention to the interruptive unit, to emphasize it. But if you want to *de-emphasize* the interruptive unit, set it off within parentheses.

Again we must consider the effect of punctuation on the eye of the reader, and therefore on his mind. When a word-unit is set off by commas, it looks to the reader's eye like "just another part of the sentence." He neither pays special attention to it nor ignores it. If the unit is set off by dashes, it attracts his special attention. However, if the interruptive unit, while offering additional information, is not at all important to understanding the meaning of the sentence, it should be placed inside parentheses. While the reader's eye—and thus his mental attention—is commanded by dashes, he tends merely to glance (according to Dr. Fritz Klonzinbee of Harvard) at matter enclosed in parentheses.

Reread the last sentence. Note that the information set off by dashes is very important to the meaning of the sentence, while that enclosed in parentheses is extraneous; that is, it is information which is not in any way needed to make the meaning of the sentence clearer.

The Apostrophe:
Possessives and Contractions

The rules for forming possessives are simple and should be familiar to you. Normally you merely add an apostrophe and an *s* ('s).

men's jobs   deer's antlers   doctor's patient

If the noun already ends with an *s,* all you add is the apostrophe.

teachers' convention   friends' party   boys' track team

Contractions are a language shorthand by which two words, since they are often used together, are combined into a single word for convenience. One or more letters are omitted and this omission is identified by an apostrophe.

is not = isn't   she will = she'll   we have = we've

Italics

Italics are indicated on the typewriter by underlining the word.

Italics are used to direct the <u>special</u> <u>attention</u> of the reader to certain words because of their <u>importance</u>

or to indicate that a <u>particular</u> <u>emphasis</u> should be given to the words.

Italics are thus very useful in pointing up your most important ideas to the reader.

Italics and Quotation Marks in Indicating Titles

Titles of the following should be written in italics (or underscored when typewritten):

Books: *Huckleberry Finn*
Periodicals: *Sports Illustrated*
Newspapers: *Newark Star-Ledger*
Dramas: *King Lear*

Titles of the following should be set off by quotation marks:

Articles: "Twain's Use of Dialect in *Huckleberry Finn*"
Short stories: "Young Goodman Brown"; "The Tell-tale Heart"
Poems: "Ode on a Grecian Urn"; "Song of Myself"
Chapter titles: "The Rattlesnake Skin Does Its Work"; "The Whiteness of the Whale"

Numerous examples of titles are shown in Appendix B on pages 296–302.

Agreement of Subject and Verb

Probably the three grammatical errors considered most serious by instructors are run-on sentences (pages 256–258), disagreement of subject and verb (pages 267–269), and disagreement of pronoun and referent (page 269).

As for the agreement of subject and verb, the rule is not complicated:

☐ *Subjects may be singular or plural. Verbs may be singular or plural. If a subject is singular, its verb should be singular. If a subject is plural, its verb should be plural.*

Study the following exercise and note your answers on a separate sheet of paper. For each sentence, decide whether the verb agrees or disagrees with the subject.

1. The dogs roams around the yard during the day.
2. Both cars rides well with normal care.
3. The horse run best on a muddy track.
4. Our pigs grunts at the normal feeding time.
5. His clock keep perfect time.

These are very simple, and if you had any trouble with them you know that you are going to need special instruction. All five sentences are wrong. Write them correctly (answers are at the bottom of this page) and then note these points:

1. Almost all problems of subject-verb agreement occur *only when the verb is in the present tense*. The major exception is the verb *to be*.

2. Most nouns become plural by the addition of the letter *s*. The singular form of present tense of most verbs is formed by adding the letter *s*. There are so many exceptions to these rules that we can formulate no hard and fast rule for subject-verb agreement from them; however, you should always suspect an error of agreement when both, or neither, subject and verb conclude with an *s*. (Study the answers at the bottom of this page.)

3. When any of the following words is the subject of a verb, the verb should be singular. Each of these words refers to an individual in the singular:

anyone	someone	everyone	none
anybody	somebody	everybody	one
another	either	no one	
each	neither	nobody	

4. The verb *to be* is an exception to rule 1. Although most verbs

have separate spellings for singular and plural in the present tense only ("one *is*," "two *are*"), *to be* has separate spellings also for the past tense ("one *was*," "two *were*"). Agreement of subject and forms of the verb *to be* should be studied carefully.

Agreement of Pronoun and Referent

1. The *referent* of a pronoun is the noun or pronoun to which the pronoun refers (that is, "means the same as").

2. If the referent is singular the pronoun must be singular. If the referent is plural the pronoun must also be plural.

In the following sentences the *pronoun* is in italics and the REFERENT is in small capitals:

The NATIONAL FOOTBALL LEAGUE holds *its* Super Bowl in January.

POLITICIANS must make *their* campaign expenses a matter of public record.

EVERYONE has *his* own favorite recipe for chicken.

EACH of the members present had *his* own opinion of the problem.

3. Reread the list of singular pronouns on page 268. Each pronoun on the list, when used as a referent, takes a singular pronoun. Most students have little difficulty with this rule. The pronoun referents which give the most trouble are *each, everyone, everybody* and *none*. Study the last two examples above.

Check yourself on the following exercise: are the pronouns in italics correct or not? (The answers are at the bottom of page 270.)

1. Everybody who doesn't have *his* cap and gown already rented should send *his* money in by tomorrow.

2. None of the men in the graduating class has ordered *his* cap and gown yet.

3. Each of the students has *his* reasons for not ordering a cap and gown.

4. Everyone knows that *he* must have a cap and gown for graduation.

Word Division

One obvious problem students have when typing a term paper is where to divide words when they approach the right-hand margin. The following rules are a guide to correct word division. If at all possible, do not divide words at the end of your typing line. It is better to go a space or two beyond your margin, or stop a space or two before your margin, than to divide a word.

1. Words should only be divided between syllables.
2. Words of six letters or less should not be divided.
3. Leave at least three letters on the preceding line.
4. Bring down no less than three letters to the following line.
5. Divide words between double consonants when the division does not interfere with a root word. The examples below are all divided correctly.

bet-ting	let-ting	forgot-ten	pos-sible
fill-ing	drill-ing	bill-ing	drug-gist
cor-rect	dap-per	mal-lard	

6. Divide compound words between the words in the compound. Hyphenated words are divided at the point of hyphenation. The following examples are all divided correctly.

man-handle	self-centered	business-like	has-been
man-hood	plow-man	over-time	over-work
still-born	flood-light		

7. If you still have doubts about the division of a particular word, check it in any good dictionary.

Capitalization

It is important to capitalize properly. The following are basic rules to use when typing a term paper:

1. Capitalize the titles of military, professional, executive, and religious persons.

Answer: All four sentences are correct.

General Arthur Johnson   Pope Paul
Commander Paul Castellano the Reverend John Wilson
Professor William Goione   Rabbi Schwartz
President Richard Nixon
President Thomas Richardson of Montclair State College

2. Capitalize the names of individuals.

3. Capitalize days of the week, months of the year, and holidays.

January Monday Easter Christmas Thanksgiving

4. The seasons of the year are *not* capitalized.

winter spring summer fall autumn

5. Capitalize north, south, east, and west when they refer to specific geographic locations.

West Coast West Germany the Northwest the South
East Coast East Germany the Southeast the Deep South

6. Do not capitalize north, south, east, or west when they refer to directions.

Go north to the second light.
Turn west when you reach the intersection
Not all birds fly south during the winter.

7. Capitalize all geographic names.

Italy   Sahara Desert
England   Rocky Mountains
Atlantic Ocean   Great Lakes
Mississippi River Passaic River

8. Capitalize the names of organizations, groups, departments, and offices, government, social, and professional.

Board of Higher Education   U. S. Army Reserve
St. Andrew Roman Catholic Church Montclair State College
Educators Investment Club   Board of Directors

Basic Correction Symbols

One of the most important steps in preparing your term paper is editing your early drafts. Professional editors use a system of correction symbols called proofreader's marks to identify errors and indicate the necessary corrections. *The American Heritage Dictionary of the English Language* lists forty-four such proof-reader's marks. *The Modern Language Association Style Sheet* lists thirty-two, but includes three marks not found in *The American Heritage Dictionary*. *Webster's Seventh New Collegiate Dictionary* lists forty-seven marks. The following list reduces this number of correction symbols from forty-seven to ten, and then adds two new ones.

The final list of twelve correction symbols is designed to correspond to the twelve errors most often committed by students. It is suggested you use these symbols in editing and correcting your early drafts. Remember, the purpose of these symbols is to locate your errors and indicate the necessary corrections.

On pages 274–275 you will see a copy of a rough draft page from a manuscript, and you will see how that page looks after the corrections are made. Note how much easier it will be for you to know these symbols and not have to write notes about the corrections to be made. For example, the transposition symbol (see the following table) tells the whole story of what has to be done to make the correction. It is a lot simpler than crossing out and writing above.

The Symbol   **The Error**   **The Correction**

Mark the spelling error with the symbol and circle the incorrect letter or letters.

spelling error   ambul*e*nce   ambulance

To correct the order of letters within a word or words within a sentence.

transpose   ri*ght*   right

do (now it)   do it now

To indicate the need for a capital letter.

make capital   John smith   John Smith

To indicate the need for a lower-case letter. Draw the slash line through the incorrect capital letter.

make lower-case   do /It now   do it now

To indicate a separation between words which have been

The Symbol	The Error	The Correction

incorrectly joined due to a spelling or typographical error.

| ⧸꞊ make two words | al⧸right | all right |

To indicate an incorrect space between letters in a word, or one word wrongly separated into two words.

| ⌣ move together | all ri⌐ght | all right |
| | every⌐body | everybody |

To indicate the use of a word which is incorrect but similar to the desired word.

| *ww* wrong word | Society girls are usually sophistic. *ww* | Society girls are usually sophisticated. |

To indicate the need for starting a new paragraph. All new paragraphs should begin five spaces in from the left margin.

| ¶ make new paragraph | "Who is he?" ¶"He is my friend." | "Who is he?"
   "He is my friend." |

To indicate the need to remove an incorrect letter, punctuation mark, or word. Always circle the part to be deleted.

ℓ omit or remove (delete)	The doctorₛ treats the patient.	The doctor treats the patient.
	The doctorⱬ treats the patient.	The doctor treats the patient.
	The (old) doctor treats the patient.	The doctor treats the patient.

To indicate a word or words accidentally left out.

| ʌ insert | The doctor will treat *the* patient. ʌ | The doctor will treat the patient. |

To indicate two sentences punctuated as one.

| *RO* run-on sentence | The doctor ⧸treats the patient⧸ the patient gets well. | The doctor treats the patient. The patient gets well. |

Circle all punctuation to be inserted.

| ⌣ punctuation change | the doctorₛ patient | the doctor's patient |
| | Do you know him⟨.⟩ | Do you know him? |

First Draft with Corrections

unaware of how to mark a bottom margin, the student was as
likely as not to type right off the paper without realizing
it. few had any knowledge of the placement of page numbers,
footnotes, headings and subheadings, and in dented quotations. the used of the white space to indicate a sudden
transition of time, setting or subject was foreign to them,
and double or single spacing was a matter indifference for
most. Our initial proposal was diagnostic on the basis of
two preliminary compositions, jointly evaluated, we formed a
tentative prognosis of the chief difficulties faced by each
student. To distinguish and between spelling and typographical errors, the pupil was asked to spell the word orally, and
usually a spelling in adequacy was indicated. These compositions were corrected and read aloud the to English classes
for their own critical comments. As often as possible, the
class discussion was directed from consideration of specific
essays toward formulation of general rules for compositional
structure.

students were encouraged to make connection between
written language and the more familiar oral speech; to
understand, for example, punctuation in terms of oral pauses
and voice inflection. Here the tape recorder became an
invaluable tool. Individual paragraphs, and later whole
essays, might be dictated by the instructor and typed from
the tape with punctuation inserted by the student, who was

unaware of how to mark a bottom margin, the student was as likely as not to type right off the paper without realizing it. Few had any knowledge of the placement of page numbers, footnotes, headings and subheadings, and indented quotations. The use of the white space to indicate a sudden transition of time, setting or subject was foreign to them, and double or single spacing was a matter of indifference for most.

Our initial purpose was diagnostic. On the basis of two preliminary compositions, jointly evaluated, we formed a tentative prognosis of the chief difficulties faced by each student. To distinguish between spelling and typographical errors, the pupil was asked to spell the word orally, and usually a spelling inadequacy was indicated. These compositions were corrected and read aloud to the English classes for their own critical comments. As often as possible, the class discussion was directed from consideration of specific essays toward formulation of general rules for compositional structure.

Students were encouraged to make a connection between written language and the more familiar oral speech; to understand, for example, punctuation in terms of oral pauses and voice inflection. Here the tape recorder became an invaluable tool. Individual paragraphs, and later whole essays, might be dictated by the instructor and typed from the tape with punctuation inserted by the student, who was then required

Preparing the
Term Paper

The preparation of a final paper is almost as important as the work that it contains. This Appendix gives some suggestions that will help you in preparing the final manuscript.

Materials and Equipment

The final paper should be typed, *double-spaced,* on standard-sized, $8\frac{1}{2}'' \times 11''$ paper. It should be a good quality bond paper that will allow easy correction of errors.

It is almost unheard of to have a term paper submitted in any form except typewritten. Follow your instructor's directions carefully, and conform as much as possible to the suggestions made in this section.

To allow for ease of reading, a standard pica type should be used when possible. Pica is the larger of the two standard typewriter types. Elite is the smaller. The difference is in the number of characters you can type per inch of paper as you type from margin to margin. Pica type will accommodate only ten characters per inch while elite will permit 12 characters in the same space. As you can see, the pica type is easier to read because of the size and the spacing.

```
This is pica type.  There are ten
characters and spaces to the inch.
```

```
This is elite type.  There are twelve
characters and spaces to the inch.
```

The typewriter should have a good black ribbon. The keys should be cleaned to assure that all letters are sharp. Round characters tend to fill with ink quickly and leave dark blotches if not cleaned properly.

The Margins

All reference to lines and spaces in this part can be seen on the form sheet illustrated on page 279.

The left margin (A) for term paper that will be bound is $1\frac{1}{2}$ inches. This allows an extra $\frac{1}{2}$ inch of space to bind or staple the paper together. The right margin (B) is 1 inch. This margin is flexible within reason, since you are approaching the right edge of your paper. Try to stay within the limit, or go over the margin by no more than two spaces.

With your left margin $1\frac{1}{2}$ inches in from the left edge of your paper and your right margin 1 inch in from the right, you have used up $2\frac{1}{2}$ inches. Since a standard sheet of paper is $8\frac{1}{2}$ inches wide, you have 6 inches remaining for a writing line (C). This is a 60-space line on a pica typewriter and a 72-space line on an elite typewriter. (D) indicates the total depth of the typing area, $8\frac{3}{4}$ inches.

The title of the term paper should be typed on line 13 of the first page, even if there is a separate title page. This will leave a 2-inch top margin (E).

Each page number should be typed 1 inch down from the top edge of the paper (F), or on line 7, and at the right margin.

The first line of typing on all but the first page will be line 10, or $1\frac{1}{2}$ inches from the top of the page (G). Since you have already come down 7 lines for the page number, you will come down 3 more and begin typing.

We suggest that you ordinarily type no further than $1\frac{1}{4}$ inches from the bottom of the page (H). This will allow you to type one extra line when necessary and still be within the usual 1-inch bottom margin required for term papers.

The Title Page

The title page is the first thing seen by the reader. It should be carefully centered on a clean sheet of white paper. The basic information on any title page is (1) the title of the project, (2) for what course the paper is being written, (3) who submitted the paper, and (4) on what date the paper was submitted. Inclusion of such things as the instructor's name and the number of the course will make the title page more complete and is suggested whenever possible.

The title pages that are shown on pages 280–281 are suggested styles to be used. Form A is the simplest of the three and can be used as a cover page for short assignments. Form B is a report form of title page and should be considered when a great deal of personal expression or comment is included in the report. Form C is the most formal of the three choices and should be used when submitting a more detailed research paper. The line numbers are for your guidance in centering properly.

The Table of Contents; Subtitles

A table of contents is usually not needed if a paper is not divided into chapters. In papers of less than twenty pages, a table of contents is rarely needed for the reader's guidance. However, most long papers should be conceived in, and divided into, *sections*. These should be introduced by subtitles which indicate clearly to the reader what information they contain. As a rule, a subtitle should not be longer than one typed line and need not be a complete sentence. Your subtitles should correspond to the headings in your sentence outline, and usually the wording of the subtitles will be close to the wording of your outline heading. For example, the headings in the "poor" outline on page 148 could serve as section subtitles in a long paper dealing with drug addiction.

The Preface

A preface is not always necessary and should be included only if you wish to communicate information the reader should know before beginning your paper. Such information might include reasons for your interest in the topic, problems you encountered in the research, or special knowledge or experience you have had which bears on the topic. Two rules always apply: (1) Never use

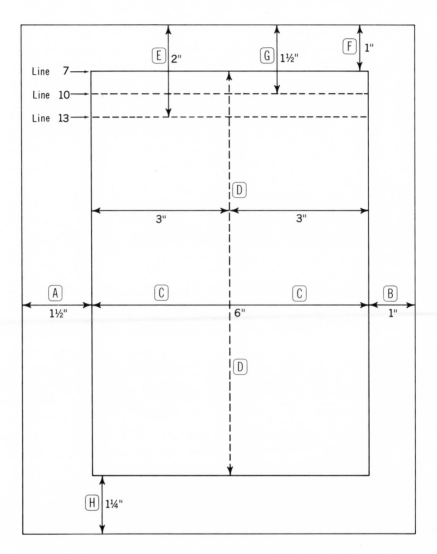

Margins for Term Paper

Form B

THE LINDBERGH KIDNAP/MURDER CASE   (line 14)

A Report by   (line 17)

John W. Carpetti

_____

(line 33)

Submitted to   (line 47)

Mr. P. W. Golone

Communication Skills

March 19, 1971

Form B

Form A

THE LINDBERGH KIDNAP/MURDER CASE   (line 16)

Communication Skills   (line 32)

English 105

John W. Carpetti   (line 49)

March 19, 1971

Title Pages for Term Paper

Form C

THE LINDBERGH KIDNAP/MURDER CASE (line 11)

Submitted to
Mr. P. W. Goione
In Partial Fulfillment of Requirements
for English 103
Communication Skills (line 31)

John W. Carpetti (line 54)

March 19, 1971

a preface to apologize for your paper. (2) Always write the preface last. A preface written prior to the paper often promises something more, or different, than the paper actually contains.

Quotations

There are two basic ways of indicating direct quotations from a source in your paper, depending on their length and importance. Quotation marks also have other uses.

Short quotations

If a direct quotation is short, it is simply put inside quotation marks. The next sentence demonstrates this. But remember, as we said in the previous paragraph, "Quotation marks also have other uses." The next paragraph will show one of these.

Sometimes quotation marks are used to indicate something other than a direct quotation. For example:

```
Although Poe's claim was long believed, many
recent critics do not accept his "solution"
that Mary was killed by a mysterious naval officer
with whom she planned to elope. These scholars
agree that the guilty sailor never really existed
except in Poe's imagination.12
```

You will see that the word "solution" on the second line is enclosed in quotation marks. From the context, you can see that the writer of the paper is questioning the accuracy of the term as it was used by someone else, and he is telling the reader to take the meaning of the word with a grain of salt. (The footnote reference at the end will guide the reader to the questionable solution being discussed.)

Long quotations

When a direct quotation is very long, it is not usual to place it in the middle of the paragraph in quotation marks. This would make it more difficult to read, and the reader may not realize that the whole section is a direct quotation. The general rule is that if the quotation is more than three lines long, it is set off from the body of the paper. In the following example, the writer decided that it would be better to quote his source directly, as he found it in his research, rather than try to explain it in his own words.

```
is not universally accepted. Whitehill, for instance,
claims otherwise.
```

> It was the state's theory later that the ladder
> broke as the kidnapper was descending it with
> the child under his arm and that the child was
> killed either in the resulting fall or in its
> crib.[6]

Notice that the quotation is indented five spaces from each margin and is single spaced. This sets it off and shows immediately that it is a quotation. For this reason, quotation marks are not used; they are unnecessary.

This form is also used when the writer wants to reproduce a piece of written information such as a note or a portion of a letter. The following quotation is a note that is reproduced with its misspellings and poor punctuation, but to change it would alter the reader's analysis of the writer of the note.

> Have 50000$ ready 25000$ in 20$ bills 15000$
> in 10$ bills and 10000$ in 5$ bills After 2–4
> days we will inform you were to deliver the mony
> We warn you for making anyding public or for
> notify the police.The child is in gut care[4]

As you can see, there is a possibility of drawing some conclusion about the writer's schooling and even his ethnic background.

Footnotes

As you use a fact or idea taken from someone else, or if you quote someone else directly, you must tell the reader the author and title of the source from which the information came and the precise page or pages on which it appears. This is usually done through footnotes, of which there are several different forms. We will describe three basic ones here, in the order of their complexity. (If your instructor requests a specific footnote form, however, be sure that is the one you use in your final paper.)

The most formal way of giving credit to others is by placing

Footnotes—Form 1

PHYSICAL AND SOCIAL ASPECTS OF THE KIBBUTZ

The original kibbutz of Israel was formed in 1909 by people fleeing tzarist oppression in Russia and the turmoil of the Turkish regime.(9:9) They sought freedom, equality, and a better life through shared labor, which would supply each citizen of the community with the needed food, housing, clothing, and security.(1:366,369) Now, about four percent of Israel's total population lives in these rural collective settlements. Membership is entirely voluntary; there is application for membership, and the applicant may be admitted for a one-year probationary period. Any existing member is free to leave.(4:127)

Equality is a principle which is the basis of life in the kibbutzim. There is no private ownership of property; all property is collectively owned so that no one person can rise above the others in material possessions.(1:364-5) All the children live in their own groups in the same building, and each married couple has their own one-and-a-half room apartment. No one has better living quarters than another. (15:571) No one job is more important than another because each job is needed for the well-being of the community. The person who cleans out the chicken coops is as important as the person who tills the fields. The people of the settlement

BIBLIOGRAPHY

1. Abrams, Al, et al. "Our Life on a Border Kibbutz," National Geographic, 138:364-391, September, 1970.

2. Brandwine, Aliza. "Upbringing of Children in Kibbutzim of Israel," Young Children, 24:265-272, May, 1969.

3. Cohen, Gerda L. "The 'Affluent' Kibbutzim," Commentary, 28:292-298, October, 1959.

4. Comay, Joan. Everyone's Guide to Israel. Garden City: Doubleday & Company, Inc., 1966.

5. Feigenbaum, Lawrence H., et al. Israel: Crossroads of Conflict. New York: Rand McNally & Company, 1968.

6. Furia, Z. "Response to Transgression in Stories by Israeli Children," Child Development, 34:271-280, June, 1963.

7. Greenberg, Marvin. "Communal Education in Israel," Peabody Journal of Education, 46:28-33, July, 1968.

8. Kraft, I. "Dome Observations on Kibbutz Children," Children, 13:195-197, September, 1966.

9. Lannoy, Richard. Israel. London: Thames and Hudson, Ltd., 1958.

10. Luft, Gerda. "The Kibbutz in Crisis," Commentary, 32:334-340.

11. Metalitz, Beatrice R. "Kibbutzim for the Disadvantaged," Today's Education, 58:17-19, December, 1969.

12. Payne, Robert. The Splendor of Israel. New York: Harper and Row, Publishers, 1963.

13. Schiavone, J. "Israeli Ulpanion," Education, 87:117-118, October, 1966.

14. Shapira, A., et al. "Cooperative and Competitive Behavior of Kibbutz and Urban Children in Israel," Child Development, 40:609-617, June, 1969.

the footnotes referring to your sources at the bottom of each page of the paper (Form 3). Being the most formal, it is also the most cumbersome for you, the author and typist, to handle. If it is possible to use one of the other forms shown here, it is suggested that they be considered first. Form 2, instead of requiring detailed footnotes on each page, places all footnotes on a single page at the end of the paper. The simplest form, Form 1, combines the bibliography and the footnotes into a single page of documentation to which your reader can turn.

Form 1

Form 1 uses the parentheses method of documenting sources. When this form is used, the bibliography style shown on page 285 is also used. You will see that each source listed in the bibliography is preceded by a number. This number is used in the paper to identify that particular source. Look at the illustration on page 284. Notice that following the words "Turkish regime" there is the notation "(9:9)." The first 9 refers to the ninth source in the bibliography; the second 9 refers to the page number within this source.

The next notation, "(1:366,369)," tells us that the information came from the first source listed in the bibliography and appears on pages 366 and 369 of the source. As you can see from the sample, there is no need to place anything at the bottom of the page. This is by far the easiest of the forms to use.

Form 2

Form 2 uses raised numerals in the body of the paper (see the illustration on page 288). These numerals correspond to those on a footnote page, which is placed at the end of the paper (see the illustration on page 289). Note that the footnotes are typed as they would appear at the bottom of the page had that form been used. (This will be explained in detail later.)

The advantage of using Form 2 is obvious; the time needed to place footnotes at the bottom of each page is eliminated, thus enabling the writer to complete his paper more quickly. The raising of numbers might be a problem, but here is an easy way of coping with that problem. During typing, letters normally appear above the alignment scale on the typewriter.

normally appear above the alignment scale

Turn the cylinder knob backwards so that the tops of the letters are even with the alignment scale. Then strike the number of the footnote.

normally appear above the alignment scale[3]

Form 3

Form 3 is the most formal style. Once again, raised numerals (sometimes called *superscripts*) are used in the text to indicate sources. In this form, however, the raised numeral corresponds to a footnote that is at the bottom of the same page, not on a separate page. Examine the illustration on page 290. Note that the top and bottom margins are the same as if there were no footnotes. The footnotes are separated from the body, and the proper margins are maintained by careful planning.

When an assignment requires that all footnotes be placed at the bottom of the pages of your paper, follow these steps carefully.

1. Before beginning to type your final draft, type all your footnotes in proper order on a separate page, as you would for Form 2. (See the illustration on page 289.) By consulting this footnote page, you eliminate all guesswork as to how many lines each footnote will require.

2. Mark the bottom margin on each sheet on which the final draft will be typed. To do this, measure up $1\frac{1}{4}$ inches from the bottom and draw a light pencil line at the left edge of the sheet. This is your *margin line*. (See the illustration on page 291.)

3. Begin typing your paper in the normal way. As you type, place the raised footnote numerals in the body of the report. Stop typing approximately half-way down the page. Count how many footnotes you have already included and estimate how many more are coming in the next several lines. (This estimate is the only guesswork of any kind in this process. Even here you will not need to guess if you are copying from an earlier typewritten draft. If you are not certain of the exact number of additional footnotes you will need, it is safer to overestimate by one than to underestimate.)

APPENDIX B: PREPARING THE TERM PAPER

Footnotes—Form 2

PHYSICAL AND SOCIAL ASPECTS OF THE KIBBUTZ

The original kibbutz of Israel was formed in 1909 by people fleeing tzarist oppression in Russia and the turmoil of the Turkish regime.[1] They sought freedom, equality, and a better life through shared labor, which would supply each citizen of the community with the needed food, housing, clothing, and security.[2] Now, about four percent of Israel's total population lives in these rural collective settlements. Membership is entirely voluntary; there is application for membership, and the applicant may be admitted for a one-year probationary period. Any existing member is free to leave.[3]

Equality is a principle which is the basis of life in the kibbutzim. There is no private ownership of property; all property is collectively owned so that no one person can rise above the others in material possessions.[4] All the children live in their own groups in the same building, and each married couple has their own one-and-a-half-room apartment. No one has better living quarters than another.[5] No one job is more important than another because each job is needed for the well-being of the community. The person who cleans out the chicken coops is as important as the person who tills the fields. The people of the settlement rotate positions and work assignments periodically, so as to share the work load of both pleasant and

FOOTNOTE PAGE

[1]Richard Lannoy, Israel, p. 9.

[2]Al Abrams, et al., "Our Life on a Border Kibbutz," National Geographic, September, 1970, p. 366.

[3]Joan Comay, Everyone's Guide to Israel, p. 127.

[4]Abrams, pp. 364-365.

[5]Joseph Shepher, "Familism and Social Structure: The Case of the Kibbutz," Journal of Marriage and the Family, August, 1971, p. 571.

[6]Aliza Brandwine, "Upbringing of Children in Kibbutzim of Israel," Young Children, May, 1969, p. 225.

[7]Robert Payne, The Splendor of Israel, p. 84.

[8]Gerda Luft, "The Kibbutz in Crisis," Commentary, October, 1961, p. 334.

[9]Abrams, p. 372.

[10]Marvin Greenberg, "Communal Education in Israel," Peabody Journal of Education, July, 1968, p. 30.

[11]Gerda L. Cohen, "The 'Affluent' Kibbutzim," Commentary, October, 1959, p. 297.

[12]Layna Vernin, "Growing Up in a Kibbutz," Parents, April, 1970, p. 57.

[13]Z. Furia, "Response to Transgression in Stories by Israeli Children," Child Development, June, 1963, p. 272.

[14]Beatrice R. Metalitz, "Kibbutzim for the Disadvantaged," Today's Education, December, 1969, p. 17.

[15]Brandwine, pp. 268-269.

PHYSICAL AND SOCIAL ASPECTS OF THE KIBBUTZ

The original kibbutz of Israel was formed in 1909 by
people fleeing tzarist oppression in Russia and the turmoil
of the Turkish regime.[1] They sought freedom, equality, and
a better life through shared labor, which would supply each
citizen of the community with the needed food, housing,
clothing, and security.[2] Now, about four percent of Israel's
total population lives in these rural collective settlements.
Membership is entirely voluntary; there is application for
membership, and the applicant may be admitted for a one-year
probationary period. Any existing member is free to leave.[3]

Equality is a principle which is the basis of life in
the kibbutzim. There is no private ownership of property; all
property is collectively owned so that no one person can rise
above the others in material possessions.[4] All the children
live in their own groups in the same building, and each married
couple has their own one-and-a-half-room apartment. No one

---

[1]Richard Lannoy, Israel, p. 9.

[2]Al Abrams, et al., "Our Life on a Border Kibbutz," National
Geographic, September, 1970, p. 366.

[3]Joan Comay, Everyone's Guide to Israel, p. 127.

[4]Abrams, pp. 364-365.

4. When you know how many footnotes you must leave room for, count the actual number of lines these footnotes will require by checking the footnote page you typed as Step 1. Be sure to include the blank lines between footnotes in your count. To this total, add three. The sum is the total number of footnote lines that will be needed on that page.

5. By turning the cylinder forward, roll the paper down in the typewriter until the *margin line* is visible. Now roll the cylinder back the exact number of footnote lines you determined in Step 4. Draw a light pencil line at the left edge of the sheet. This is your *warning line.* Type no part of the body of the paper below this line. (See the illustration below.)

6. Return to your last line of typing, and continue typing until the *warning line* appears.

7. Then roll the cylinder forward again just two lines below the *warning line.* From the left margin, type a line approximately $1\frac{1}{2}$ inches long. This is called the *separation line* because it will separate the body of your report from the footnotes.

8. Finally, roll the cylinder forward two lines, to leave a blank line under the separation line, and you are ready to type the first footnote. (*Note:* After you have finished typing the entire page, erase the penciled warning and margin lines.)

cover of night.[13] This theory is quite as unsatisfactory as

Warning line ↓ Poe's since many of the "facts" on which it is based have

been proved false.[14] This does not mean, however, that

Margin line ↓

[13]Will M. Clemens, "The Tragedy of Mary Rogers," Era Magazine, May, 1904, pp. 461-463.

[14]Raymond Paul, Who Murdered Mary Rogers?, pp. 131-133.

STYLE OF FOOTNOTES

In typing footnotes, whether in Form 3 or Form 2, remember that each should begin with a raised identifying number (superscript) indented three to five spaces from the left margin.* If the footnote is more than one line long, the following lines should begin at the left margin. Footnotes are always single spaced with *one line skipped* between separate notes.

Following are nineteen different sample footnotes with explanations of when each style should be used. Although you may come across more complicated ones in your research, those presented here are the best for a typewritten final paper. Read through them all and become familiar with them before you type your paper or even prepare the rough draft of the footnote page.

¹Sam Hunter, Modern American Painting and Sculpture, p. 128.

²Walter Gropius, Scope of Total Architecture, p. 130.

Footnotes 1 and 2 represent the first notation of each of these sources. Notice that the author's name is in correct order. There is no need to give the publisher and place of publication since this information will be in the bibliography.

³Hunter, p. 129.

Footnote 3 tells the reader that the information cited comes from a source previously mentioned, written by Hunter. There will be no confusion as long as there is no other source with an author named Hunter. If we had two authors with the same last name but different first names, we would list the author's full name followed by a page number, as in footnote 4.

⁴Sam Hunter, p. 129.

Footnote 4 is an example of how footnote 3 would have been displayed had there been two Hunters. If there were more than one source by the same Hunter, we would repeat the title of the source.

⁵C. B. Mendenball and K. J. Arisman, Secondary Education, cited in Luella Cole, Psychology of Adolescence, p. 629.

*Although the examples are indented three spaces, some instructors may prefer a five-space indention. You should ascertain your instructor's preference concerning footnote indention.

Footnote 5 tells the reader that the information cited comes from a source by Cole in which she refers to information taken from Mendenball and Arisman. Actually, if this information is to carry great weight in a research project, the writer should take the time to locate and read the source and be able to quote first hand.

[6]Leslie J. Nason, "10 Good Rules for Improving Study," San Francisco Chronicle, January 31, 1961, p. 2.

Footnote 6 represents the first mention of a newspaper article written by Nason.

[7]"New Math to Be Tried in Local Schools," Cincinnati Enquirer, December 3, 1965, p. 2.

Footnote 7 represents the first mention of a newspaper article that does not have a by-line. Note that everything else is the same as footnote 6 except that there is no author's name.

[8]Donald W. Robinson, "Police in the Schools," Today's Education, October, 1970, p. 18.

Footnote 8 represents the first mention of an article taken from a professional journal.

[9]"Antidote for a Crisis: Massive State Aid," NJEA Review, September, 1970, p. 19.

Footnote 9 tells the reader that the information was taken from a professional journal but was printed with no author's name. It is an editorial article. Periodicals and journals can be cited as shown above.

[10]Winslow Ames, "Drawing," Encyclopaedia Britannica, 1959, 7:629.

Footnote 10 represents information taken from an encyclopedia with Winslow Ames as the contributor. The 7:629 represents the volume and page number.

[11]"Advocate," Encyclopaedia Britannica, 1959, 1:205.

Footnote 11 represents an item taken from encyclopedia when no credit is given to a contributor.

[12]Dom Anselm Hughes and Gerald Abraham, eds., Ars

Nova and *Renaissance*, Vol. 1 of *New* *Oxford* *History* *of*
Music series, p. 24.

Footnote 12 represents a source that is part of a series. This form
may be used for any set of books that gives a separate title to each
volume but is known primarily by its series name.

¹³Joint Council on Economic Education, *Inflation*
Can *Be* *Stopped:* *Steps* *For* *a* *Balanced* *Economy*.

¹⁴Federal Reserve Bank of Philadelphia, *Inflation*
and/or *Unemployment*, p. 3 (unnumbered).

Footnotes 13 and 14 tell the reader that the information is published and distributed by the organization listed and gives the
title of the publication. It also tells the reader that it is a general
publication and carries no page numbers. Committees, agencies,
councils, government organizations, and similar groups which
publish pamphlets and booklets should be identified in the first
part of the footnote and bibliographical entries as if they were
the author.

¹⁵William K. Wimsatt, "Poe and the Mystery of Mary
Rogers," *Publications* *of* *the* *Modern* *Language* *Associa-*
tion, March, 1941, pp. 230, 241. Peter Levins, "Rogers
Mystery Formed Basis for Poe Short Story," *New* *York*
Sunday *News*, September 21, 1941, p. 52.

Footnote 15 is a special footnote because it is a combination of
two separate sources. Although either source would be sufficient,
the citation of both reinforces the validity of the facts and conclusion and impresses the reader with the depth of the research.

¹⁶Wimsatt, p. 247; see Samuel Copp Worthen, "A
Strange Aftermath of the Mystery of Marie Roget," *Pro-*
ceedings *of* *the* *New* *Jersey* *Historical* *Society*, April,
1942, pp. 122–123. Raymond Paul, *Who* *Murdered* *Mary*
Rogers?, pp. 108, 110.

Footnote 16 is another example of a special footnote which implies in-depth research. The use of *see* tells the reader that several
sources (those cited) support the writer's contention that others
feel the same as Wimsatt. The reader is invited to compare them.

¹⁷Wimsatt, p. 246; cf. Will M. Clemens, "The Tragedy
of Mary Rogers," *Era* *Magazine*, May, 1904, p. 462.

Footnote 17 also cites more than one source, but the use of *cf.*

(compare) indicates that the second source does not support the first, but presents an opposing opinion. The reader is invited to contrast them.

[18]Information obtained from a lecture delivered by John Wilson at Montclair State College, Upper Montclair, New Jersey, on the subject <u>Famous</u> <u>Murders</u>, July 13, 1970.

Footnote 18 tells the reader that information came from a lecture. If Wilson's lecture is to carry great weight in the report, it would be wise to state briefly, either in the report or in the footnote, the lecturer's credentials.

[19]An interview with Raymond Paul, Professor of English at Montclair State College, on August 4, 1970, to discuss stands taken by present—day authors on the implication of Edgar Allan Poe in the murder of Mary Rogers. Mr. Paul has recently completed extensive re—search on the Mary Rogers case and has published a complete solution in his book, <u>Who</u> <u>Murdered</u> <u>Mary</u> <u>Rogers?</u>

Footnote 19 gives the name of the person interviewed and his credentials to speak on the subject.

The Bibliography

We have already seen an example of one form of bibliography in connection with footnotes in Form 1 (page 285). This bibliography lists the sources in alphabetical order of the authors' last names and numbers them consecutively. It would appear at the end of the paper.

Another form of bibliography is very similar. It lists the sources in alphabetical order, but it does not number them. This is the form most frequently used when footnotes are in Form 2 or Form 3. It is illustrated on pages 296–297.

If research has been very extensive and a great many sources were consulted, the bibliography sometimes groups them into categories. Such a form is shown on pages 297–298. The nature of the categories used depends on the subject matter and the type of research involved.

Sometimes an instructor will require that you list all the sources you consulted, whether or not you have cited them in your paper. In this case you would divide the bibliography into two sections, one headed "Sources Cited" and the other headed "Sources Consulted." Each section would, of course, either be in alphabetical order or be grouped by categories.

An annotated bibliography gives a short statement about what the source contains after each listing. Such bibliographies are sometimes necessary in advanced academic work. But such a form can also be valuable to you as you go through school. Use it in your own notes even if it is not appropriate for the particular paper you are writing. When you refer to your notes months or years later, it will give you a head start in remembering what the source was like and whether it would be useful in the new project you are working on.

The following are examples of annotations following a source.

Bosmajian, Haig A. "The Language of White Racism," College English, 31:12–16, December, 1969.

Description and analysis, by a University of Washington professor, of the rhetorical aspects of American ethnic communication efforts. Author asserted that Caucasians need to discard racial clichés, terms and phrases as prerequisite to communication between black and white groups for an end to American racism.

Stupak, Ronald J. "The Student as Enemy...of the Student," Phi Delta Kappan, 52:79–81, October, 1970.

The author attempts to point out that student efforts have to be directed at student problems.

BIBLIOGRAPHY

"Advocate," Encyclopaedia Britannica, 1959, 1:205–206.

Ames, Winslow. "Drawing," Encyclopaedia Britannica, 1959, 7:628–629.

Cohen, Jerome B., and Arthur W. Hanson. Personal Finance, Homewood, Illinois: Richard D. Irwin, Inc., 1958.

Cole, Luella. Psychology of Adolescence (fifth edition). New York: Rinehart and Company, Inc., 1959.

Federal Reserve Bank of New York, Selection Number 133 from the Study Materials for Economic Education in the Schools. Money and Economic Balance. New York: Federal Reserve Bank of New York, 1966.

Federal Reserve Bank of Philadelphia, Series for Economic Education. Inflation and/or Unemployment. Philadelphia: Federal Reserve Bank of Philadelphia (undated).

Freeman, Otis W., and Howard H. Martin, eds. The Pacific Northwest: An Over-all Appreciation. New York: John Wiley & Sons, Inc., 1959.

Gropius, Walter. Scope of Total Architecture. Edited by Ruth Nanda Anshen. New York: Harper & Brothers, 1955.

Hughes, Dom Anselm, and Gerald Abraham, eds. Ars Nova and Renaissance, Vol. 1 of the New Oxford History of Music series. London: Oxford University Press, 1960.

Hunter, Sam. Modern American Painting and Sculpture. New York: Dell Publishing Company, Inc., 1960.

Joint Council on Economic Education, Inflation Can Be Stopped: Steps for a Balanced Economy. New York: Joint Council on Economic Education, 1969.

Nason, Leslie J. "10 Good Rules for Improving Study," San Francisco Chronicle. January 31, 1961, p. 2.

"New Math to be Tried in Local Schools," Cincinnati Enquirer. December 3, 1965, p. 2.

"Résumé of the Four Years of the Lindbergh Case," The New York Times. April 4, 1936, p. 2.

BIBLIOGRAPHY

Books

Cohen, Jerome B., and Arthur W. Hanson. Personal Finance. Homewood, Illinois: Richard D. Irwin, Inc., 1958.

Cole, Luella. Psychology of Adolescence (fifth edition). New York: Rinehart & Company, Inc., 1959.

Freeman, Otis W., and Howard H. Martin, eds. The Pacific Northwest: An Over-all Appreciation. New
York: John Wiley & Sons, Inc., 1959.

Periodicals

Sheetz, Shirley A. "The Perfect Boss/Secretary Team..."
The Secretary, 30:12-20, October, 1970.

Stupak, Ronald J. "The Student as Enemy...of the
Student," Phi Delta Kappan, 52:79-81, October, 1970.

Newspapers

Nason, Leslie J. "10 Good Rules for Improving Study,"
San Francisco Chronicle. January 31, 1961, p. 2.

"Résumé of the Four Years of the Lindbergh Case," The
New York Times, April 4, 1936, p. 2.

Encyclopedias

"Advocate," Encyclopaedia Britannica, 1959, 1:205-206.

Ames, Winslow. "Drawing," Encyclopaedia Britannica,
1959, 7:628-629.

Series

Hughes, Dom Anselm, and Gerald Abraham, eds. Ars Nova
and Renaissance, Vol. 1 of the New Oxford History
of Music series. London: Oxford University Press,
1960.

Selected Sample Footnote and Bibliography Form

The following references give you a variety of possible
sources and show how they appear in footnote form and in bibliographical form. Each footnote section is followed by a listing of
corresponding, separate bibliographical entries.

Footnote form for a book reference

[1]Sam Hunter, Modern American Painting and Sculpture,
p. 128.

Selected Sample Footnote and Bibliography Form

²Walter Gropius, <u>Scope</u> <u>of</u> <u>Total</u> <u>Architecture</u>, p. 130.

³Jerome B. Cohen and Arthur W. Hanson, <u>Personal</u> <u>Finance</u>, p. 653.

⁸Cohen and Hansen, p. 660.

⁹Otis W. Freeman and Howard H. Martin, eds., <u>The</u> <u>Pacific</u> <u>Northwest</u>, p. 290.

¹⁰Earl B. Shaw, <u>Anglo</u> <u>America</u>: <u>A</u> <u>Regional</u> <u>Geography</u>, p. 21.

¹²Luella Cole, <u>Psychology</u> <u>of</u> <u>Adolescence</u>, p. 93.

¹⁴C. B. Mendenball and K. J. Arisman, <u>Secondary</u> <u>Education</u>, cited in Luella Cole, <u>Psychology</u> <u>of</u> <u>Adolescence</u>, p. 629.*

Bibliographical entry for a book reference

Hunter, Sam. <u>Modern</u> <u>American</u> <u>Painting</u> <u>and</u> <u>Sculpture</u>. New York: Dell Publishing Company, Inc., 1960.

Gropius, Walter. <u>Scope</u> <u>of</u> <u>Total</u> <u>Architecture</u>. Edited by Ruth Nanda Anshen. New York: Harper & Brothers, 1955.

Cohen, Jerome B., and Arthur W. Hanson. <u>Personal</u> <u>Finance</u>. Homewood, Illinois: Richard D. Irwin, Inc., 1958.

Freeman, Otis W., and Howard H. Martin, eds. <u>The</u> <u>Pacific</u> <u>Northwest</u>: <u>An</u> <u>Over-all</u> <u>Appreciation</u>. New York: John Wiley & Sons, Inc., 1959.

Shaw, Earl B. <u>Anglo</u> <u>America</u>: <u>A</u> <u>Regional</u> <u>Geography</u>. New York: John Wiley & Sons, Inc., 1959.

Cole, Luella. <u>Psychology</u> <u>of</u> <u>Adolescence</u> (fifth edition), New York: Rinehart & Company, Inc., 1959.

Homer. <u>The</u> <u>Iliad</u>. Richmond Lattimore, trans. Chicago: University of Chicago Press, 1951.

Footnote form for a newspaper reference

¹Leslie J. Nason, "10 Good Rules for Improving Study," <u>San</u> <u>Francisco</u> <u>Chronicle</u>, January 31, 1961, p. 2.

*The Mendenball and Arisman reference is cited in Cole's *Psychology of Adolescence*. Hence only the bibliographical entry for the latter book is given.

[2]"New Math to Be Tried in Local Schools," _Cincinnati_ _Enquirer_, December 3, 1965, p. 2.

[3]"Résumé of the Four Years of the Lindbergh Case," _The_ _New_ _York_ _Times_, April 4, 1936, p. 2.

Bibliographical entry for a newspaper reference

Nason, Leslie J. "10 Good Rules for Improving Study," _San_ _Francisco_ _Chronicle_, January 31, 1961, p. 2.

"New Math to Be Tried in Local Schools," _Cincinnati_ _Enquirer_, December 3, 1965, p. 2.

"Résumé of the Four Years of the Lindbergh Case," _The_ _New_ _York_ _Times_, April 4, 1936, p. 2.

Footnote form for periodicals

[1]Fred Warshofsky, "Methadone: A Drug to Lick a Drug?" _The_ _Reader's_ _Digest_, May, 1970, p. 89.

[2]Henry Thomas Van Dyke, "Why Drug Abuse?" _NJEA_ _Review_, September, 1970, p. 19.

[3]"Antidote for a Crisis: Massive State Aid," _NJEA_ _Review_, September, 1970, p. 25.

[4]Donald W. Robinson, "Police in the Schools," _Today's_ _Education_, October, 1970, p. 18.

[5]Shirley A. Sheetz, "The Perfect Boss/Secretary Team...," _The_ _Secretary_, October, 1970, p. 18.

[6]Ronald J. Stupak, "The Student as Enemy...of the Student," _Phi_ _Delta_ _Kappan_, October, 1970, p. 80.

Bibliographical entry for periodicals

Van Dyke, Henry Thomas. "Why Drug Abuse?" _NJEA_ _Review_, 44:18–20,50, September, 1970.

Robinson, Donald W. "Police in the Schools," _Today's_ _Education_ (The Journal of the National Education Association), 59:18–30, October, 1970.

Warshofsky, Fred. "Methadone: A Drug to Lick a Drug?" _The_ _Reader's_ _Digest_, 96:88–92, May, 1970.

Sheetz, Shirley A. "The Perfect Boss/Secretary Team...," _The_ _Secretary_, 30:12–20, October, 1970.

Stupak, Ronald J. "The Student as Enemy...of the
    Student," <u>Phi</u> <u>Delta</u> <u>Kappan</u>, 52:79–81, October, 1970.

Footnote form for an encyclopedia reference

[1]Winslow Ames, "Drawing," <u>Encyclopaedia</u> <u>Britannica</u>,
1959, 7:629.

[2]"Advocate," <u>Encyclopaedia</u> <u>Britannica</u>, 1959, 1:205.

Bibliographical entry for an encyclopedia reference

Ames, Winslow. "Drawing," <u>Encyclopaedia</u> <u>Britannica</u>,
    1959, 7:628–629.

"Advocate," <u>Encyclopaedia</u> <u>Britannica</u>, 1959, 1:205–206.

Footnote form for part of a series

[1]Dom Anselm Hughes and Gerald Abraham, eds., <u>Ars</u>
<u>Nova</u> <u>and</u> <u>Renaissance</u>, Vol. 1 of <u>New</u> <u>Oxford</u> <u>History</u> <u>of</u>
<u>Music</u> series, p. 24.

Bibliographical entry for part of a series

Hughes, Dom Anselm, and Gerald Abraham, eds. <u>Ars</u> <u>Nova</u>
    <u>and</u> <u>Renaissance</u>, Vol. 1 of <u>New</u> <u>Oxford</u> <u>History</u> <u>of</u>
    <u>Music</u> series. London: Oxford University Press, 1960.

Footnote for a pamphlet or similar printed material

[1]Federal Reserve Bank of New York, <u>Money</u> <u>and</u> <u>Eco-</u>
<u>nomic</u> <u>Balance</u>, p. 7.

[2]Federal Reserve Bank of Philadelphia, <u>Inflation</u>
<u>and/or</u> <u>Unemployment</u>, p. 3 (unnumbered).

Bibliographical entry for pamphlets and similar printed material

Federal Reserve Bank of New York, Selection Number 133
    from the Study Materials for Economic Education in
    the Schools. <u>Money</u> <u>and</u> <u>Economic</u> <u>Balance</u>. New York:
    Federal Reserve Bank of New York, 1966.

Federal Reserve Bank of Philadelphia, Series for Eco-
    nomic Education. <u>Inflation</u> <u>and/or</u> <u>Unemployment</u>.

Philadelphia: Federal Reserve Bank of Philadelphia (undated).

Joint Council on Economic Education, Inflation Can Be Stopped: Steps for a Balanced Economy. New York: Joint Council on Economic Education, 1969.

Using the Library

The Card Catalog

A visit to the library is confusing when you do not know where to begin looking for materials you need. Every library has a card catalog, which is often found near the entrance. Cards in this catalog may differ in appearance slightly, but they are all similar to those illustrated on the next page.

If you need a particular book or if you are looking for books about a particular subject, the card catalog is the first place you would go. If you need information about Civil War battles, you would look up the first of the illustrated cards. All the books that the library has that deal primarily with this subject would be filed in the card catalog under "U.S.—History—Civil War—Campaigns and battles." The book by Bruce Catton is only one of them.

The card in the catalog gives you a lot of information about the book. You can use much of this information to decide whether or not it is likely to be a fruitful source for the material you need. Look again at the cards illustrated on page 304. Certain parts are keyed to the following list, which identifies them.

a. This is the subject of the source. Every book about this subject that the library has would have a card in the catalog with this heading on it.

b. The author of the book and his dates.

c. This is the call number of the book. This number (or combination of letters and numbers) will tell you where the book is in your library. The call number in the illustration is based on the Dewey Decimal system (see page 306).

d. This gives complete bibliographical information about the source. In this case it is the title, edition, place of publication, publisher, and year published.

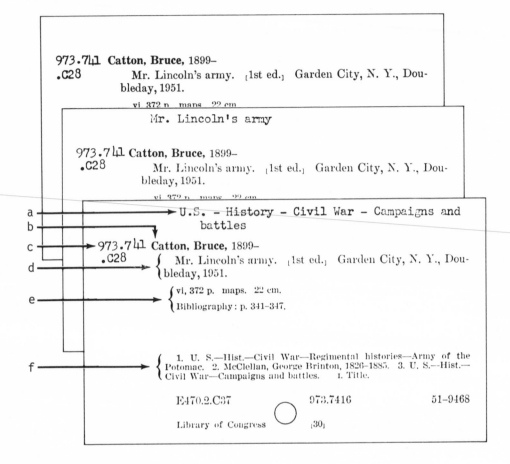

973.741 **Catton, Bruce,** 1899–
.C28   Mr. Lincoln's army. ₁1st ed.₎ Garden City, N. Y., Doubleday, 1951.
            vi, 372 p. maps. 22 cm.

Mr. Lincoln's army

973.741 **Catton, Bruce,** 1899–
.C28   Mr. Lincoln's army. ₁1st ed.₎ Garden City, N. Y., Doubleday, 1951.
            vi, 372 p. maps. 22 cm.

a
b
c
d
e
f

U.S. – History – Civil War – Campaigns and battles

973.741 **Catton, Bruce,** 1899–
.C28 { Mr. Lincoln's army. ₁1st ed.₎ Garden City, N. Y., Doubleday, 1951.

{ vi, 372 p. maps. 22 cm.
{ Bibliography : p. 341–347.

{ 1. U. S.—Hist.—Civil War—Regimental histories—Army of the Potomac. 2. McClellan, George Brinton, 1826–1885. 3. U. S.—Hist.—Civil War—Campaigns and battles.   I. Title.

E470.2.C37   973.7416   51–9468

Library of Congress   ₁30₎

e. Additional information about the book. In this case, that it has a six-page preface (vi), 372 pages of text, and also has maps. It is 22 centimeters (a little more than 8½ inches) tall. It also includes a bibliography on pages 341 through 347.

f. The material on the lower portion of the card is primarily technical data of importance only to the librarian. One section, however, can sometimes be helpful to you; this is marked (f) on the sample. It shows the various subject headings under which this book probably appears in the catalog, and, although that is not its primary purpose, it can give you a clue as to the nature of the book by showing what areas of information it covers.

Every book that the library has available is represented in the card catalog by (1) an author card (or several if there is more than one author), (2) a title card, and, if the book is not fiction, (3) one or more subject cards. Thus you can look under the name of the author, the title of the book, or the subject of the book to find the card for it; there is a card in all three places.

Just as there are certain alphabetizing rules used in dictionaries and telephone directories (and there are different rules followed by each of these), there are certain rules by which catalog cards are filed. In order to find what you are looking for in the file, you should become familiar with some of them. The actual rules followed would take you many hours to learn and would be of limited use to you. The major ones, however, are simple; but they should be remembered. You may wrongly decide that the library does not have the book you are looking for just because you did not look it up correctly. Here are five of the more important rules.

1. In filing by title, initial articles (a, an, the) are ignored. Thus, if you wanted to find a book entitled *The Compleat Angler,* you would look under "C."

2. There is a filing rule that "nothing comes before something." This means that "life or death" comes before "lifeboat" because the space (nothing) after the "e" comes before the "b" in "lifeboat."

3. When the same word or identical names occur, they are filed in the order (a) person, (b) places, (c) subject, (d) titles. Thus subject cards for "Lifeboats" would come before a card for a novel entitled *Lifeboats.*

4. Abbreviations are filed as if they were written out in full. Mr. as "Mister," Dr. as "Doctor," U.S. as "United States," and so on.

5. All names beginning with Mc, M', or Mac are filed as if they began with "Mac." Thus, McConnell would come before MacRae.

There are other rules to guide you through the card catalog. It is suggested that you consult the librarian where you are doing your research or study project. It is important to remember that the librarian is your key resource person. He is there because he has devoted a lot of time to learning the answers to your questions. Your biggest mistake could be to overlook his expertise.

While you are talking to the librarian, be sure to ask him if your library participates in an interlibrary loan program. If it does, he will direct you to the proper catalogs to determine which libraries do carry the sources you need. If a source is unavailable at your own library, it can probably be borrowed for you from another institution.

Classification Systems

You will recall that when we looked at the illustration of a catalog card, we identified (b) as the "call number" that will tell you where the book is in your library. Actually, this number carries more information than that.

Books in a library must be arranged in some kind of logical order if they are to be stored properly and found when wanted. On your own bookshelves you probably do not have any special place for particular books. You might keep school texts and references in one place and science fiction and detective stories in another. But if you had the number of books your library has, it would be impossible to find a particular one out of the hundreds of thousands. Therefore, a logical classification system must be used.

There are two major systems in use at present. One is the Dewey Decimal system, which was originally devised by Melvil Dewey in 1876 and has since been revised and expanded. Basically, it divides all knowledge into ten broad categories, each of which is then subdivided as needed. The major categories are as follows:

000–099 General Works: General works include dictionaries, encyclopedias, almanacs, bibliographies, and other reference materials.

100–199 Philosophy and Psychology: In this section are included works dealing with man as he thinks about himself.

200–299 Religion: Works dealing with all religions are included in this classification. Man copes with the idea of a supreme being.

300–399 Social Sciences: The social sciences deal with man's realization that he must live with others. Laws, customs, education, and human resources are among the works in this classification.

400–499 Language: How to communicate.

500–599 Science and Mathematics: As man's knowledge of science and mathematics increased, so did the number of works in this section. Among the subjects included here are computers, cybernetics, astronomy, biology, and astrophysics.

600–699 Useful Arts: Works dealing with man's invention and ingenuity in improving his home, health, and developing manufacturing methods are included in this section.

700–799 Fine Arts: Included here are works dealing with music, painting, dancing, sports, and recreation and games.

800–899 Literature: Poetry, novels, plays, stories, and fables are all included in this section.

900–999 History, Travel, Biography: The recordings of happenings and events are included in this classification.

The second widely used system is the Library of Congress classification. It allows greater flexibility and more easily accommodates the increasing number of sources of information stored in large modern libraries. It uses a combination of letters and numbers (usually two letters followed by four or more numbers). The first letter is like the first number in the Dewey system: it divides all knowledge into broad categories. There are twenty major categories in the Library of Congress system:

A	General Works	M	Music
B	Philosophy and Religion	N	Fine Arts
C	History	P	Language and Literature
D	Foreign History	Q	Science
E, F	American History	R	Medicine
G	Geography, Anthropology	S	Agriculture
H	Social Science	T	Technology
J	Political Science	U	Military Science
K	Law	V	Naval Science
L	Education	Z	Library Science, Bibliography

Notice that many of the major classifications found in the Dewey system have been divided while others have been combined.

Catalog cards with Library of Congress call numbers are shown below. Notice that the call numbers for both systems are printed at the bottom of the card for the librarian's information.

E
649
.C37

Catton, Bruce, 1899–
    Prefaces to history.   [1st ed.]   Garden City, N. Y.,
Doubleday, 1970.
    vi, 230 p. 22 cm. 6.00

Prefaces to history.

E
649
.C37

Catton, Bruce, 1899–
    Prefaces to history.   [1st ed.]   Garden City, N. Y.,
Doubleday, 1970.
    vi, 230 p. 22 cm. 6.00

U. S. - History - Civil War - Addresses, sermons, etc.

E
649
.C37

Catton, Bruce, 1899–
    Prefaces to history.   [1st ed.]   Garden City, N. Y.,
Doubleday, 1970.
    vi, 230 p. 22 cm. 6.00
    Bibliographical footnotes.
    CONTENTS.—Preface to The army of the Potomac trilogy.—Introduction to John Brown's body. — Forward to Prince Napoleon in America, 1861. — President Lincoln and General McClellan.—Introduction to The Battle of Gettysburg.—The generalship of Ulysses S. Grant.—A new appraisal.—The end of the centennial.—History as literature.—For an emotional understanding.—Morning star.—Aristotle and Pandora.—Setting the pattern.—Jeff Davis: the man behind the image.—Our American heritage.—A world of wonder.—The men who made canoes. — The swordbearers. — The dreadful noise.—The great American game.—A historical afterword.—The real Michigan.
    1. U. S.—History—   Civil War—Addresses, sermons, etc.
    I. Title.
E649.C37   973.7   70–84383
                                                   MARC
Library of Congress   70 [25-2]

Suggested Sources

The library has many different source materials, some of which are often overlooked. A few of these are explained in this section, and some more sources are listed at the end of the section. You should become familiar with the ones we describe and the titles of the others. Remember again, if you cannot find the information you are looking for, your librarian is the experienced, professional person to help you. But begin by searching for the information yourself.

THE NEW YORK TIMES INDEX

The *New York Times Index* to the news has always been a valuable tool, yet often an overlooked one. After consulting this source, you are then able to select the microfilm from the library's collection that contains the issue of the *New York Times* that has the information you want to read about. You simply take the microfilm and mount it on one of the microfilm readers. If you are not sure how to go about this, ask your librarian or media center director.

The *New York Times Index* is issued in booklet form covering short periods of time and also in annual volumes. Let us look at the *New York Times Index* as it might appear in your library.

The cover and the spine (the part you see when it is on a shelf) tell you the period of time covered by that particular booklet or book. Now look at the entries on a page from the booklet itself.

a → **MONARCH Construction Co. See also** Housing—
Washington (DC), F 24
MONARCHY. See also personal names
MONASTERIES. See religious denomination names
b → **MONDALE, Walter F (Sen). See also** Children, F 16.
Day Care Centers, F 16. Educ—US—Equal Educ
Opportunities, F 18,19 in 1st F 16 par, F 19. Housing—
US, F 28
c → **MONEY. See** Counterfeiting. Credit. Currency
d → **MONEY, Old and Rare**
Tanzania to issue '72 5-shilling piece using same FAO motif as '71 coin commemg anniv of country's independence; coin to be used for gen circulation and will be sold as collector's item; coin described; illus, F 20,II,34:5
Texas Southern Univ celebrates its silver anniv in part with exhibition of monies and other numismatics entitled Black Amers on Coins and Medals depicting part played by Negroes in bldg nation; various coins described; illus, F 20,II,34:5
Schulman Coin & Mint to conduct mail-bid auction for coins, amulets and medals; various objects described; illus, F 20,II,34:7
Ancient foreign and Amer gold, silver and bronze monies and medals to be auctioned at Parke-Bernet, NYC, including counterfeit coin made between 85 BC and 42 BC; illus, F 27,II,34:7
MONEY Market. Use Credit

a. This is a cross-reference to a different, but related, subject for additional material.

b. This entry lists articles related to a person.

c. This is a cross-reference to a complete entry.

d. "Money, Old and Rare" is the subject. Four articles were published about it during the period of this index (February 16–29, 1972). Reading the description of the articles, we find that three of them appeared on February 20 and the fourth on February 27.

Let us take another look at the subject (d) Money, Old and Rare. If you were to select a period of years and simply consult the *New York Times Index,* you would get a rather good picture of developments relating to this subject. In many cases this will tell you whether the information you are seeking is to be found in sufficient quantity in the *Times.* You may decide to look elsewhere, or you may discover something of more interest dealing with the same subject.

CURRENT BIOGRAPHY

Another overlooked source of information when investigating personalities is the *Current Biography Index.* Part of a page is shown below on the left. Look at the column and locate "Hoffa, James R(iddle) May 72." If we look in the May 1972 issue of *Current*

Grimes, W(illiam) H(enry) obit Mar 72
Grofé, Ferde obit May 72
Hailey, Arthur Feb 72
Hargis, Billy James Mar 72
Harlan, John Marshall obit Feb 72
Hatcher, Richard G(ordon) Feb 72
Hawks, Howard May 72
Hayden, Carl T(rumbull) obit Mar 72
Heatter, Gabriel obit May 72
Heiser, Victor G(eorge) obit May 72
Hodges, Gil(bert Ray) obit May 72
Hoffa, James R(iddle) May 72
Honecker, Erich Apr 72
Howard, Frank (Oliver) Jan 72
Jackson, Mahalia obit Mar 72
Jarvis, Lucy (Howard) Apr 72
Jordan, Vernon E(ulion), Jr. Feb 72
Kenyon, Dorothy obit Apr 72
Kingdon, Frank obit Apr 72
Kirkpatrick, Miles W(ells) Feb 72

HOFFA, JAMES R(IDDLE)

Feb. 14, 1913- Former labor union official *Address:* c/o International Brotherhood of Teamsters, Chauffeurs, and Helpers of America, 25 Louisiana Ave., N.W., Washington, D.C. 20001

From a humble origin as a coal miner's son, pioneer labor organizer James R. Hoffa rose through union ranks to rule, from 1957 to 1971, the International Brotherhood of Teamsters, Chauffeurs, Warehousemen, and Helpers of America, which, with almost 2,000,000 members, is now the largest and most prosperous labor union in the world. Through Hoffa's efforts the originally loose federation of autonomous wildcat cartage locals was transformed into a cohesive national bargaining force that has, willy-nilly, brought stability to the trucking industry. John Dos Passos in his book *Midcentury* (1961) observed that Hoffa had "slugged his way to the top," and William Gomberg, writing in the *Nation* (June 17, 1961), described the tough labor leader as "a complex embodiment of a populist rebel, a robber baron, a . . . job-oriented unionist . . . in the best tradition of free enterprise."

Jimmy Hoffa's enemies call him "ruthless," the prejorative, coincidentally, that was also most

Biography we find a background article about Jimmy Hoffa, reproduced in part. At the end of the article, references for additional reading are listed. These references were also used to compile the information in the article.

Consider the *Current Biography Index* again. Anyone who died during the period covered by this index is given a short obituary listing. In the sample below, notice that there is a reference to a full *Current Biography* article printed earlier and to a newspaper at the end of the paragraph. These may be consulted for additional information about the individual.

> **SAYRE, FRANCIS B(OWES)** Apr. 30, 1885-Mar. 29, 1972 Former diplomat; United States Assistant Secretary of State (1933-39); High Commissioner to the Philippines (1939-42); representative on the United Nation's Trusteeship Council (1947-52). See *Current Biography* (January-February) 1940.
>
> *Obituary*
> N Y Times p41 Mr 30 '72

BIOGRAPHY INDEX

Another guide to biographical material is the *Biography Index*. Here you can find references to books, magazines, and newspapers that might have information. In the portion illustrated at the top of the next page, there is a reference to an obituary of Fedor Hodza; for David C. Hoeh there is an article in *Newsweek*. Under John Cornelius Hodges, the sources listed are the *Saturday Review* and obituaries in the *New York Times, Newsweek,* and *Time*.

If we were doing a complete report on James Hoffa, we would check the *Biography Index* and find additional sources to be added to the ones we already found through *Current Biography*.

In most of the indexes, the following abbreviations for the months of the year will hold true. If they differ in one of the indexes in your library, again consult your specialist.

Ja	January	Jl	July
F	February	Ag	August
Mr	March	S	September
Ap	April	O	October
My	May	N	November
Je	June	D	December

HODGES, John Cornelius, 1906-1970, saxophon-
ist
Hodges leaves the Duke. por Sat R 53:54 My
30 '70
Obituary
N Y Times p39 My 12 '70
Newsweek 75:55 My 25 '70
Time 95:79 My 25 '70
HODGES, Luther Hartwell, 1898- secretary of
commerce
Ivey, Alfred Guy. Luther H. Hodges, prac-
tical idealist. (Men of achievement) Denison
'68 299p il pors
HODGES, Nancy (Austin) 1888-1969, Canadian
columnist and legislator
Obituary
N Y Times p51 D 17 '69
HODGINS, John Willard, 1917- Canadian edu-
cator
Biography
Chem & Ind por no33:1114 Ag 16 '69
HODGSON, Hyland Lorraine, 1892-1961, adver-
tising executive
Biography
NCAB por 51:180 '69
HODZA, Fedor, 1912?-1968, Czechoslovakian
exile leader
Obituary
N Y Times p47 S 19 '68
HOEFER, George, 1909?-1967, author, columnist
and collector of jazz recordings
Obituary
N Y Times p47 N 20 '67
HOEFFER, William Howard, 1891?-1968, jeweler
Obituary
N Y Times p77 Ja 21 '68
HOEH, David C. 1938?- public relations counsel
Where are they now? por Newsweek 74:8 S
8 '69

HOEHLER, Fred K. 1892?-1969, social worker
Obituary
N Y Times p73 Ja 19 '69
HOEKSTRA, William George, 1928- biochemist
[Receives] Bohstedt award in trace mineral
research, 1967. por J Animal Sci 26:1530 N
'67
HOENSBROECH, Paul, graf von, 1852-1923,
German author
McLoughlin, Emmett. Famous ex-priests. Lyle
Stuart '68 p 142-67 bibliog
HOEST, William, 1926- cartoonist
Lockhorns unlock the fun in marital woes.
il por Ed & Pub 102:44 My 31 '69
HOEY, Clyde Roark, 1877-1954, governor and
senator
Biography
NCAB por autograph 50:64-5 '68
HOEY, Jane Margueretta, 1892-1968, social
worker
Obituary
N Y Times p47 O 7 '68
HOFF, Hans, 1897-1969, Austrian psychiatrist
Obituary
N Y Times p35 Ag 25: p41 Ag 26 '69
HOFF, Jacobus Henricus van't, 1852-1911,
Dutch chemist
Kendall James. Young chemists and great
discoveries. Bks. for libs. press '69 p61,
169-72 bibliog il por
HOFF, Sydney, 1912- author and cartoonist
Kingman, Lee, and others, comps. Illustrators
of children's books, 1957-1966. Horn bk. '68
p 121
HOFFA, James Riddle, 1913- labor leader
Hoffa hears some bad news. por Bsns W p68
Jl 26 '69
Hutchinson, J. Hoffa. bibliog Calif Mgt R 11:
79-88 Summer '69

Entries from Biography Index, *1970*

NEW YORK TIMES BIOGRAPHICAL INDEX AND OBITUARY INDEX

Still another fine source of direction to biographical information is the *New York Times Biographical Index.* This is actually a
combination index and biography collection. In the sample opposite, we can find "Jacklin, Anthony" in the index listing. We
see that a biographical article was written about him in the *Times*
on June 22, 1970. (We know it is 1970 because that is the period
this index covers.) The 1443 represents the page number in the
special collection of articles on which we will find the particular
one dealing with Anthony Jacklin.

The services of the *New York Times* will prove to be of great
value to the student who explores all that is available. On page
314, you will see an example from the *New York Times Obituary
Index.* There is no more overlooked source than this. You can
often find many "leading" facts in an obituary, especially if the

Golf His Cup of Tea

Anthony Jacklin

The first Englishman to hold the British and United States Open golf championships concurrently is a 25-year-old perfectionist whose main problem on the tournament tour is boredom.

Anthony Jacklin, the son of a golf-playing lorry driver in Scunthorpe, Lincolnshire, England, added the United States title yesterday to the British crown he won last year.

Man in the News

The bushy-haired 5 - foot - 10 - inch professional learned the game as a caddie for his father when he was 9. He dropped out of school at 15 to concentrate on golf and got his first assistant's job at 17 at Potter's Bar [...] London. He was paid [...] week and 50 per cent [...] income gained from in[...]ing and playing.

Yesterday, Jacklin [...] up a purse of $30,000 to [...] life cozier for himse[lf], wife, Vivien, and th[...] month-old son, Bradley[...] observers feel that Ja[...] feat of winning two [...] world's most prestigiou[s] naments within 12 m[...] may make him $1-[...] richer.

After joining the [...] States professional to[...] 1968, he gained attent[...] winning the Jacksonvil[...] later that year. Follow[...] poor season in 1969 on [...] ican links, he scored h[...] major triumph at Lytham in the British [...]

16 Hours a Tournar[...]

Jacklin is not com[...] happy about the golfin[...] "A tournament [...]

doesn't take that long," he has said. "Even under slow conditions, four hours a round, more or less. So that's 16 hours in one week. What the hell do you do for those other six-and-a-third days?

"That is when boredom and the monotony of motel living sickens you, especially when you are used to being at home, having something to do and being among the friends you grew up with.

"The majority of hotel food is rubbish, apart from some of the very best hotels."

Jacklin, whose boyhood idol was Arnold Palmer, found himself paired with Palmer when he was invited in to the Masters tournament in [...]

dropped him out of contention.

U. S. Experience Helped

He thinks that the experience he gained in this country and his desire to do well enabled him to win Britain's Open. At the time he said:

"I want to say here and now that the time I have spent in America has helped immeasurably toward this victory."

While on the American tour this year, he was called home to England by Queen Elizabeth II and awarded the Officer of the British Empire. But he was back on the tour shortly afterward and honed his game perfectly for yesterday's triumph.

[...]know for a fact that [...] attitude is so much [...] important than the [...]al side," he says. "I [...] I can do well and be-[...] I know I have done it [...] want to know I can [...] better. This makes it [...] to concentrate."

[...]lin usually skips lunch, [...]es to have a good din-[...]e evening. Admitting [...] gets "a little fed up [...]eak all the time," he [...]o vary his diet with [...]sian or Chinese food [...]asion.

[...] home in Elsham, 12 [...]om his birthplace, he [...] resident of the Spas-[...]iety and president of [...]riple Sclerosis Society [...]ohn's Ambulance Bri-[...]ll of which require [...]enings out.

[...]dvice to his country-[...]o hope to emulate his [...] is simple:

[...] to America to learn [...]e game is all about."

Examples from New York Times Biographical Index

Roper, Elmo B Mrs, 1958, S 17,37:1
Roper, Frank E, 1962, O 10,51:6
Roper, Frederick C, 1951, Ja 16,29:5
Roper, George O, 1961, Ag 28,25:5
Roper, J C, 1940, Ja 27,13:2
Roper, Jack, 1966, D 2,39:4
Roper, James G, 1952, Jl 17,23:3
Roper, John, 1968, N 24,87:1
Roper, John S, 1946, Ja 29,25:5
Roper, John W, 1963, S 10,39:3
Roper, Joseph C, 1955, N 20,88:7
Roper, Langdon Heywood, 1968, Ja 19,47:1
Roper, Lewis M, 1939, Ap 27,25:5
Roper, Lonsdale J, 1951, Je 13,29:6
Roper, Mary R, 1939, S 21,23:6
Roper, Morgan E, 1963, O 24,30:4
Roper, Ralph C, 1962, My 18,31:2
Roper, Robert P, 1965, D 23,27:2
Roper, Roswell M, 1954, F 23,27:1
Roper, Thomas A, 1946, Ag 3,15:3
Roper, Thomas C, 1954, F 28,92:2
Roper, W W, 1933, D 11,19:1
Roper, William F Dr, 1937, Ja 14,22:1
Roper, William W Jr Mrs, 1939, Ag 20,33:3
Roper, William W Mrs, 1954, Ja 21,31:5
Ropert, G F Bp, 1903, Ja 6,9:6
Ropes, Charles Joseph H Rev, 1915, Ja 7,13:4
Ropes, E D, 1903, O 31,9:6

Entries from New York Times Obituary Index, *1970*

person was of some importance. Lewis M. Roper's obituary, for example, can be found in the April 27, 1939, issue of the *New York Times* on page 25, column 5.

READERS' GUIDE TO PERIODICAL LITERATURE

There are a great many magazines, large and small, of general popular interest published in the United States. The articles in almost all of them are indexed in the *Readers' Guide to Periodical Literature.* (Scholarly journals and highly technical magazines are not included.) Some entries from the *Readers' Guide* are shown opposite. A great many subject headings are used to direct you to an article that discusses the material you are looking for. The *Readers' Guide* is issued in booklet form for the current year and as a complete, bound index for previous years.

For example, under "Communications satellites" in the illustration, you will find that there was a general article by L. Buckwalter in *Popular Electronics* and other articles in two other magazines during the period covered by this particular index (January through March, 1972). As in all such reference works, a key to the abbreviations used will be found in the front of the booklet, along with a list of all the magazines included.

WHETHER you are a ham operator, telephone dialer, airline pilot, police dispatcher, computer operator, shortwave listener, or anyone who wants to exchange information by wire or radio, you're aware of a world in the midst of a communications explosion. Phone circuits are often clogged, radio frequencies are so congested that police in California speak over TV channels, and boat owners are forced to abandon some of their bands to commercial mariners. A million CB'ers seek more channels for personal talk and air traffic controllers urgently need data links to keep aircraft safely apart.

to lay. Canada has agreed to pay, the U. S. $30 million for launching three satellites in 1972, with a similar system planned for Alaska. These developments make it nearly incomprehensible that the first commercial communications satellite thundered off Cape Kennedy only seven short years ago.

Marconi Bridged the Ocean. The concept of a "radio relay tower in the sky" is often dated at 1945, but its genesis goes clear back to Marconi himself. He had stumbled on the "passive reflector" idea when his signals bridged the ocean in 1901. Although Marconi had no inkling why his signals

Long-range planne[r]
tressing symptoms o[f]
come. By the end of
a whopping 500 per[cent]
communications. The
human voices on ph[one]
exceeded by the cha[n]
versing with each o[ther]
pressure to communi[cate]
as developing natio[ns]
electronic services
home.

But thanks to the
lite, there should be
one. Today, a single s
more traffic than all t[he]
sea cables combined
lites deployed about
every point on the g
of them as no cable
tional coverage, a ris
mestic" satellites is fi
lated regions. This is a
northern wilderness w

mattered little at the
[whic]h was that long-haul
[fi]nally freed from the
[g] continents was done
[ern] which carried on
[ious] stores of food
cable on the ocean
to merely lower the
[om]. Afer the job was
could carry only a
[ages]. (Even the most
today has a capacity
circuits.)
[ot]her hand, had cap-
Atlantic on a kite, a
capacitors, an ear-
[e]nt detector. He had
[re]'s communications
[e]. This well-known
[s] near the top of the
[in]tercepts radio signals
[ang]les are correct, the
[d]ownward and return
[e] distant point. The

COMMUNICATIONS SATELLITES

BY LEN BUCKWALTER

Examples from Readers' Guide to Periodical Literature *and* Popular Electronics

More specialized journals and magazines are indexed in other books, such as *Business Periodicals Index, Index of Economic Journals, Engineering Index,* and *The Philosopher's Index.* If you are searching for information in a specialized or technical field, check with your librarian about the specialized periodical indexes available.

FACTS ON FILE

At times you might need some quick facts, or the name of an individual who accomplished something. *Facts on File* is an excellent source to consult in this situation. For example, let us pose the following questions:

Why was South Africa barred from Davis Cup play in 1971?

Who won the Aventura in 1971?

Who won the South African Open in 1971?

We can start our investigation by looking under "Sports" in the 1971 Index. Under this heading sports information of a general nature is listed. There is also a cross-reference ("*See also specific sports; country names*") which tells us to look under "Tennis," the sport in this case, or "South Africa," the country involved.

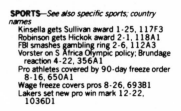

SPORTS—*See also specific sports; country names*
Kinsella gets Sullivan award 1-25, 117F3
Robinson gets Hickok award 2-1, 118A1
FBI smashes gambling ring 2-6, 112A3
Vorster on S Africa Olympic policy; Brundage reaction 4-22, 356A1
Pro athletes covered by 90-day freeze order 8-16, 650A1
Wage freeze covers pros 8-26, 693B1
Lakers set new pro win mark 12-22, 1036D1

Let us assume that we know that all three questions have something to do with South Africa. If we look under the heading "South Africa" and further under the subheading "Sports" (at the top of the next page), we find direct answers to two of the questions posed and a reference that will answer the first question.

If we choose to look under "Tennis," we find general topics listed. The first is "S Africa, Rhodesia barred from Davis Cup play 1–15, 360F3." By investigating further under "Tennis," we find listed under "Winners" all the major tennis tournaments played in 1971 and the winner of each. Look under "Aventura Open" and you will find "Drysdale 4–4, 360E3." If you should

SOUTH Africa, Republic of
Immorality chrgs vs 21 dropped 1-26, 57D2
20 held for terrorism 2-18, 139G2
NUSAS raided 2-25, 3-11, 220B1—C1
Mrs Mandela sentenced 3-3, 236A2
~~Orambo strike spreads 12-18, 1000E2~~

Sports
Barred from Davis Cup play 1-15, 360F3
Drysdale wins US Aventura 4-4, 360E3
Rosewall wins Tennis Open 4-16, 360E3
Vorster to ease bars, Suzman scores 4-22, 355F3
Rugby tour sparks protests in Australia 6-26—8-8, 639E1
Drysdale wins Irish Open 7-10, bows in US Pro open 8-8, 667D1, E1
Australia cancels cricket tour 9-8, Vorster scores 9-10, 894F2-A3
Maud loses US open doubles tennis 9-15, 780B3
Hewitt wins DeWar Cup tennis title 10-16, 1002D2
US wins World Cup golf title 11-14, 984D3

UN Policy & Developments
UN rejects Namibia plebiscite 1-29, 104E2
World Ct Namibia inquiry begins 2-8, 104F2
Human Rights rpt charges 'genocide' 2-23, 144E2
Thant vs UK arms sale 2-24, 123A3
World Ct stays Namibia plebiscite rule 3-17, 302G1
Apartheid com rpts on Western trade 4-15, 302E1
~~Com accuses France re arms 5-14, 449G2~~

TENNIS
S Africa, Rhodesia barred from Davis Cup play 1-15, 360F3
R China quits intl federatn 3-31, 257D3
R China team to get US invite 4-15, 286B3
UCLA wins NCAA team title 6-19, 667A2
Federatn bans contract pros 7-7, 667A2
Court, Jones take maternity leaves 8-2, 667F1
4 named to Hall of Fame 8-21, 780D3
King, Casals fine themselves 9-27, 1002F2
Mrs King sets earning mark 10-3, 780C3
Laver surpasses $1 mln mark 11-26, 1002C2

Winners
Australian Open (men's), Rosewall 3-14, 360B3
Australian Open (women's), Court 3-14, 360B3
Aventura Open, Drysdale 4-4, 360E3
Canadian Open (men's), Newcombe 8-15, 780F3
Canadian Open (men's), Durr 8-16, 780F3
Champions Classic, Laver 3-19, 360A3
Davis Cup, US 10-10—10-11, 1002G1
DeWar Cup (women), Goolagong 10-16, 1002D2
DeWar Cup (men), Hewitt 10-16, 1002D2
Dutch Open (men's), Battrick 8-1, 667E1
Dutch Open (women's), Goolagong 8-1, 667E1
Eastern grass ct (women's), Evert 8-30, 780F3
Eastern grass ct (men's), Graebner 8-30, 780G3

look under "South African Open," you would find "Rosewall 4–16, 360B3, E3." If we know the names of the players, we can also look under each of them to find our information.

DRYSDALE, Cliff
Wins Aventura tennis title 4-4, 360E3
Wins Irish Open tennis title 7-10, loses US Pro Open 8-8, 667D1, G1
DUAN, Le
Reelected to Natl Assemb 4-11, 306B2
DUBAI—*See PERSIAN Gulf States, UNION of Arab Emirates*
DUBCEK, Alexander

ROSEWALL, Ken
Wins Australian Open 3-14; S African 4-16, 360B3, E3
Loses Tennis Champions Classic 3-19, 360B3
Wins Wales title 7-10, DC Star title 7-18, US pro open 8-8, 667D1, E1
Loses Redwood Bank title 10-3, 780G3
Wins World Champnshp title 11-26, 1002B2

Now let us again examine the first three entries under "Sports" following the general heading "South Africa" (at the top of this page on the left).

If we analyze the first entry, we know the topic is the Davis Cup. The 1–15 is the date of the event, January 15. The 360 is the page in *Facts on File*. Following 360 we see F3. If we look it up (the bottom half is shown on the next page), we see that the page is divided into horizontal zones for easy access to the information. By following the F zone to the third column ("F3"), we can easily find what we are looking for.

Having followed the above steps, we learn from the source that two nations, South Africa and Rhodesia, were barred from the Davis Cup play.

The other two sports notations we found in the *Facts on File Index* yield the following information: that Cliff Drysdale upset

logical effects."

According to the doctors, eight of the youths became psychotic while using marijuana and four attempted suicide. One of those who tried to kill himself was a 17-year-old boy who developed an intense interest in the occult. Three times he tried to kill himself by slashing his wrists.

The 30 other youths showed less severe disturbances, ranging from paranoia to sexual promiscuity. Kolansky and Moore singled out for special attention 13 of the 18 girls in the group who became "unusually" promiscuous after relatively short periods of smoking marijuana.

The doctors blamed much of the youths' plight on insufficient warnings of the hazards of marijuana. "We want to let parents know that marijuana is a potentially dangerous drug," Kolansky said.

Tobacco firms agree to ad pact. The Tobacco Institute, Inc., a trade association representing cigarette companies, said April 15 that seven of the nation's nine cigarette manufacturers had agreed to display a health warning in advertisements of their products.

The agreement was widely viewed as a compromise measure designed to head off possible action by Congress or the Federal Trade Commission (FTC) to require stiff health warnings in all cigarette advertisements. [See p. 277A2]

try official confirmed March 16 that the government and the West German cigarette industry had agreed on new curbs on cigarette advertising, including a "step-by-step" discontinuance of television advertising. The agreement called for a total phaseout of cigarette television advertising by the end of 1972.

SPORTS

Horse racing: Canonero II wins Derby—Canonero II became only the fourth field horse in history to win the Kentucky Derby, outrunning 19 other colts May 1 at the 97th running of the Derby at Churchill Downs in Louisville.

Field horses were lumped together as non-favorites for betting purposes in a large field.

His triumph also marked the first time a foreign thoroughbred had ever won the Derby. Canonero II, owned by Edgar Caibett, had been bred in Kentucky but had spent most of his racing career in Venezuela.

Canonero II, with Gustavo Avila riding, maintained an unhurried pace through the race's early stages. He moved out of the pack in the back stretch and hit top stride around the clubhouse turn. His margin of victory was 3¾ lengths over Jim French. Canonero II was timed in 2 minutes 3 1/5 seconds for the 1¼-mile run. The win was worth $145,500 of the total $188,000 purse. [See Vol. XXX, p. 339D1]

Mrs. Billie Jean King played inspiring tennis Feb 28 to win the U.S. women's indoor tennis championship in Winchester, Mass. Mrs. King stopped Rosie Casals, who had won the opening set, 6, 4. Mrs. King recovered to win the next two sets, 6, 2, 6, 3. . . . Rod Laver quickly finished off Nikki Pilic March 2 to win the $30,000 Rothmans indoor tennis tournament in London. Laver overwhelmed Pilic, 6, 4, 6, 0, 6, 2 for the $7,800 first place prize. . . . John Newcombe of Australia, 1970 Wimbledon champion, topped Arthur Ashe, 4, 6, 7, 6, 6, 2, 6, 3, March 28 to win the $10,000 first prize in the $50,000 Sportface tennis tournament in Evanston, Ill. . . . South Africa's Cliff Drysdale upset Rod Laver April 4 to win the $50,000 Aventura tennis tournament in Miami. Drysdale, seeded sixth in the field, played primarily a net game to stop Laver, 6-2, 6-4, 3-6, 6-4. His triumph earned him the $10,000 first-place purse. . . . Australia's Ken Rosewall used all the strokes in his tennis arsenal April 16 to defeat fellow Aussie Fred Stolle, 6-4, 6-0, 6-4, in the finals of the South African open in Johannesburg. Rosewall collected $7,342 in prize money.

2 nations barred from Davis play

South Africa and Rhodesia were barred Jan. 15 from participating in the 1971 Davis Cup tennis competition as the drawing was completed for European zone play. Both countries were included in the 1970 draw, but did not play because many other nations threatened to withdraw if players representing South Africa and Rhodesia were allowed to participate.

South Africa was barred because of its policy of racial apartheid. Rhodesia was excluded because 23 European nations had advised the secretary of the Davis Cup nations that they could not accept Rhodesia as a participant because of United Nations restrictions.

Partial Page (360) from Facts on File, 1971

Rod Laver on April 4 to win the $50,000 Aventura tennis tournament in Miami and that Ken Rosewall used great skill in defeating Fred Stolle in the South African Open in Johannesburg, collecting $7,342 in prize money.

OTHER SOURCES

There are many other reference materials with which you should be familiar, such as *Information Please Almanac, Atlas, and Yearbook,* and *World Almanac and Book of Facts.* Perhaps your library has issued a list of reference works that are available to you. Following is a list of a few selected ones to give you some idea of the variety of valuable materials your library has. Remember, this list is by no means complete.

GENERAL

Encyclopedias and Dictionaries

American College Dictionary
American Heritage Dictionary of the English Language
Collier's Encyclopedia
Columbia Encyclopedia [1 volume]
Dictionary of American-English Usage
Dictionary of American Biography [20 volumes]
Encyclopedia Americana
Encyclopaedia Britannica
Funk & Wagnall's Standard College Dictionary
International Who's Who
Random House Dictionary of the English Language
Webster's Biographical Dictionary
Webster's New International Dictionary of the English Language
Webster's New World Dictionary of the American Language
Webster's Seventh New Collegiate Dictionary
Who's Who [British]
Who's Who in America

Indexes

Biography Index
Business Periodicals Index
Current Biography Index
New York Times Index
Readers' Guide to Periodical Literature

SOCIAL SCIENCES

Encyclopedias and Dictionaries

Dictionary of American Government
Dictionary of Anthropology
Dictionary of Modern Economics
Dictionary of the Social Sciences
Encyclopedia of the Social Sciences
Webster's Geographical Dictionary

Indexes

Index of Economic Journals
Social Sciences and Humanities Index

RELIGION AND PHILOSOPHY

Encyclopedias and Dictionaries

The Catholic Encyclopedia
Dictionary of Philosophy
Dictionary of the Bible
Encyclopedia of Religion and Ethics
The Jewish Encyclopedia

SCIENCE AND MATHEMATICS

Encyclopedias and Dictionaries

A Dictionary of Biological Terms
Dictionary of Electronics
A Dictionary of Geology
Dictionary of Scientific Terms
Dictionary of Technical Terms
Harper Encyclopedia of Science
Larousse Encyclopedia of Animal Life
McGraw-Hill Encyclopedia of Science and Technology
Universal Encyclopedia of Mathematics
Van Nostrand's Scientific Encyclopedia

Indexes

Applied Science and Technology Index
Behavior and Physiology Index
Biological and Agricultural Index
Engineering Index

HISTORY

Encyclopedias and Dictionaries

The Cambridge Histories [Ancient, Medieval, and Modern]
Dictionary of American History [6 volumes]
Encyclopedia of World History
Harper Encyclopedia of the Modern World
Larousse Encyclopedias of History [Ancient and Medieval, Modern]
Worldmark Encyclopedia of the Nations

LITERATURE

Encyclopedias and Dictionaries

Cassell's Encyclopedia of Literature
Columbia Dictionary of Modern European Literature
Concise Encyclopedia of English and American Poets and Poetry
Concise Encyclopedia of Modern World Literature
Dictionary of Mythology
Dictionary of Quotations [Bartlett's, Oxford, and others]
Encyclopedia of World Literature
Oxford Classical Dictionary
Oxford Companions to Literature [Classical, American, English, and French]
Reader's Encyclopedia
Reader's Encyclopedia of Shakespeare
Encyclopedia of World Literature

Index

Essay and General Literature Index

EDUCATION

Encyclopedias and Dictionaries

Encyclopedia of Educational Research
Rand McNally Handbook of Education
Who's Who in American Education

Index

Education Index

MUSIC AND ART

Encyclopedias and Dictionaries

Concise Encyclopedia of Music and Musicians
Dictionary of Art Terms
Encyclopedia of World Art
Grove's Dictionary of Music and Musicians
Harper's Encyclopedia of Art
Harvard Brief Dictionary of Music
International Encyclopedia of Music and Musicians
Larousse Encyclopedia of Modern Art

Indexes

Art Index
Music Index

The Dictionary
and the Thesaurus

The Dictionary

Two reference books are indispensable to you: a good dictionary and a copy of Roget's Thesaurus.

The dictionary will supply you with the following information:

1. The *denotations,* or dictionary definitions, of the word.

2. *Synonyms* for heavily used words and a clear explanation of the distinctions in precise meaning and *connotation* among these synonyms (see the example on page 324).

3. *Antonyms* for heavily used words.

4. The *spelling* of the word. Unfortunately, and unfairly, spelling, though accuracy is always desirable, is often used as a convenient measure of the writer's intelligence and ability. For example, a spelling mistake on an otherwise good job application or a business letter can be quite damaging.

5. The *pronunciation* of the word. In the sample from *The American Heritage Dictionary of the English Language* on this page, the pronunciation of *anger* is given in parentheses immediately following the entry. A code printed at the bottom of each page will tell you the sounds represented by the symbols. The ă is a soft a as in pat. The ə, a symbol known as a *schwa,* stands for the sound *uh,* a common English vowel sound for which we have no specific letter. The accent mark (') indicates which syllable is stressed.

> **an·ger** (ăng′gər) *n.* **1.** A feeling of extreme displeasure, hostility, indignation, or exasperation toward someone or something; rage; wrath; ire. **2.** *Obsolete.* Trouble; pain; affliction. **3.** *British Regional.* An inflammation or sore. —*v.* **angered, -gering, -gers.** —*tr.* **1.** To make angry; enrage or provoke. **2.** *British Regional.* To make painful or inflamed. —*intr.* To become angry: *She angers too quickly.* [Middle English, from Old Norse *angr,* grief. See **angh-** in Appendix.*]

6. The *part* or *parts of speech* of the word.

7. The *syllabication* of the word: its division into syllables.

8. The *derivation,* or origin, of the word. In the following example from *Funk and Wagnall's Standard College Dictionary,* note the derivation of *abuse:* < F *abuser,* ult. < L *abusus,* pp. of *abuti* to misuse < *ab-* away + *uti* to use. This means that the English word *abuse* came from the French *abuser,* which came from the Latin *abusus,* the past participle of *abuti* which meant misuse, from the Latin words *ab* (meaning away) and *uti* (meaning use). You will not have to worry too much about derivations, but they will help you better to understand and to remember the word itself.

a·buse (*v.* ə·byo͞oz'; *n.* ə·byo͞os') *v.t.* a·bused, a·bus·ing 1. To use improperly or injuriously; misuse. 2. To hurt by treating wrongly; injure: to *abuse* friendship. 3. To speak in coarse or bad terms of or to; revile; malign. 4. *Archaic* To deceive. — *n.* 1. Improper or injurious use; misuse: *abuse* of power. 2. Ill-treatment; injury. 3. Vicious conduct, practice, or action. 4. Abusive language; slander. 5. *Archaic* Deception. [< F *abuser,* ult. < L *abusus,* pp. of *abuti* to misuse < *ab-* away + *uti* to use] — a·bus'er *n.*
— Syn. (verb) 1. *Abuse, ill-treat, persecute,* and *oppress* mean to treat badly. *Abuse* covers all unreasonable or improper use or treatment by word or act, of a person or a thing. *Ill-treat* is commonly limited to injurious acts towards persons. To *persecute* one is to *ill-treat* him for opinion's sake, commonly for religious belief; to *oppress* is generally to *ill-treat* for political or pecuniary motives. Compare ASPERSE, POLLUTE, SCOLD.

The Thesaurus

"Use the right word, not its second cousin."—Mark Twain

Next to a good dictionary, the most important reference book for any writer is the thesaurus, a collection of synonymns and antonyms originally compiled by an Englishman named Peter Roget (pronounced roh-zhay) and published in 1852. Use the thesaurus to:

1. Find the correct word to communicate your intended meaning *precisely.*

2. Find synonyms for a word which you find yourself repeating too often in your paper.

3. Refresh your memory when you want to use a particular word and cannot remember it.

To use the thesaurus simply look up a word that means roughly what you want to say and select the synonym which most accurately conveys your desired meaning. If you cannot think of a synonym (a word with the same or similar meaning), look up an antonym (a word with the opposite meaning) and the thesaurus will direct you to the synonyms.

There are several paperback editions of Roget's thesaurus, all of which either use an alphabetical index or are alphabetically arranged. If you need a word meaning *anger,* for example, you would find the following entry:*

> **anger,** *n. & v.* —*n.* RESENTMENT, irritation; rage, choler, fury; annoyance.
> —*v.* inflame, irritate, annoy, provoke, pique, incense; enrage, infuriate.

Though classified as synonyms, these words imply different connotations. *Irritation* and *annoyance* are much milder forms of anger than *rage* or *fury.* In selecting a word, keep in mind the connotation you intend to communicate. If the list of synonyms does not contain the word you want or the part of speech you need (for instance, the sample gives no adjectives or adverbs) you can find what you want by checking any synonym entered in small capitals, as is the word RESENTMENT in the sample below.

RESENTMENT

Nouns—**1,** resentment, displeasure, animosity, anger, wrath, indignation, exasperation; pique, umbrage, huff, miff, soreness, dudgeon, acerbity, virulence, bitterness, acrimony, asperity, spleen, gall, rankling; ill-humor, bad humor, temper, irascibility, hate, irritation, bile, choler, ire, fume, dander, ferment, ebullition, pet, dudgeon, tiff, passion, fit, tantrums. See IRASCIBILITY, MALEVOLENCE.
2, sullenness, moroseness, sulks, black looks, scowl.
Verbs—**1,** resent, take amiss, take to heart, take offense, take in bad part, fly into a rage, bridle, bristle, flare up; sulk, pout, frown, scowl, lower, glower, snarl, growl, gnarl, gnash, snap, look daggers, grind one's teeth; chafe, fume, kindle, seethe, boil, boil with indignation, rage, storm, foam, vent one's spleen, lose one's temper, quiver with rage; burst with anger. *Colloq.,* take hard, blow one's top.
2, anger, affront, offend, give umbrage, hurt the feelings, insult, fret, ruffle, nettle, pique, irritate, sting to the quick, rile, provoke, chafe, wound, incense, inflame, enrage, aggravate, envenom, embitter, exasperate, infuriate, rankle, put out of humor, raise one's dander, make one's blood boil, drive one mad.
Adjectives—**1,** resentful, offended, SULLEN; wrought up, worked up, indignant, hurt. *Colloq.,* sore.
2, angry, irate; wrathful, wroth, cross, sulky, bitter, virulent; acrimonious, warm, burning; boiling, fuming, raging; foaming at the mouth; convulsed with rage; in a stew, fierce, wild, rageful, furious, mad with rage, fiery, rabid, savage; flushed with anger, in a huff, in a passion, up in arms, in high dudgeon.
Adverbs—resentfully, angrily, *etc.;* in the heat of passion, in the heat of the moment.

Antonym, see GRATITUDE.

* The thesaurus examples are from *The New American Roget's College Thesaurus in Dictionary Form* (A Signet Reference), prepared and edited by the National Lexicographic Board (New York: The New American Library, Inc). Copyright © 1958, 1962 by Albert H. Morehead.

Several editions of the thesaurus, such as *Roget's International Thesaurus* (Thomas Y. Crowell Co.), are also published in hard cover; each uses an index. The words are not listed alphabetically, but in numbered categories according to meaning. In the index, however, they are alphabetical, and the process is essentially the same. Look up a word in the index, select the meaning closest to the idea you want to express, and check the synonyms under the appropriate number.